First World War
and Army of Occupation
War Diary
France, Belgium and Germany

4 DIVISION
10 Infantry Brigade,
Brigade Machine Gun Company
and Brigade Trench Mortar Battery
17 January 1916 - 31 January 1919

WO95/1485

The Naval & Military Press Ltd
www.nmarchive.com
Published in association with The National Archives

Published by

The Naval & Military Press Ltd

Unit 10 Ridgewood Industrial Park,

Uckfield, East Sussex,

TN22 5QE England

Tel: +44 (0) 1825 749494

www.naval-military-press.com

www.nmarchive.com

This diary has been reprinted in facsimile from the original. Any imperfections are inevitably reproduced and the quality may fall short of modern type and cartographic standards.

Contents

Document type	Place/Title	Date From	Date To
Heading	10 Inf Brigade Brigade Machine Gun Company 1916 Jan To 1918 Jan Bde Trench Mortar Bty's 1917 Feb To 1919 Jan		
Heading	4th Division 10th Bde M.G.C. January To December 1916		
Heading	10th Brigade Machine Gun Company 17th To 31st January 1916		
Heading	War Diary Of 10th Brigade Machine Gun Company From 17th Jan 1916 To Jan 31st 1916 Volume IA		
War Diary	H.Q & 2 Sections in billets at Mailly-Maillet 2 Sections in trenches between K 34a.0.0. & K.23.C 55	17/01/1916	20/01/1916
War Diary	H.Q. & 2 Sections in Billets 2 Sections in Trenches	21/01/1916	23/01/1916
War Diary	2 Sections in trenches H.Q. & 2 Sections in Billets	24/01/1916	31/01/1916
Heading	10th Brigade. Machine Gun Company February 1916		
Heading	War Diary Of 10th Brigade Machine Gun Coy From Feb 1st 1916 To Feb 29th 1916 Volume I		
War Diary	H.Q. & 2 Sections in Billets in Mailly-Maillet 2 Sections in trenches W. of Serre	01/02/1916	06/02/1916
War Diary	Billets at Halloy	07/02/1916	29/02/1916
Heading	10th Brigade Machine Gun Company March 1916		
Heading	War Diary Of 10th Brigade Machine Gun Coy From March 1st To March 31st 1916 Volume III		
War Diary	Halloy	01/03/1916	01/03/1916
War Diary	Billets at S. Amand	02/03/1916	12/03/1916
War Diary	S. Amand	13/03/1916	19/03/1916
War Diary	H.Q. Nos 2. 3 & 4 in billets in Berles au Bois No 1 in billets in Bienvillers. Reference maps. France sheets 51c & 57d 1/40000 also 1/10,000 sheets 57d Fonquevillers & 51c Ransart.	20/03/1916	31/03/1916
Heading	10th Brigade 4th Division 10th Brigade Machine Gun Company April 1916		
Heading	War Diary Of 10th Brigade Machine Gun Company From April 1st 1916 To April 30th 1916 Volume I		
War Diary	H.Q. & Nos 2.3.4 Sections billets at Berles No 1 Billets at Bienvillers No 3 Section two guns in line before Monchy No 1 section one guns in line before Monchy	01/04/1916	05/04/1916
War Diary	No 1 Section Billets & Trenches at Bienvillers H.Q. & Nos 2.3.4 Billets & Trenches at Billets	06/04/1916	18/04/1916
War Diary	H.Q. & 3 Sections at Berles-au-Bois 1 Section at Bienvillers 4 Guns in trenches.	19/04/1916	24/04/1916
War Diary	H.Q. & Nos 1.2 Sections at Bienvillers No 3 in trenches No 4 in Bienvillers & trenches	25/04/1916	30/04/1916
Heading	10th Brigade Machine Gun Company May 1916		
Heading	War Diary Of 10th Brigade Machine Gun Company From May 1st 1916 To May 31st 1916 Volume V		
War Diary	Berles to Hombercamp	01/05/1916	01/05/1916
War Diary	Humbercamp to Halloy	02/05/1916	02/05/1916
War Diary	Halloy to Barly	03/05/1916	03/05/1916
War Diary	Barly	04/05/1916	04/05/1916
War Diary	Barly to Le Plooy	05/05/1916	05/05/1916

War Diary	Le Plouy	06/05/1916	08/05/1916
War Diary	Le Plouy to Mesnil-Domqueur	09/05/1916	09/05/1916
War Diary	Mesnil Domqueur	10/05/1916	20/05/1916
War Diary	Line of March	21/05/1916	21/05/1916
War Diary	Argenvillers	22/05/1916	31/05/1916
Heading	10th Brigade Machine Gun Company June 1916		
Heading	War Diary Of 10th Brigade Machine Gun Company From June 1st 1916 To June 30th 1916 Volume 5		
War Diary	Argenvillers	01/06/1916	02/06/1916
War Diary	Yvrench	04/06/1916	08/06/1916
War Diary	Line of March	09/06/1916	11/06/1916
War Diary	Bertrancourt	12/06/1916	13/06/1916
War Diary	Bertrancourt-Mailly & Trenches	14/06/1916	14/06/1916
War Diary	Mailly-Maillet & Trenche	15/06/1916	23/06/1916
War Diary	Mailly-Maillet Trenches	24/06/1916	26/06/1916
War Diary	Bertrancourt	27/06/1916	30/06/1916
Heading	10th Brigade Machine Gun Company July 1916		
Heading	War Diary No 10 Company Machine Gun Corps From July 1st 1916 To July 31st 1916		
War Diary	Beaumont-Hamel	01/07/1916	01/07/1916
War Diary	Trenches	02/07/1916	04/07/1916
War Diary	Trenches to Camp P.17.	05/07/1916	14/07/1916
War Diary	Bertrancourt	17/07/1916	18/07/1916
War Diary	Line of March	19/07/1916	20/07/1916
War Diary	Beauval	21/07/1916	23/07/1916
War Diary	Proven	24/07/1916	27/07/1916
War Diary		29/07/1916	31/07/1916
Heading	10th Brigade Machine Gun Company August 1916		
Heading	War Diary No 10 Company M.G. Corps From August 1 To August 31		
War Diary	Company H.Q. & reserve gun teams on Bank of Yser Canal About C2.5. Central 13 Guns in Position in the line From C22C78 to C14d 45.	01/08/1916	03/08/1916
War Diary	Camp at A 22d	04/08/1916	10/08/1916
War Diary	Coy H.Q. & reserve of No 1 Section on Canal Bank detachment at Elverdinge chateau & trenches	11/08/1916	20/08/1916
War Diary	Trenches	20/08/1916	23/08/1916
War Diary	Trenches Near Zillebeke	24/08/1916	31/08/1916
Heading	10th Brigade Machine Gun Company September 1916		
Heading	No 10 Company Machine Gun Corps War Diary Original Copy From September 1st 1916 To September 30th 1916		
War Diary	Erie Camp G.11.C	01/09/1916	03/09/1916
War Diary	To Camp	04/09/1916	16/09/1916
War Diary	On the Move	17/09/1916	17/09/1916
War Diary	Rainneville	18/09/1916	22/09/1916
War Diary	On the Move	23/09/1916	24/09/1916
War Diary	Sailly-Le-Sec	25/09/1916	28/09/1916
War Diary	To Daours	29/09/1916	30/09/1916
Heading	10th Brigade Machine Gun Company October 1916		
Heading	War Diary No 10 Company Machine Gun Corps Original Copy From October 1st-October 31st 1916		
War Diary	Daours	01/10/1916	08/10/1916
War Diary	Moved to Line	09/10/1916	11/10/1916
War Diary	Trenches Near Les Boeufs	12/10/1916	17/10/1916
War Diary	Dugouts About A 38.	18/10/1916	26/10/1916

War Diary	Sandpits-Corbie	27/10/1916	27/10/1916
War Diary	Corbie	28/10/1916	30/10/1916
War Diary	Bellifontaine	31/10/1916	31/10/1916
Heading	10th Brigade Machine Gun Company November 1916		
War Diary	Bellifontaine Onicourt	01/11/1916	12/11/1916
War Diary	Onicourt	13/11/1916	30/11/1916
Heading	10th Brigade Machine Gun Company December 1916		
Heading	10th M.G. Company Original War Diary For The Month Of December 1916		
War Diary	Onicourt	01/12/1916	02/12/1916
War Diary	Line of March	03/12/1916	04/12/1916
War Diary	Camp 112	05/12/1916	06/12/1916
War Diary	Camp 107	07/12/1916	08/12/1916
War Diary	Trenches S of Saillisel	09/12/1916	14/12/1916
War Diary	Trenches	15/12/1916	15/12/1916
War Diary	Camp 16	16/12/1916	23/12/1916
War Diary	Trenches	24/12/1916	30/12/1916
War Diary	Camp 111	31/12/1916	31/12/1916
Heading	4th Division 10th Infantry Bde 10th M.G.C. January To August 1917		
Heading	War Diary 10th Machine Gun Company For The Month Of January 1917		
War Diary	Camp 111 L 2a	01/01/1917	15/01/1917
War Diary	Camp 111 Suzanne Trenches C21 b 26 to C26 b 07	16/01/1917	17/01/1917
War Diary	Transport at Moulin De Fargny A 29 a Central	18/01/1917	23/01/1917
War Diary	Suzanne	24/01/1917	24/01/1917
War Diary	Bray	25/01/1917	25/01/1917
War Diary	Camp 112	26/01/1917	31/01/1917
Heading	War Diary Of 10th M.G. Coy From 1-28 February 1917		
War Diary	Camp 112	01/02/1917	02/02/1917
War Diary	Suzanne	03/02/1917	10/02/1917
War Diary	Trenches 1st Line Transport At Y Wood	10/02/1917	14/02/1917
War Diary	Trenches	15/02/1917	26/02/1917
War Diary	Camp 12	27/02/1917	28/02/1917
Heading	War Diary 10th M.G. Company March 1st-31st 1917		
War Diary	Camp 12 Chipilly	01/03/1917	06/03/1917
War Diary	Remaisnil	07/03/1917	20/03/1917
War Diary	Ourton	21/03/1917	31/03/1917
Heading	10th Company M.G.C. War Diary Month April 1917		
War Diary	Ourton	01/04/1917	06/04/1917
War Diary	Chelers	07/04/1917	08/04/1917
War Diary	Line E of Arras North of La Scarpe	09/04/1917	09/04/1917
War Diary	Line	09/04/1917	11/04/1917
War Diary	Line E of Fampoux	11/04/1917	12/04/1917
War Diary	Line	12/04/1917	12/04/1917
War Diary	Line N of Fampoux	16/04/1917	24/04/1917
War Diary	Nicholas	24/04/1917	24/04/1917
War Diary	& Nicholas Denier	25/04/1917	25/04/1917
War Diary	Denier-Ambrines	26/04/1917	26/04/1917
War Diary	Ambrines	27/04/1917	29/04/1917
War Diary	Arras & Trenches	30/04/1917	30/04/1917
War Diary	Trenches	30/04/1917	30/04/1917
Heading	War Diary 10th M.G. Company May 1917		
War Diary	Line	01/05/1917	02/05/1917
Map			
War Diary	Line	02/05/1917	08/05/1917

Map			
War Diary	Line	09/05/1917	13/05/1917
War Diary	Billets	14/05/1917	21/05/1917
War Diary	Billets in Houvigneul	22/05/1917	31/05/1917
Heading	War Diary 10th Machine Gun Company June 1-June 30 1917		
War Diary	Houvin-Houvigneul	01/06/1917	12/06/1917
War Diary	Arras	13/06/1917	18/06/1917
War Diary	Trenches	18/06/1917	30/06/1917
Heading	10th Machine Gun Coy Original-War Diary-July 1917 Vol 18		
War Diary	Arras Sector	01/07/1917	31/07/1917
Heading	10th Machine Gun Company War Diary For The Month Of August 1917 Vol 19		
War Diary	Field	01/08/1917	31/08/1917
Map			
Heading	4th Division 10th Infantry Bde 10th M.G.C. September To December 1917		
Heading	10th Infantry Brigade Original War Diary For September 1917 Vol 20		
War Diary	Field	01/09/1917	30/09/1917
Heading	10th Machine Gun Coy Original War Diary For Month Of October 1917 Vol 21		
War Diary	In The Field	01/10/1917	01/10/1917
War Diary	Field	01/10/1917	03/10/1917
War Diary	In The Field	04/09/1917	30/09/1917
Map			
Miscellaneous			
Map			
Miscellaneous			
Map			
Miscellaneous			
Heading	10th Machine Gun Coy War Diary For Month Of November Vol 22		
War Diary	Field	01/11/1917	30/11/1917
Map	Map "A"		
Map			
Heading	10th Machine Gun Coy War Diary For Month Of December		
War Diary			
War Diary	In The Field	01/12/1917	31/12/1917
Map			
Heading	War Diary		
Heading	4th Division 10th M.G.C. January 1918		
Heading	10th Machine Gun Coy Original War Diary For Month Of January		
War Diary	In The Field	01/01/1918	31/01/1918
Heading	4th Division 10th Infantry Bde 10th Trench Mortar Battery February To September Less May To July 1917		
Heading	War Diary Of 10th Trench Mortar Battery For February 1917		
War Diary	Camp 112	01/02/1918	01/02/1918
War Diary	Camp 18	03/02/1918	05/02/1918
War Diary	B.16 d 08. (Bouchevanes)	10/02/1918	17/02/1918
War Diary	Camp. 12	21/02/1918	26/02/1918

Heading	War Diary 10th Trench Mortar Battery March 1st To 31st 1917		
War Diary	Camp 12 (Chipilly)	01/03/1917	01/03/1917
War Diary	Corbie	04/03/1917	04/03/1917
War Diary	Montonvillers	05/03/1917	05/03/1917
War Diary	Beauval	06/03/1917	06/03/1917
War Diary	Remaisnil	07/03/1917	18/03/1917
War Diary	Ourton	20/03/1917	20/03/1917
War Diary	Arras	29/03/1917	31/03/1917
Heading	War Diary Of 10th Trench Mortar Battery From 1st To 30th April 1917		
War Diary		01/04/1917	30/04/1917
Heading	War Diary August 1917 10th Trench Mortar Battery		
War Diary	In The Field Near Roeux	01/08/1917	31/08/1917
Map			
Heading	War Diary 10th Trench Mortar Battery Volume From 1st To 30th September 1917		
War Diary		01/09/1917	30/09/1917
Heading	4th Division 10th D.M.B. 1918 Jan-1919 Jan		
Heading	10th Trench Mortar Battery War Diary January 1918		
War Diary	Arras	01/01/1917	03/01/1917
War Diary	Cambrai Road Sector	04/01/1917	19/01/1917
War Diary	Arras	19/01/1917	27/01/1917
War Diary	Monchy Sector	27/01/1917	31/01/1917
Heading	10 Trench Mortar Battery War Diary February 1918		
War Diary	Monchy Sector	01/02/1917	06/02/1917
War Diary	Arras	07/02/1917	28/02/1917
Heading	War Diary March 1918 10 Trench Mortar Battery		
War Diary	Arras	01/03/1918	15/03/1918
War Diary	Tilloy	16/03/1918	16/03/1918
War Diary	Neuville Vitasse Road	18/03/1918	18/03/1918
War Diary	Roeux	19/03/1918	27/03/1918
War Diary	Feuchy	28/03/1918	31/03/1918
Heading	10 Trench Mortar Battery War Diary April 1918		
War Diary	Near Feuchy	01/04/1918	09/04/1918
War Diary	Near Lillers	12/04/1918	13/04/1918
War Diary	Near Robecq	14/04/1918	18/04/1918
War Diary	L'Ecleme	19/04/1918	21/04/1918
War Diary	Near Robecq	22/04/1918	22/04/1918
War Diary	L'Ecleme	23/04/1918	24/04/1918
War Diary	Near Robecq	26/04/1918	30/04/1918
Heading	War Diary May 1918 10 Trench Mortar Battery		
War Diary	Near Robecq	01/05/1918	01/05/1918
War Diary	L'Ecleme	03/05/1918	05/05/1918
War Diary	Near Robecq	06/05/1918	14/05/1918
War Diary	L'Ecleme	15/05/1918	18/05/1918
War Diary	Near Robecq	19/05/1918	27/05/1918
War Diary	L'Ecleme	28/05/1918	31/05/1918
Heading	The 10th Trench Mortar Battery War Diary June 1918		
War Diary	L'Ecleme	01/06/1918	01/06/1918
War Diary	Pacaut Sector	11/06/1918	13/06/1918
War Diary	L'Ecleme	14/06/1918	18/06/1918
War Diary	Riez de Vinage Sector	19/06/1918	23/06/1918
War Diary	Riez de Vinage Sector	22/06/1918	30/06/1918
Heading	War Diary 10 Trench Mortar Battery July 1918		
War Diary	L'Ecleme	01/07/1918	06/07/1918

War Diary	In the Line in Pacaut Sector	07/07/1918	19/07/1918
War Diary	L'Ecleme	20/07/1918	26/07/1918
War Diary	In the Line Vinage Sector	27/07/1918	28/07/1918
War Diary	In the Line in Vinage Sector	29/07/1918	31/07/1918
Miscellaneous	4th Division "A"	11/09/1918	11/09/1918
War Diary	Bellerive	01/08/1918	09/08/1918
War Diary	L'Ecleme	10/08/1918	15/08/1918
War Diary	Le Cauroy	17/08/1918	23/08/1918
War Diary	Lecleme	24/08/1918	24/08/1918
War Diary	Raimbert	25/08/1918	25/08/1918
War Diary	Petit Houvin	26/08/1918	26/08/1918
War Diary	Le Pendu	27/08/1918	28/08/1918
War Diary	Arras Cambrai Rd	29/08/1918	31/08/1918
Heading	War Diary September 1918 10 Trench Mortar Battery		
War Diary	In the Line Near Vis En Artois	01/09/1918	02/09/1918
War Diary	Monchy Le Preux	03/09/1918	03/09/1918
War Diary	Averdoingt	04/09/1918	18/09/1918
War Diary	In the Line Near Eterpigny	18/08/1918	29/08/1918
War Diary	Near Monchy Le Preux	30/08/1918	30/08/1918
Heading	War Diary October 1918 10 Trench Mortar Battery		
War Diary	Orange Hill Near Monchy Le Preux	01/10/1918	05/10/1918
War Diary	Wanquetin	05/10/1918	10/10/1918
War Diary	St Olle	11/10/1918	11/10/1918
War Diary	Naves	13/10/1918	17/10/1918
War Diary	Villers En Cauchies	18/10/1918	21/10/1918
War Diary	Saulzoir	21/10/1918	31/10/1918
Heading	War Diary 10 Trench Mortar Battery November 1918		
War Diary	Saulzoir	01/11/1918	05/11/1918
War Diary	Preseau	06/11/1918	18/11/1918
War Diary	Valenciennes	19/11/1918	30/11/1918
Heading	War Diary December 1918 10 Trench Mortar Battery		
War Diary	Valenciennes	01/12/1918	31/12/1918
War Diary	War Diary January 1919 10th Trench Mortar Battery		
War Diary	Valenciennes	01/01/1919	05/01/1919
War Diary	Binche	06/01/1919	31/01/1919

10 INF BRIGADE.

BRIGADE MACHINE GUN
COMPANY.

1916 JAN TO 1918 JAN.

BDE TRENCH MORTAR BTY'S

1917 FEB TO 1919 JAN.

1485

10 INF BRIGADE.

BRIGADE MACHINE GUN
COMPANY.

1916 JAN TO 1918 JAN.

BDE TRENCH MORTAR BTY'

1917 FEB TO 1919 JAN.

1485

4th Division

10th Bde

M. G. C.

January to December

1916

~~Jan 1918~~

10th Brigade.

4th Division.

10th BRIGADE.

MACHINE GUN COMPANY

17th to 31st JANUARY 1916

Confidential

WAR DIARY

of

10th Brigade Machine Gun Company

from 17th Jan 1916 to Jan 31st 1916.

Volume I A

G. S. Alison Capt.

Page 1

Instructions regarding War Diaries and Intelligence Summaries are contained in F. S. Regs., Part II. and the Staff Manual respectively. Title Pages will be prepared in manuscript.

WAR DIARY
or
~~INTELLIGENCE SUMMARY~~
(Erase heading not required.)

Army Form C. 2118

Place	Date	Hour	Summary of Events and Information	Remarks and references to Appendices
H.Q. & 2 Sections in billets at MAILLY-MAILLET 2 Sections in trenches between K. 34a. 0.0 & K 23 c 5.5	1916 ~~17 Nov~~ 17 Jan		Nos 3 & 4 sections relieved Nos 1 & 2 sections in the trenches. 4 Emplacements in Divisional second line Nos 6. 7. 8 & 9 4 Guns in front line system (i) ROB-ROY joins NAIRNE STREET. (ii) ROB-ROY joins LE CATEAU AVENUE (iii) FLAG AVENUE (iv) DELAUNAY AVENUE. Nos 1 & 2 sections returned to billets. Nothing else to record	Departures 18th Lieut J. M Low & 1 OR on leave till Jan 29th 18th 3. O.R to hospital sick 19th 2 O.R to hospital sick 20th 1. O.R to hospital
	18 Jan		No reports from trenches on operations. Fine day but dull. A distinct improvement is now visible in the state of trenches which are now for the most part passable.	Arrivals 20th 1 O.R to hospital.
	19 Jan		No reports to record. Dull day, some rain	
	20 Jan		No reports from trenches Bad day as regards weather	

1875 Wt. W593/826 1,000,000 4/15 J.B.C. & A. A.D.S.S./Forms/C. 2118.

Page 2

Instructions regarding War Diaries and Intelligence Summaries are contained in F. S. Regs., Part II. and the Staff Manual respectively. Title Pages will be prepared in manuscript.

WAR DIARY
or
INTELLIGENCE SUMMARY
(Erase heading not required.)

Army Form C. 2118

Place	Date 1915	Hour	Summary of Events and Information	Remarks and references to Appendices
H.Q. & 2 sections in Billets 2 sections in trenches.	Jan 21		Relief day. Nos 1 & 2 sections relieved Nos 3 & 4 sections in the trenches. Same positions as before except that Emplacement No 10 is now occupied instead of No 9. Nothing to record in trenches Weather very bad. foggy, some rain, & cold	**Departures.** 21st 1. o.r. to Hospital Sick 22nd 1 o.r. (attached from A & SH) to hospital sick **Arrivals.** 21st 2Lieut Coatsworth & 1 o.r. from leave 22nd 2 o.r. from hospital
	Jan 22nd		Report from No 1 section. Fire opened from No 6 Emplacement on party of Germans about R. 36. a range about 2000x one reported hit. Weather again inclement.	
	Jan 23rd		No reports on operations to record Working party sent up to the line this night. for work in right sector. (FLAG AVENUE) The improvement in state of trenches still continues Weather fine Early. dull later, some rain	

1875 Wt. W593/826 1,000,000 4/15 J.B.C. & A. A.D.S.S./Forms/C. 2118.

Army Form C. 2118.

WAR DIARY
or
INTELLIGENCE SUMMARY
(Erase heading not required.)

Instructions regarding War Diaries and Intelligence Summaries are contained in F. S. Regs., Part II. and the Staff Manual respectively. Title Pages will be prepared in manuscript.

Page 3

Place	Date 1915	Hour	Summary of Events and Information	Remarks and references to Appendices
2 Sections in trenches #9 — 2 sections in billets	Jan 24		No reports on operations from trenches armour piercing test carried out by No 2 Gun of No 3 Section Weather fair but dull & rather cold.	Departures 25th. Capt G. M. Alison & 3 or. on leave.
	Jan 25.		Seven German aeroplanes passed over flying N.W. Relief day Nos 3 & 4 sections relieved Nos 1 & 2 in trenches. Emplacements as before. Weather, fair	Arrivals. 26th 2 or. from Hospital 1 or. from leave
	Jan 26.		Nothing to report from trenches. Fine day but cloudy	
	Jan 27		No reports from trenches on operations. Gas alarm at 8 pm. proved groundless Fine day but dull	

1875 Wt. W593/826 1,000,000 4/15 J.B.C. & A. A.D.S.S./Forms/C. 2118.

Page 4

Instructions regarding War Diaries and Intelligence Summaries are contained in F. S. Regs., Part II. and the Staff Manual respectively. Title Pages will be prepared in manuscript.

WAR DIARY
or
INTELLIGENCE SUMMARY
(Erase heading not required.)

Army Form C. 2118

Place	Date	Hour	Summary of Events and Information	Remarks and references to Appendices
2 sections in trenches HQ & 2 sections in billets	Jan 28th		Gas alarm at 8 a.m. proved groundless. No reports on operations from trenches. Fine day misty early	Departures –
	Jan 29th		Gas alarm at 7 a.m. Gas shells distinctly smelt in MAILLY Relief Nos 1 & 2 sections relieved Nos 3 & 4 sections LA SIGNY Fme heavily shelled during relief. Fine, misty early	Jan 30. Arrivals. Lt J. M. Low from leave.
	Jan	30.	No reports on operations. Gas alarm 3 pm groundless Fine day but dull & cold	
	Jan	31.	Nothing to report. German artillery active. Fine day & warm, though dull	

1875 Wt. W593/826 1,000,000 4/15 J.B.C. & A. A.D.S.S./Forms/C. 2118.

10th Brigade.

4th Division.

10th BRIGADE.

MACHINE GUN COMPANY

FEBRUARY 1 9 1 6

Confidential

WAR DIARY

of

10th Brigade Machine Gun Coy

from Feb. 1st 1916 to Feb. 29th 1916

Volume I

G. S. Alison Capt.

Army Form C. 2118

Instructions regarding War Diaries and Intelligence Summaries are contained in F. S. Regs., Part II. and the Staff Manual respectively. Title Pages will be prepared in manuscript.

Page 5

WAR DIARY
or
~~INTELLIGENCE SUMMARY~~
(Erase heading not required.)

Place: H.Q. & 2 Sections in billets in MAILLY-MAILLET. 2 Sections in trenches N. of SERRE

Date	Hour	Summary of Events and Information	Remarks and references to Appendices
~~Jan~~ Feby	1st	Fine day. Sunny & warm. Cold early. No reports from trenches.	Departures Wednesday Feby 2nd 4 o.r. on leave
Feby	2nd	Very cold early. Nos 3 & 4 sections relieved Nos 1 & 2 in the trenches. Nothing to report	Arrivals. Nil.
Feby	3rd	Fine day. No report from trenches.	
Feby	4th	Very wet day. O.C. 12th Brigade Machine Gun Company & officers came to inspect the line to take over	
Feby	5th	Fine morning. Machine Gun Company 12th Brigade came up to relieve the Company. Relief carried out punctually & satisfactorily. Bombs dropped by aeroplane on MAILLY	

1875 Wt. W593/826 1,000,000 4/15 J.B.C. & A. A.D.S.S./Forms/C. 2118.

Instructions regarding War Diaries and Intelligence Summaries are contained in F. S. Regs., Part II. and the Staff Manual respectively. Title Pages will be prepared in manuscript.

WAR DIARY
or
INTELLIGENCE SUMMARY
(Erase heading not required.)

Army Form C. 2118

Place	Date	Hour	Summary of Events and Information	Remarks and references to Appendices
Sunday	Feby 6th		Company proceeded by march to billets at HALLOY Route. BEAUSSART – BERTRANCOURT – BUS – AUTHIE – THIEVRES – FAMECHON – HURTEBISE FME – HALLOY	Departures. Feby 7th 2 or to hospital Feby 10th 1 or to hospital. Feby 12th 2/Lt THOMPSON & 3 or on leave
BILLETS AT HALLOY	Feby 7th Feby 8th Feby 9th Feby 10th Feby 11th Feby 12th		Training carried out by sections. Time devoted largely to range practice in which satisfactory progress was made, though hindered considerably by rainy & cold weather. Gun drill practised continually. Advanced drill attempted Tactical training impossible owing to the heavy state of the country.	Arrivals. Feby 6th Capt ALISON & 2 or from leave Feby 10th 1 or from Hospl. Feby 11th 1 or from Leave

1875 Wt. W593/826 1,000,000 4/15 J.B.C. & A. A.D.S.S./Forms/C. 2118.

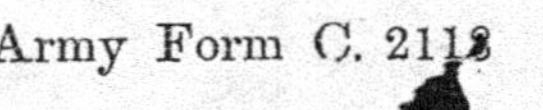

Instructions regarding War Diaries and Intelligence Summaries are contained in F. S. Regs., Part II. and the Staff Manual respectively. Title Pages will be prepared in manuscript.

WAR DIARY
or
INTELLIGENCE SUMMARY
(Erase heading not required.)

Army Form C. 2118

Place	Date	Hour	Summary of Events and Information		Remarks and references to Appendices
Billets at Halloy	Feby. 13		Sunday. Parade for Divine Service & inspection by company officers of billets & Equipment.	Departures Feby 13th 1 OR to Hpll ~~Feb [illegible]~~	
	Feby 14 Feby 15 Feby 16 Feby 17 Feby 18th Feby 19th		Training continued on lines of programme on previous page. Weather rather worse, consequently progress not very fast. Range now used 300x in length. Improvement in this branch very noticeable	Feby 20th [illegible] 2 OR to leave Arrivals Monday 14th 1 OR from Hpll 15th 1 OR from base reinforcements 17th 1 OR from Hpll 18th 1 OR from leave 19th 1 OR from leave	
	Feby 20th		Sunday Divine Service & inspections as usual.		

1875 Wt. W593/826 1,000,000 4/15 J.B.C. & A. A.D.S.S./Forms/C. 2118.

Instructions regarding War Diaries and Intelligence Summaries are contained in F. S. Regs., Part II. and the Staff Manual respectively. Title Pages will be prepared in manuscript.

WAR DIARY
or
INTELLIGENCE SUMMARY
(Erase heading not required.)

Army Form C. 2118

Place	Date	Hour	Summary of Events and Information	Remarks and references to Appendices
Billets at HALLOY	Feby	21	Training continued	Departures 21st 1 or to Hptl 24th 1 or to Hptl 28th 2 or to Hptl 29 1 or to Hptl at G. H. Q. Arrivals. 21st 1 or from Hptl 22nd 1 or from Hptl 2 or from U. K. Reinforcements 27th 2Lt MATSON leave extended till 5th March
	"	22		
	"	23		
	"	24		
	"	25		
	"	26		
	Feby	27	Sunday. Usual Church Parade & inspections	
	Feby	28	Training Continued	
	Feby	29		

1875 Wt. W593/826 1,000,000 4/15 J.B.C. & A. A.D.S.S./Forms/C. 2118.

10th Brigade.

4th Division.

10th BRIGADE.

MACHINE GUN COMPANY

MARCH 1 9 1 6

1

Confidential

WAR DIARY

of

10th Brigade Machine Gun Coy

from March 1st to March 31st 1916.

Volume III

G. S. Alison Capt

Instructions regarding War Diaries and Intelligence Summaries are contained in F. S. Regs., Part II. and the Staff Manual respectively. Title Pages will be prepared in manuscript.

Page 9

WAR DIARY
or
INTELLIGENCE SUMMARY
(Erase heading not required.)

Army Form C. 2118

Place	Date	Hour	Summary of Events and Information	Remarks and references to Appendices
	MARCH			Departures
HALLOY	1		Training continued.	4th 1 or to hospl
	2		Company moved to new billeting area at S. AMAND Route. Hurlebise Fme – FAMECHON – PAS – HENU	12th 1 or to hospl.
Billets at S. Amand	3, 4, 5		Sectional training continued. A good range was here unobtainable, & little progress could be made in this direction. The snowy weather hindered work.	Arrivals.
	6		Sunday. Usual church parades & inspections.	4th 1 o.r. from Hpl.
	7, 8, 9, 10, 11		Training continued to best advantage possible. This district, offers little or no facility for training. The weather continues bad.	7th 1 o.r. from Hptl.
	12		Sunday. Usual Sunday programme adhered to.	9th 1 o.r. from Hptl.

1875 Wt. W593/826 1,000,000 4/15 J.B.C. & A. A.D.S.S./Forms/C. 2118.

Army Form C. 2118

WAR DIARY
or
INTELLIGENCE SUMMARY
(Erase heading not required.)

Instructions regarding War Diaries and Intelligence Summaries are contained in F. S. Regs., Part II. and the Staff Manual respectively. Title Pages will be prepared in manuscript.

Page 10

Place	Date	Hour	Summary of Events and Information		Remarks and references to Appendices
	MARCH.			Departures.	
S. AMAND	13th		Training continued.		
"	14th			19th Two o.r. to Hptl including Q.M.S. Whiting.	
	15th	—	Company Route march.		
"	16th	—	Capt Alison & other Officers visit the line with a view to taking over. Training continued.	19th 2Lt BARWOOD & 2 or on leave to U.K.	
"	17th		Section Officers visit the line, around BERLES-au-Bois & BIENVILLERS.		
"	18th		This day was devoted to the final preparations of Guns & Gear to return to the line.	Arrivals. 19th 2Lt MATSON from Sick leave.	
	19th		The Company proceeded to take the place in the line of the 110th Bde. Machine Gun Company.	13th 1 or from Hptl	
			Route - HOMBERCAMP - LA CAUCHIE - BAILLEULMONT - BERLES	17th 1 o.r. from Hptl.	
			Company disposed as follows.	13th 3 o.r. from Base Reinforcements	
			H.Q. & Nos 2. 3. 4 sections at BERLES.		
			No 1 section detached at BIENVILLERS.		
			Transport & Q.M. Sergeant's establishment at POMMIER.		

1875 Wt. W593/826 1,000,000 4/15 J.B.C. & A. A.D.S.S./Forms/C. 2118.

Army Form C. 2118

Instructions regarding War Diaries and Intelligence Summaries are contained in F. S. Regs., Part II. and the Staff Manual respectively. Title Pages will be prepared in manuscript.

Page 11

WAR DIARY
or
INTELLIGENCE SUMMARY
(Erase heading not required.)

Place	Date	Hour	Summary of Events and Information	Remarks and references to Appendices
~~Billets~~ H.Q. Nos 2. 3 & 4 in billets in BERLES au BOIS No 1 " in BIENVILLERS Reference maps. FRANCE Sheets 57c & 57D 1/40000 also 1/10,000 Sheets 57D FONQUEVILLERS & 57c RANSART	MARCH 20th		Trenches in this line have not been adapted for machine gun fire. No emplacements suitable for Vickers Guns having been constructed in the front line, & very few of the erections in the Divisional Second line being made to take Vickers guns. All positions therefore have to be made.	Departures & Arrivals Nil
	21st		Working Parties from all sections proceed with work in the trenches.	
			No 2 section work on emplacements & dug outs in NEWARK STREET about W 29 a 24	
			No 3 section on emplacements in Divisional line CALVAIRE W. 22 a 47 VICKERS VILLA ~~about~~ & PETROL VILLA	
			No 4 section on dug-outs & emplacements in support line off NEVER-ENDING STREET about W. 28 d 88	
			No 1 section on emplacement in support line behind trench 86 about E 4 a 88	

1875 Wt. W593/826 1,000,000 4/15 J.B.C. & A. A.D.S.S./Forms/C. 2118.

Instructions regarding War Diaries and Intelligence Summaries are contained in F. S. Regs., Part II. and the Staff Manual respectively. Title Pages will be prepared in manuscript.

Page 12

WAR DIARY

or

INTELLIGENCE SUMMARY

(Erase heading not required.)

Army Form C. 2118

Place	Date	Hour	Summary of Events and Information	Remarks and references to Appendices
Billets in BERLES & BIENVILLERS	MARCH 22nd		Work continued on the same lines as 21st MARCH	Departures
	23rd		Working parties as for previous day. Trenches for most part wide & straight necessitating construction of traverses	24th 1 or to Hptl
	24th		As for 23rd	25th 1 o.r. reinforcement returned to BASE; 1 or to Hptl.
	25th		as for 23rd	29th 1 or. to Hptl.
	26th		Sunday. Church Parades. No working parties sent up tonight.	29th 2Lt POTTER & 2 or on leave; Arrivals
	27th		Work resumed as before	29th 1 or. from Hptl.
	28th		Emplacement in NEWARK STREET progressing. Dugouts completed.	
	29th		NEVER ENDING STREET Emplacement is not progressing very fast.	

1875 Wt. W593/826 1,000,000 4/15 J.B.C. & A. A.D.S.S./Forms/C. 2118.

Army Form C. 2118

WAR DIARY
or
INTELLIGENCE SUMMARY
(Erase heading not required.)

Instructions regarding War Diaries and Intelligence Summaries are contained in F. S. Regs., Part II. and the Staff Manual respectively. Title Pages will be prepared in manuscript.

Page 13

Place	Date	Hour	Summary of Events and Information	Remarks and references to Appendices
Trenches. No 3 Section BERLES – BIENVILLERS	30th		Working Parties No 16654 Pte H Lawrence No 4 Section killed while working. buried in Graveyard at BERLES-au-BOIS.	
	31st		Relief day. No 3 Section puts one gun in the NEWARK STREET Emplacement. H 29 a 24 Work continued.	

1875 Wt. W593/826 1,000,000 4/15 J.B.C. & A. A.D.S.S./Forms/C. 2118.

10th Brigade.

4th Division.

10th BRIGADE.

MACHINE GUN COMPANY

APRIL 1 9 1 6

Confidential

WAR DIARY

of

10th Brigade Machine Gun Company

from April 1st 1916 to April 30th 1916.

Volume I

G. S. Alison Capt.

Instructions regarding War Diaries and Intelligence Summaries are contained in F. S. Regs., Part II. and the Staff Manual respectively. Title Pages will be prepared in manuscript.

Page 14

WAR DIARY
or
INTELLIGENCE SUMMARY
(Erase heading not required.)

REGISTRY MACHINE GUN CORPS RECORD OFFICE. Date 3. 7. 16 No. R6/192.

Army Form C. 2118

Place	Date	Hour	Summary of Events and Information		Remarks and references to Appendices
H.Q. & Nos 2. 3. 4 sections billets at BERLES No 1 billet at BIENVILLERS No 3 section two guns in line before MONCHY No 1 " one gun in line before MONCHY	April	1st	Position off NEVER-ENDING STREET now completed. Map reference 1/40000 RANSART Sheet H. 28. d 88. Work on divisional second line progressing.	Departures. 2nd 1 OR to U.K. for transfer to Signal Service R.E. 4th 1 OR to Hpl.	
		2nd	Sunday. Church Parades. Inspections carried out. Working Parties continued		
		3rd	Position off NEVER ENDING STREET occupied. There are now in trenches. Right Section 1 Gun in support line behind Trench 86 about 24 d 88. No 1 Section Left Section. 1 Officer 1 Gun in NEWARK STREET 1 Gun off NEVER ENDING STREET.	Arrivals. 1st 2/Lt BARNWOOD & 1 OR from leave. 3rd 1 OR from Hpl. 4th 1 OR from Hpl.	
		4th 5th	Work continued. Work in divisional second line on PETROL VILLA & VICKERS VILLA has been almost abandoned. These positions were badly sited & water is deep, rendering work impossible.		

1875 Wt. W593/826 1,000,000 4/15 J.B.C. & A. A.D.S.S./Forms/C. 2118.

WAR DIARY
or
INTELLIGENCE SUMMARY
(Erase heading not required.)

Army Form C. 2118

Instructions regarding War Diaries and Intelligence Summaries are contained in F. S. Regs., Part II. and the Staff Manual respectively. Title Pages will be prepared in manuscript.

Page 15

Place	Date	Hour	Summary of Events and Information	Remarks and references to Appendices
No 1 Section Billets – Trenches at BIENVILLERS H.Q. – Nos 2.3.4 Billets Trenches at BERLES	6th		Relief. No 2 section relieves No 3 in trenches. A third position is now occupied. ESSEX HOUSE in Divisional 2nd line. East of BERLES – BIENVILLERS ROAD	Departures. 6th 3 o.r. to U.K. on leave
	7th		Work continued. Direct hit obtained by German field gun on emplacement off NEVERENDING Street. Tripod completely destroyed.	Arrivals 6th 2 o.r. from Base Reinforcements.
	8th		Work on line continued. Usual routine adhered to. Nothing to report on.	7th 1 o.r. from H.P.H.
	9th	Sunday		10th 2/Lt POTTER & 2 o.r. from leave
	10th			
	11th			
	12th		Relief. No 3 relieves No 2. Positions as before.	

1875 Wt. W593/826 1,000,000 4/15 J.B.C. & A. A.D.S.S./Forms/C. 2118.

Page 16

Instructions regarding War Diaries and Intelligence Summaries are contained in F. S. Regs., Part II. and the Staff Manual respectively. Title Pages will be prepared in manuscript.

WAR DIARY
or
INTELLIGENCE SUMMARY
(Erase heading not required.)

Army Form C. 2118

Place	Date	Hour	Summary of Events and Information		Remarks and references to Appendices
No 1 Section Billets & trenches at BIENVILLERS H.Q. No 2.3.4 at BERLES	13th		Usual routine followed.	Departures.	
	14th		Works on emplacements continued.	13th 1 or. to Hptl.	
	15th		No reports to enter.		
	16th			Arrivals.	
				13th 1 or. from Hptl.	
	17th		An enterprise carried out by 1. R. Irish Rifles & 1. R. Norwick Regt at 4 p.m. German trenches entered & raided after a short bombardment.	15th 1 or. to Hptl.	
			Machine Guns ordered to hold their fire unless suitable targets appeared. No targets were seen.	17th 3 or from Base	
	18th		No 2 section relieves No 3 in trenches.		

1875 Wt. W593/826 1,000,000 4/15 J.B.C. & A. A.D.S.S./Forms/C. 2118.

Army Form C. 2118

Instructions regarding War Diaries and Intelligence Summaries are contained in F. S. Regs., Part II. and the Staff Manual respectively. Title Pages will be prepared in manuscript.

Page 7

WAR DIARY
or
~~INTELLIGENCE SUMMARY~~

(Erase heading not required.)

Place	Date	Hour	Summary of Events and Information	Remarks and references to Appendices
H.Q. & 3 Sections at BERLES-au-BOIS 1 Section at BIENVILLERS 4 Guns in trenches	19th 20th 21st 22nd 23rd		Usual routine followed Work in trenches continued Construction of proof emplacements started but much hampered by delay in obtaining material at NEWARK STREET & NEVERENDING On 22nd German trenches bombarded by our Guns opposite MONCHY. Heavy retaliation on our trenches. Hit on parapet close by our position in NEWARK STREET. Gun & team saved by a large & specially built traverse	Departures 21st 2 O.R. ranks (corporals) to base for further training Arrivals 21st 2 O.R. from Base
	24th		Relief day. No 3 section relieved No 2 in the lines No 4 Section proceeded to BIENVILLERS to relieve No 1. No 1 returned to BERLES. Company now disposed as under. H.Q. & Nos 1 & 2 ~~4~~ Sections in BERLES No 3 section in trenches No 4 in BIENVILLERS & trenches. An Extra Gun was put into trenches this day in left sector as a flying gun for use in emergency, situated close to H.Q. of 1. R. Irish Fusiliers. No particular instruction given to this gun	

1875 Wt. W593/826 1,000,000 4/15 J.B.C. & A. A.D.S.S./Forms/C. 2118.

Instructions regarding War Diaries and Intelligence Summaries are contained in F. S. Regs., Part II. and the Staff Manual respectively. Title Pages will be prepared in manuscript.

Page 18

WAR DIARY
or
~~INTELLIGENCE~~ SUMMARY
(Erase heading not required.)

Army Form C. 2118.

Place	Date	Hour	Summary of Events and Information	Remarks and references to Appendices
H.Q. & Nos 1.2. Sections at BIENVILLERS No 3 in Trenches No 4 in BIENVILLERS & trenches	25th		additional Guns sent this night to ~~Bn~~ H.Q. 1. R. Irish Fus. as flying gun Normal routine followed	Departures.
	26th		Usual routine followed	30th 1 O.R. to Hosp.
	27th		Work continued	29th 3 O.R. on leave
	28th		No report to make.	
	~~[illegible]~~		One of four covered emplacements ~~near~~ BIENVILLERS - MONCHY road demolished by shell fire 28th	Arrivals
	~~[illegible]~~	29th	Orders received that the company is to be relieved by 110th Bde M.G. Coy. on night May 1-2nd.	Nil.
			O.C. 110th Bde M.G. Coy arrived to inspect the line.	
	30th		110th B. M.G.C. arrived up at nightfall, to relieve.	

1875 Wt. W593/826 1,000,000 4/15 J.B.C. & A. A.D.S.S./Forms/C. 2118.

10th Brigade.

4th Division.

10th BRIGADE.

MACHINE GUN COMPANY

M A Y 1 9 1 6

Confidential

WAR DIARY

of

10th Brigade Machine Gun Company

from May 1st 1916 to May 31st 1916.

Volume V

G. S. Alison Capt.

Instructions regarding War Diaries and Intelligence Summaries are contained in F. S. Regs., Part II. and the Staff Manual respectively. Title Pages will be prepared in manuscript.

Page 19

WAR DIARY
or
~~INTELLIGENCE SUMMARY~~
(Erase heading not required.)

Army Form C. 2118.

Place	Date	Hour	Summary of Events and Information	Remarks and references to Appendices
	MAY.			Departures
BERLES to HUMBERCAMP	1.		Relief of No 3 Section carried out by 110th B.M.G.C. in morning. " No 4 " " " in evening. Company proceeded at 8.15 pm to bivouac at HUMBERCAMP via POMMIER. Two limbers broke down, considerable delay caused.	4th Capt G.N. Alison to Hospital. Arrivals 1st 1 pte. Hptl to 4th Divnl Reserve Coy.
HUMBERCAMP to HALLOY	2nd		Moved off at 9.30 am to billets in HALLOY Route GAUDIEMPRÉ – PAS – GRENAS – HALLOY	2nd 1 pte 1. R. Irish Fus taken on strength
HALLOY to BARLY	3rd		Moved off at 9.30 a.m. to billets in BARLY Route HALLOY – DOULLENS – HEM – OCCOCHES – BARLY.	4th 2 ptes 1. R. Irish Fus taken on strength.
BARLY	4th		Remained in billets at BARLY. Capt ALISON to Hptl Lieut A. Low. taken over Command	

1875 Wt. W593/826 1,000,000 4/15 J.B.C. & A. A.D.S.S./Forms/C. 2118.

Page 9

Instructions regarding War Diaries and Intelligence Summaries are contained in F. S. Regs., Part II. and the Staff Manual respectively. Title Pages will be prepared in manuscript.

WAR DIARY
or
INTELLIGENCE SUMMARY
(Erase heading not required.)

Army Form C. 2118

Place	Date	Hour	Summary of Events and Information	Remarks and references to Appendices
BARLY to LE PLOUY	5th		Moved off at 10 a.m. to billets in LE PLOUY Route MEZEROLLES – LE MEILLARD – PROUVILLE – BEAUMETZ – LONGVILLERS – MESNIL-DOMQUEUR – DOMQUEUR – LE PLOUY.	Departures. 5th 3 o.r. on leave. 8th 1 o.r. to Hptl.
LE PLOUY	6th		Billets at LE PLOUY. Day spent in setting kit & wagons & in minor repairs.	Arrivals.
"	7th		Billets at LE PLOUY. Church Parade & Inspections	9th 3 o.r. from leave.
"	8th		Training commenced in grounds of CHATEAU du PLOUY	
LE PLOUY to MESNIL-DOMQUEUR	9th		Moved at 11.30 a.m. to billets at MESNIL-DOMQUEUR.	

1875 Wt. W593/826 1,000,000 4/15 J.B.C. & A. A.D.S.S./Forms/C. 2118.

Page 20

Instructions regarding War Diaries and Intelligence Summaries are contained in F. S. Regs., Part II. and the Staff Manual respectively. Title Pages will be prepared in manuscript.

WAR DIARY
or
INTELLIGENCE SUMMARY
(Erase heading not required.)

Army Form C. 2118

Place	Date	Hour	Summary of Events and Information	Remarks and references to Appendices
MESNIL-DOMQUEUR	10th		Training Commenced. Programme for day — { 7.30am-8 Coy drill; 9-12.30pm { Gun drill, advanced drill, Stoppage, Mechanism } } Weather good.	Departures 10th 2 O.R. to Base for further training.
—	11th			
—	12th		Capt Alison from Hptl on 12th & resumes command	13th 2/Lt COATSWORTH & 2 O.R. on leave
—	13th		Route march. MESNIL-DOMQUEUR — LONGVILLERS — CRAMONT — COULONVILLERS — MAISON-ROLLAND — LE PLOUY — DOMQUEUR — MESNIL-DOMQUEUR. Morning wet, but fine later	Arrivals 12th Capt G. N. Alison from Hptl
—	14th		Church Parade & Inspections. Day fine but dull.	13th 1 O.R. from Base (Signaller)

1875 Wt. W593/826 1,000,000 4/15 J.B.C. & A. A.D.S.S./Forms/C. 2118.

Army Form C. 2118

WAR DIARY
or
INTELLIGENCE SUMMARY
(Erase heading not required.)

Instructions regarding War Diaries and Intelligence Summaries are contained in F. S. Regs., Part II. and the Staff Manual respectively. Title Pages will be prepared in manuscript.

Page 21

Place	Date	Hour	Summary of Events and Information	Remarks and references to Appendices
MESNIL – DOMQUEUR.	15th		Training continued.	Departures.
	16th		Programme as before	16th C.Q.M.S. Whiting on leave, 1 OR to H.Q.M.
	17th			17 1 OR. to H.Q.M.
	18th		Training continued. Weather much improved. Brigade sports took place in the afternoon.	20 4 OR. to H.Q.M.
	19th		Training continued.	Arrivals.
	20th		Route-march. Route as under. MESNIL – FRANSU – DOMQUEUR – Moulin DE CRAMONT – Le MENAGE – CRAMONT – MESNIL. Capt Alison & 4 officers visited 4th Army School of Instruction to witness the final day.	15th 1 OR from H.Q.M. 17. 1 OR. from H.Q.M. 19th 2Lt H. E. BOYLE R. I. Fus. & M.G.C. from Base to complete establishment
Line of March.	21st		Company moved to billets in ARGENVILLERS near St. RIQUIER training area. Route as under, MESNIL – DOMLEGER. – CONTEVILLE S/Sea – YVRENCH – YVRENCHEUX – GAPENNES – ARGENVILLERS	

1875 Wt. W593/826 1,000,000 4/15 J.B.C. & A. A.D.S.S./Forms/C. 2118.

Army Form C. 2118

Instructions regarding War Diaries and Intelligence Summaries are contained in F. S. Regs., Part II. and the Staff Manual respectively. Title Pages will be prepared in manuscript.

Page 22

WAR DIARY
or
~~INTELLIGENCE SUMMARY~~
(Erase heading not required.)

Place	Date	Hour	Summary of Events and Information		Remarks and references to Appendices
ARGENVILLERS	MAY			Departures	
	22nd		Company training on S. RIQUIER training area	22nd 2 o.r. to Hptl.	
	23rd			25 1 o.r. to Hptl	
	24th		Brigade training	27 Lt C.R. BUCKH[illegible]	
	25th			2 o.r. on leave to U.K.	
	26		Company training.	30 3 o.r. on leave	
	27				
	29		Divisional training.	Arrivals.	
	30		Company training.	22nd 1 o.r. from Hptl.	
	31			24th 8 o.r. from Base.	
				1 o.r. from Hptl.	
				26th 1 o.r. from Base	
				1 o.r. from Hptl.	
				27th 1 o.r. from Hptl.	

1875 Wt. W593/826 1,000,000 4/15 J.B.C. & A. A.D.S.S./Forms/C. 2118.

10th Brigade.

4th Division.

10th BRIGADE.

MACHINE GUN COMPANY

J U N E 1 9 1 6

Confidential

WAR DIARY

of

10th Brigade Machine Gun Company

from June 1st 1916 to June 30th 1916

Volume ~~VI~~ 5

G. S. Allison Capt

Page 23

Instructions regarding War Diaries and Intelligence Summaries are contained in F. S. Regs., Part II. and the Staff Manual respectively. Title Pages will be prepared in manuscript.

WAR DIARY
or
~~INTELLIGENCE SUMMARY~~
(Erase heading not required.)

Army Form C. 2118

Place	Date	Hour	Summary of Events and Information	Remarks and references to Appendices
ARGENVILLERS	JUNE			Departure.
	1		Company training on St RIQUIER training area	7th Lt A Low & 2 O.R. on leave.
	2.		Divisional training.	
	3.		Company training.	Arrival.
YVRENCH	4.		Company moved to billets in YVRENCH. to be attached temporarily to 12th Infantry Brigade.	2nd 1 O.R. from base Reinforcements
	5.		Day devoted to work in billets. Weather shows signs of breaking	
	6.		Weather most unfavourable in morning. Company training in afternoon. Limbers included in training. Training of drivers appears to need much attention.	
	7		Tactical Exercise carried out according to scheme prepared by G.S. 4th Divn Company in attack Principles — open warfare.	

1875 Wt. W593/826 1,000,000 4/15 J.B.C. & A. A.D.S.S./Forms/C. 2118.

Page 26

Army Form C. 2118

Instructions regarding War Diaries and Intelligence Summaries are contained in F. S. Regs., Part II. and the Staff Manual respectively. Title Pages will be prepared in manuscript.

WAR DIARY
or
~~INTELLIGENCE SUMMARY~~
(Erase heading not required.)

Place	Date	Hour	Summary of Events and Information	Remarks and references to Appendices
YVRENCH	8 JUNE		Company training.	13th 3 o.r. on leave
Line of march	9th June		moved to temporary billets at GORGES Route CONTEVILLE — DOMLEGER — BEAUMETZ - GORGES.	9th Lt C.R. BUCKWORTH & 2 o.r. for leave
Line of march	10th		moved to temporary billets at BEAUVAL. Route FIENVILLERS — CANDAS — BEAUVAL	
Line of march	11th		moved to rejoin 10th Brigade in bivouac at BERTRANCOURT. Route - BEAUQUESNE - MARIEUX - AUTHIE - BERTRANCOURT.	
BERTRANCOURT	12th		} Company parades	
"	13th		} Normal routine.	

1875 Wt. W593/826 1,000,000 4/15 J.B.C. & A. A.D.S.S./Forms/C. 2118.

Page 25

Instructions regarding War Diaries and Intelligence Summaries are contained in F. S. Regs., Part II. and the Staff Manual respectively. Title Pages will be prepared in manuscript.

Map reference 57D NE. & SE 1: 20.000

WAR DIARY
or
~~INTELLIGENCE SUMMARY~~
(Erase heading not required.)

Army Form C. 2118.

Place	Date	Hour	Summary of Events and Information	Remarks and references to Appendices
BERTRANCOURT -MAILLY & trenches	14th		Company moved this day as under. H.Q. & Nos 1 & 3 sections to MAILLY-MAILLET. Nos 2 & 4 to trenches to relieve sections of 92nd & 86th Bde M.G. Companies respectively. Positions as under No 2 section TAUPIN Trench about K 33. b 4 6 SACKVILLE STREET " K 34 b 5 2 VALLADE Trench " K. 34 a 95 15 VALLADE " " K 34 d 2 6 No 4 section ELLES SQUARE " K 33 d 38 FORT HOYSTED " K 33 d 24. FIFTH AVENUE " Q 4 a 52 FOURTH AVENUE " Q 4 b 15 25	Departures & Arrivals Nil.

1875 Wt. W593/826 1,000,000 4/15 J.B.C. & A. A.D.S.S./Forms/C. 2118.

Army Form C. 2118.

Instructions regarding War Diaries and Intelligence Summaries are contained in F. S. Regs., Part II. and the Staff Manual respectively. Title Pages will be prepared in manuscript.

Page 26

Map reference: As for preceding page

WAR DIARY
or
INTELLIGENCE SUMMARY
(Erase heading not required.)

Place	Date	Hour	Summary of Events and Information		Remarks and references to Appendices
MAILLY-MAILLET Trenches	15		These three days were employed in working on the strengthening of ~~dug~~ shelters & emplacements in the line with a view to forthcoming operations.	Departures	
				18. 1 or to Hpl	
				20 1 or to Hpl	
"	16		These positions had been taken over in an unsatisfactory condition from the point of view of shelter from bombardment.	Arrivals	
			On the 17th Officers & N.C.O.s accompanied the Company	16 ~~to~~ Lt A. LOW from leave in U.K.	
"	17		Officer to view the German lines from an observation post.	17. 1 o.r. from leave in U.K.	
"	18		Nos 1 & 3 sections relieved Nos 2 & 4 sections in the line. Nos 2 & 4 sections returned to billets in MAILLY-MAILLET.	18 1 o.r. from base	
"	19		Work in line as for 15th–17th	21. 1 o.r. from leave in U.K.	
"	20		In addition Nos 2 & 4 sections provided parties nightly for work on the assembly trenches, deepening these		
"	21		& providing ladders & shelters for guns & gear.		

1875 Wt. W593/826 1,000,000 4/15 J.B.C. & A. A.D.S.S./Forms/C. 2118.

Instructions regarding War Diaries and Intelligence Summaries are contained in F. S. Regs., Part II. and the Staff Manual respectively. Title Pages will be prepared in manuscript.

Map reference 57 D NE & SE 1: 20000

WAR DIARY
or
~~INTELLIGENCE SUMMARY~~

(Erase heading not required.)

Army Form C. 2118.

Place	Date	Hour	Summary of Events and Information	Remarks and references to Appendices
MAILLY-MAILLET & Trenches	22nd		Work as for last three days.	
	23rd		Work as for 22nd.	Arrival 24th 10r. from base
			The following extract is taken from 10th Bde operation orders dated June 23rd with reference to forthcoming operations:—	
			"M. G. Company.	
			The 2 guns with each front line Bn (2nd Seaforth Highrs & 2nd R. Dublin Fus) will be with the outer flank platoons to bring converging fire across the front or to cover the flanks & will be under the orders of Battalion Commanders	
			The 8 guns in rear of front line Bns will take up positions East of 11th Bde objective to sweep the final objective with fire.	
			4 guns will go forward with Bde H. Q. after capture of final objective these 4 guns will be detailed 1 to each strong post	
			8 guns will take up positions in support about the line N. & S. through R. 1. Central covering the ground west of the final objective."	

1875 Wt. W593/826 1,000,000 4/15 J.B.C. & A. A.D.S.S./Forms/C. 2118.

Instructions regarding War Diaries and Intelligence Summaries are contained in F. S. Regs., Part II. and the Staff Manual respectively. Title Pages will be prepared in manuscript.

Map reference 57D NE TSE 1: 20000

Army Form C. 2118

WAR DIARY
or
~~INTELLIGENCE SUMMARY~~
(*Erase heading not required.*)

Place	Date	Hour	Summary of Events and Information	Remarks and references to Appendices
MAILLY-MAILLET Trenches	June 24th		Preliminary bombardment by our artillery. Long range machine gun fire opened on enemy approaches Gas released against German trenches at 10 p.m. Machine gun fire opened to cover the noise of escaping gas. Fire later directed behind German lines to keep enemy to his trenches ~~[illegible]~~ & to catch fugitives. Heavy hostile barrage put down on our trenches about K. 34 b & d. Our gun at K 34 d 2.6. narrowly escaped destruction.	Departures 24th 1 OR to Hospl 26th 1 OR to Hospl
	25th		Bombardment continued. Long range machine gun fire employed to prevent enemy repairing gaps in his wire cut by our artillery.	
	26th		2.30 a.m. Gas again directed against enemy trenches. Same programme adopted as on 24th. Barrage followed at 3.15 a.m.	

Instructions regarding War Diaries and Intelligence Summaries are contained in F. S. Regs., Part II. and the Staff Manual respectively. Title Pages will be prepared in manuscript.

Page 29

Army Form C. 2118.

WAR DIARY
or
~~INTELLIGENCE SUMMARY~~
(Erase heading not required.)

Map reference FRANCE Sheet 57D 1:40000
57D NE 1 & 2 1:20000

Place	Date	Hour	Summary of Events and Information	Remarks and references to Appendices
MAILLY-MAILLET & trenches	June 26	continued	Billets in MAILLY-MAILLET shelled. Nos 1 & 3 sections relieved from trenches by 11th Bde M.G. Coy. Company proceeded to billets at BERTRANCOURT to await the attack.	Arrivals & departures Nil.
BERTRANCOURT	27th		Bombardment continued. Rest in billets.	
"	28th		Bombardment continued. Attack postponed.	
"	29th		Bombardment continues. Rest in billets.	
"	30th		Company proceeded to position of assembly at 5 pm. as per Extract of 10th Bde operation order quoted below "M.G. Coy From BERTRANCOURT TO TENDERLOIN. Starting Point P.4.a.5.8. at 4.30pm. to march by gun teams from P.12 c.9.1"	

1875 Wt. W593/826 1,000,000 4/15 J.B.C. & A. A.D.S.S./Forms/C. 2118.

10th Brigade

4th Division

10th BRIGADE MACHINE GUN COMPANY

JULY 1916

WAR DIARY.

No 10 Company. Machine Gun Corps.

From. JULY 1st 1916.

To JULY 31st 1916.

Original Copy.

1/8/16

A. Low. Capt.
Comdg No 10. Company
M. G. Corps.

Army Form C. 2118

WAR DIARY
or
INTELLIGENCE SUMMARY
(Erase heading not required.)

Instructions regarding War Diaries and Intelligence Summaries are contained in F. S. Regs., Part II. and the Staff Manual respectively. Title Pages will be prepared in manuscript.

Page 30

Map Reference 57D NE & SE 1:2000

Place	Date	Hour	Summary of Events and Information	Remarks and references to Appendices
Trenches between SERRE & BEAUMONT-HAMEL	JULY 1		Company took part in offensive of 4th Division against the German line between SERRE & BEAUMONT HAMEL.	
			10th Brigade ordered to follow 11th Brigade through German front line & attack the Corps line on the front L 32 d 2 6 – R 2 b 3 0 approx	
			Company in assembly in Shelter 41 TENDERLOIN STREET reference Q 4 c 6 6	
		9 a.m.	2nd Seaforths & 2nd R. Dublin Fus advanced accompanied by 2 guns (No 2 section) under Lt J.M. Low & 2 guns under Lt C Malton (No 4 Section) respectively, in front line	
			Eight guns followed the leading battalions from left to right thus	
			2 guns (No 2 section) under Lt C.R. Buckworth on left	
			2 guns (No 1 section) under Lt H.H. Coltsworth	
			2 guns " " under Lt A.C. Potter	
			2 guns (No 4 section under Lt A. Low on right	
			4 guns (No 3) under Lt H. P. Barwood & 2/Lt H. E. Boyle remained in Bde reserve	

1875 Wt. W593/826 1,000,000 4/15 J.B.C. & A. A.D.S.S./Forms/C. 2118.

Instructions regarding War Diaries and Intelligence Summaries are contained in F. S. Regs., Part II. and the Staff Manual respectively. Title Pages will be prepared in manuscript.

Page 31

WAR DIARY
or
INTELLIGENCE SUMMARY
(Erase heading not required.)

Army Form C. 2118 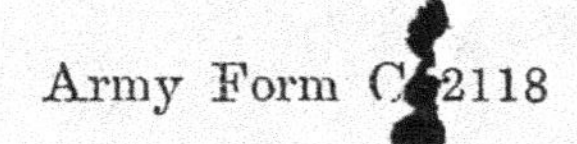

Place	Date	Hour	Summary of Events and Information	Remarks and references to Appendices
	July 1.		Lt J. M. Low was wounded & his guns disappeared, one was brought back by a party of Seaforths that night in a very shaken condition. Of the other guns only those under Lt Buckworth reached the German line at all. This officer behaved with great gallantry & got his guns into action in the German 3rd line: Lt. Col. Hopkinson 2nd Seaforths speaks most warmly of his work. The German machine guns appeared quite unaffected by the bombardment & absolutely cut the attack to pieces. At the close of the day we were ordered to consolidate our old front line. Seven guns were left in the line & the remainder withdrawn to Tenderloin. Total losses in material ——→ 4 Vickers guns destroyed 4. tripods 1 lost 3 destroyed about 50 belts & boxes lost & destroyed	CASUALTIES. Capt G. N. Alison Seaforth Highrs & M. G. C. Killed. Lt C. R. Buckworth Seaforths & M. G. C. Killed Lt J. M. Low. Seaforths. & M. G. C. missing. 2Lt COATSWORTH M. G. C. Wounded Other ranks Killed 2 Wounded 15. Missing 7.

1875 Wt. W593/826 1,000,000 4/15 J.B.C. & A. A.D.S.S./Forms/C. 2118.

Instructions regarding War Diaries and Intelligence Summaries are contained in F. S. Regs., Part II. and the Staff Manual respectively. Title Pages will be prepared in manuscript.

Page 31

Reference Map 57D NE. 1:20000

WAR DIARY
or
~~INTELLIGENCE SUMMARY~~
(Erase heading not required.)

Army Form C. 2118

Place	Date	Hour	Summary of Events and Information	Remarks and references to Appendices
	JULY			
Trenches	2nd		Orders received from Brigadier to withdraw half the Company from the line into Camp near MAILLY-MAILLET (P.17 b) Six guns were accordingly left in the line situated as under. 2 in VALLADE TRENCH S of SUCRERIE - SERRE Road 1 S of REDAN N. of WATLING STREET 1 in 4th AVENUE. 2 in reserve in TENDERLOIN STREET. Lt H. R BARWOOD & 2/Lt BOYLE remained in charge of these guns 2/Lt POTTER, 2/Lt MATSON with H.Q & seven guns in bivouac.	Arrivals 4th 50 O.R. reinforcements from Base
	3rd		Nothing to record. Everything was quiet in our front. Activity on our right was very visible.	
	4th		10th Brigade shifts its front to the right. Left battalion was relieved by a battalion of 12th Brigade, & moved to the right in relief of the left battalion 86th Brigade. Machine guns as a consequence were shifted. Positions now as under. 1 gun in 4th Avenue. 1 gun in PELK ST. 2 guns in LUNA TR 1 — ESSEX — 2 guns in AUCHONVILLERS defences	

1875 Wt. W593/826 1,000,000 4/15 J.B.C. & A. A.D.S.S./Forms/C. 2118.

Army Form C. 2118

WAR DIARY
or
~~INTELLIGENCE~~ SUMMARY
(Erase heading not required.)

Instructions regarding War Diaries and Intelligence Summaries are contained in F. S. Regs., Part II. and the Staff Manual respectively. Title Pages will be prepared in manuscript.

Page 32

Map Reference Sheet 57D NE 1: 20000

Place	Date	Hour	Summary of Events and Information		Remarks and references to Appendices
Trenches & Camp in P.17.	JULY			8th 2/Lt R.W.A. PAINTER & 2/Lt V.H. WILLOUGHBY from Base.	
	5th		Nothing to record. All remains quiet on our front.		
	6th		Fire kept up by machine guns & artillery on the German wire.		
	7th		Relief. Six guns from P.17 under 2/Lt POTTER & 2/Lt MATSON relieved the guns in the line under Lt BARWOOD. Positions remain the same.	10th Lt H.G. Smith from Base.	
	8th, 9th, 10th, 11th, 12th		No activity on our front. A show of activity was kept up. On 8th a smoke discharge was made. The personnel & guns in reserve at P.17 occupied in training. The draft from the base show an utter lack of any training or discipline.		
	13th		A display of activity was made on the night 13th 14th. At 10 p.m. gas was discharged apparently with success.		
	14th		At 3 a.m. a discharge of smoke was made, accompanied by one hour's concentrated bombardment & continuous fire by machine guns. Fire continued in bursts throughout the day.		

1875 Wt. W593/826 1,000,000 4/15 J.B.C. & A. A.D.S.S./Forms/C. 2118.

Army Form C. 2118

WAR DIARY
or
~~INTELLIGENCE SUMMARY~~
(Erase heading not required.)

Instructions regarding War Diaries and Intelligence Summaries are contained in F. S. Regs., Part II. and the Staff Manual respectively. Title Pages will be prepared in manuscript.

Page 33 Map Reference Sheet 57D N.E. 1: 20000

Place	Date	Hour	Summary of Events and Information	Remarks and references to Appendices
Trenches	15.		Lt BARWOOD, 2Lt BOYLE & eight guns from P.17. relieved guns in line. Positions now slightly altered & one added. ESSEX STREET moved to CRIPPS CUT. LANWICK STREET is now occupied. All guns now in line have good mined dug-outs & further accommodation is to be made.	16th 2Lt A. LAWDER from base. 18 Two O.R. (Corporals) from base
	16.		Nothing to record. O.C. 12th Bde M G Company & officers visited the line.	19 One O.R. (Sergeant) from base
BERTRANCOURT	17.		Company relieved by 12th Bde Company in the line & moved to billets & bivouacs in BERTRANCOURT.	20 20 O.R. from base
	18		Training in BERTRANCOURT	
LINE of MARCH	19		(as above)	
	20		Moved at 3pm. from BERTRANCOURT to billets in BEAUVAL. ROUTE LOUVENCOURT — VAUCHELLES — MARIEUX — BEAUQUESNE BEAUVAL.	

1875 Wt. W593/826 1,000,000 4/15 J.B.C. & A. A.D.S.S./Forms/C. 2118.

Army Form C. 2118

WAR DIARY
or
INTELLIGENCE SUMMARY
(Erase heading not required.)

Instructions regarding War Diaries and Intelligence Summaries are contained in F. S. Regs., Part II. and the Staff Manual respectively. Title Pages will be prepared in manuscript.

Reference map. Sheets 27 & 28 1:40000 & Sheet 28 NW. 1:20,000.

Place	Date	Hour	Summary of Events and Information	Remarks and references to Appendices
BEAUVAL	21.		Day spent quietly in view of late arrival in billets yesterday. Short inspection.	24th 1 O.R. reinforcement from base.
	22.		Nothing done in morning.	
	-23		Company entrained at CANDAS during night 22-23rd & morning 23rd. No 1 section entrained with 1/R. Warwick Regt.	
			No 4 " " " 2/Seaforth Highrs.	
			No 3 " " " 1/R. Irish Fus.	
			No 2 " " " 2/R. Dublin Fus.	
			Detrained at HOPOUTRE Station (POPERINGHE) & moved to billets in PROVEN.	
PROVEN	24th		} Nothing done except inspection, squad drill & some gentle training.	
"	25th		25th Company Officers proceeded to the trenches to take over from the 1st Guards Brigade M.G. Company.	

1875 Wt. W593/826 1,000,000 4/15 J.B.C. & A. A.D.S.S./Forms/C. 2118.

Instructions regarding War Diaries and Intelligence Summaries are contained in F. S. Regs., Part II. and the Staff Manual respectively. Title Pages will be prepared in manuscript.

Page 35

Army Form C. 2118

WAR DIARY
or
~~INTELLIGENCE SUMMARY~~

(Erase heading not required.)

Map reference sheet 28 NW. 2 1:10,000 & sheets 27 & 28 1:40000

Place	Date	Hour	Summary of Events and Information	Remarks and references to Appendices
PROVEN	26		Moved at 8am to temporary bivouac in A 30.b near Hospital Farm.	26th 1 OR to Hptl.
			Three section officers proceeded to line to take over sectors at 7.30	
			Company proceeded to relieve 1st Guards Bde M. G. Company at 8pm. Arrived at CANAL BANK about C 25 C 98 at 10 pm.	
			Relief complete by 2am 27th	
	27th		13 Guns in position. manned by half teams.	
			Company H. Q, & reserve half gun teams on CANAL BANK.	
			Accomodation on CANAL BANK. Good	
			in Trenches moderate to bad.	
			Positions as under	

Right Group (No 2 Section)	Centre Group (No 1 Section)	Left Group (No 3 Section)	Reserve Group (No 4 Section)
X Roads Farm (C 22 c 38)	Hill Top Farm (C 21 d 10)	FOCH FARM (C 20 b 1. ½)	WILSON FM East (C 26 d 58)
Threadneedle Street (C 21 d 30)	View Farm (C 21 c 98)	LONE WILLOW (C 20 b 81)	WILSON FM North C 26 c 31
X 9 Trench (C 27 a 74)	Sowthorpe Road (C 21 a 41)	KNARESBRO CASTLE (C 14 d 81)	CANAL BANK EAST
& one gun in reserve on CANAL BANK	B16 Trench (C 21 a 98)	CLIFFORD TOWERS (C 21 a 38)	1 in reserve

1875 Wt. W593/826 1,000,000 4/15 J.B.C. & A. A.D.S.S./Forms/C. 2118.

Instructions regarding War Diaries and Intelligence Summaries are contained in F. S. Regs., Part II. and the Staff Manual respectively. Title Pages will be prepared in manuscript.

36

Map reference 28NW2 1:10,000.

WAR DIARY
or
~~INTELLIGENCE SUMMARY~~
(Erase heading not required.)

Army Form C. 2118

Place	Date	Hour	Summary of Events and Information	Remarks and references to Appendices
Company H.Q. & reserve team on CANAL BANK about C25 central. 13 guns in line between C22c78 & C14d54	28th		all quiet nothing to report.	29th 2 or to Hptl.
	29th		One gun withdrawn from the line & added to brigade reserve on the CANAL BANK. Delete Gowthorpe Road C21a41 from list of positions occupied.	31st 2 or to Hptl Sick & 1 or wounded.
	30th		The positions in the line are mostly very weak. Only three can be visited by day, & thus supervision is very hard to exercise. Relief carried out.	
	31st		Gun in X Roads Farm destroyed by a heavy shell. Sentry wounded badly. Unfortunately the best man in No 2 Section had been picked out for promotion.	

1875 Wt. W593/826 1,000,000 4/15 J.B.C. & A. A.D.S.S./Forms/C. 2118.

10th Brigade.

4th Division.

10th BRIGADE

MACHINE GUN COMPANY

AUGUST 1 9 1 6

WAR DIARY.

No 10 Company M. G. Corps.

From ~~[illegible]~~ AUGUST I

To AUGUST 31.

Original Copy.

A. Lowe.
Capt
Comdg No 10 Company
M.G.C.

1/9/16

Army Form C. 2118.

page 37

WAR DIARY
or
~~INTELLIGENCE~~ SUMMARY.
(Erase heading not required.)

Instructions regarding War Diaries and Intelligence Summaries are contained in F. S. Regs., Part II. and the Staff Manual respectively. Title pages will be prepared in manuscript.

Map Reference 28 NW. 2 1:10000

Place	Date	Hour	Summary of Events and Information	Remarks and references to Appendices
Company H.Q. in reserve gun teams on Bank of YSER CANAL about C 2 S Central. 13 guns in position in the line from C 22 c 78 to C 14 d 4 5	AUGUST.			
	1st		Nothing to report. all quiet on our front.	2nd Lt O.R. to Hospital.
	2nd		O.C. 12 Company M.G.C. came up to take over the line.	
	3rd		12th Company M.G.C. arrived up to relieve this company at 11.30 pm. (1½ hours late)	
			Relief was consequently extremely late, last section not being relieved until 2 am (4th).	
			No 4 section on relief put 4 guns into position in reserve lines. 2 guns in L2 Work about C 23 b 24. 2 guns in L6 Work about C 16 a 09.	
			Lt W. L. Boyle remained in charge of these guns & was billeted in the CHATEAU, ELVERDINGHE.	
			The remainder of the company marched back to Camp in A 22 d on South of ELVERDINGHE — POPERINGHE road.	

Army Form C. 21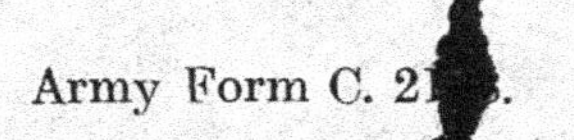.

WAR DIARY
or
~~INTELLIGENCE SUMMARY~~.
(Erase heading not required.)

Instructions regarding War Diaries and Intelligence Summaries are contained in F. S. Regs., Part II. and the Staff Manual respectively. Title pages will be prepared in manuscript. Map Reference sheet 28.

Place	Date	Hour	Summary of Events and Information	Remarks and references to Appendices
				Departures –
Camp	4th		Sections arrived in camp independently. First section (No1) at about 4. am	7th. 40 o.r. to Base.
at A22.d			No 3 about 4.30am. No2 about 5am & No 4 about 6am.	9th 1 o.r. to Hptl.
			First day spent in sleep & cleaning up of persons & gear.	
	5th		Inspection of all guns & gear by company officer. Parade under	Arrivals –
			Section officers – special attention to gun drill.	4th 1 o.r. from Hptl.
	6th		Demand received from Base for return of all surplus personnel	7th 1 o.r. from Hptl.
			40 other ranks were accordingly despatched on the following day.	
			Gun drill under section arrangements in the morning.	
			18 other ranks were attached to the company for instruction in	
			machine gun work, rations & discipline, this day.	
	7th		Training continued.	
	8th		on lines of previous day. Gun drill & elementary range practice.	
	9th		Gas alarm on morning of 9th at 12 m.n. Gas distinctly smelt & helmets put on.	
	10th		Company officers proceeded to line to take over from 11th Coy. M.G.C.	
			Line moderately satisfactory. But fourteen guns in action	
			This makes an intolerable strain upon the personnel	

P. 38

Army Form C. 2118.

WAR DIARY
or
~~INTELLIGENCE~~ SUMMARY.
(*Erase heading not required.*)

Instructions regarding War Diaries and Intelligence Summaries are contained in F. S. Regs., Part II. and the Staff Manual respectively. Title pages will be prepared in manuscript.

Reference Map Sheet 28 N.W. 2 1:10000

Place	Date	Hour	Summary of Events and Information	Remarks and references to Appendices
Coy H.Q. & reserves of No 1 section on Canal Bank, detachment at ELVERDINGE CHATEAU, & trenches.	11th		Company proceeded at dusk to line to relieve 11th Coy M.G.C. 3 section officers went on ahead to take over. Company arrived at Canal Bank at 10 p.m. Relief completed by 12 m.n. Positions as under. Left Group. No 2 section. P1. (C.7c. 2½ ½). P3. (C 7 c. 2. 2½). F2 (C 13 a 8.7.) F1. (C 13 b 1.4) Right Group No 3 section D1. C14 a 8.0. D3. C14 a 5.2. Y1. C 19 b 3.8½. N1. C [illegible] 20 a 0 5. Support Group No 4 section P3a B12 d 9½.3. O1 C 13 a 5.½. O2. C 13 a 2 3½. Z1 B 12 c 4½ 5. Reserve Group No 1 section X1 C19 a 1½ 2. X2. C19 a 2 5. 2 guns in reserve at Company H.Q. Coy H.Q. at Canal Bank about C19 c 6 6 [?]	Departures 11th 2 or to Hptl.

T2134. Wt. W708–776. 500000. 4/15. Sir J. C. & S.

Army Form C. 2118.

Instructions regarding War Diaries and Intelligence Summaries are contained in F. S. Regs., Part II. and the Staff Manual respectively. Title pages will be prepared in manuscript.

P 39

WAR DIARY
or
~~INTELLIGENCE SUMMARY~~.
(Erase heading not required.)

Map Reference 28 NW2. 1:10000

Place	Date	Hour	Summary of Events and Information	Remarks and references to Appendices
As for previous pages	12th – 18th		Nothing to report. Work done confined to cleaning up of positions & dugouts, most of which were not satisfactory. Range cards & Emplacement orders checked & altered where necessary (necessity arose in most positions). Trees & other obstructions cleared for field of fire apparently none had noticed these obstructions. Indirect fire opened almost nightly from X2. Target most popular was the road just South of Pilkem. Good results are thought to have been obtained on more than one occasion.	12th 1 or. accidentally injured. 14 1 or. to Hplt. Lieut Thompson wounded to Hplt. 15. 1 or to Hplt. 17. 1 or. to Hplt 1 or to UK. on leave 18 1 or. to Hplt.
			14th Lieut Thompson (Transport officer) wounded by shell fire at night.	
	19		Company Commander of 113th Coy M.G.C. came up to reconnoitre the line.	
	20th		Nothing to report during the day. 113th Coy. M.G.C. came up to relieve the Company at night. Four officers arrived up at 5pm to take over the line.	
			113th Company came up by train, limbers by march route.	

T2134. Wt. W708–776. 500000. 4/15. Sir J. C. & S.

WAR DIARY
or
~~INTELLIGENCE SUMMARY.~~

Army Form C. 2118.

Instructions regarding War Diaries and Intelligence Summaries are contained in F. S. Regs., Part II. and the Staff Manual respectively. Title pages will be prepared in manuscript.

P 40

Map Reference Sheet 28 N.W. & 28 NE → 1:20000

(*Erase heading not required.*)

Place	Date	Hour	Summary of Events and Information	Remarks and references to Appendices
	August			
Trenches	20		113th Coy arrived extremely late about 11 p.m. Relief began in good order but was not completed until very late. The last gun team (No 2 section) did not get limbered up till 3.30 am 21st.	
	21st		The Company marched back to billets in M. Camp on POPERINGHE – WATOU road. Last section arrived in 7.30 am.	
	22nd		Company officers & O.C. Nos 1 & 4 sections proceeded to line to reconnoitre new trenches. Visited H.Q. of 9th Canadian Company M.G.C. at I.21 b 8.½. 2/Lt POTTER proceeded to left Group. 2/Lt PAINTER to Right Group.	

T2134. Wt. W708–776. 500000. 4/15. Sir J. C. & S.

Instructions regarding War Diaries and Intelligence Summaries are contained in F. S. Regs., Part II. and the Staff Manual respectively. Title pages will be prepared in manuscript.

41

Map Reference Sheets 28 NW. & NE 1:20000

Army Form C. 2118.

WAR DIARY
or
~~INTELLIGENCE SUMMARY.~~
(*Erase heading not required.*)

Place	Date	Hour	Summary of Events and Information	Remarks and references to Appendices
Trenches	23		Company proceeded to relieve 9th Canadian M.G.C.	
			Nos 1 & 4 sections + one gun No. 3 section proceeded to line, (by train to YPRES ASYLUM, thence by march route)	
			No 2 & No 3 (less one gun) proceeded to camp in G.11.d.	
			No 1 Section (Left Group) — S.P. 12 I 24 d ½ 4; Halifax I 24 c 7½ 2½; Rudkin House A. I 24 c ½ 2½; — B. I 24 c 2½ 3; Square wood I 29 b 9.7; Officers' dugout at Halifax	
			No 4 Section Right Group — Fosse Way I 23 c 2 ½; Knoll Farm I 29 a 8½ 6½; Metropolitan Tr. I 29 a 6½ 1; S.P. 10 I 28 b 5 6.; Officers dugout at Metropolitan	
			The positions in Left Group constructed on good lines, i.e. tunnelled dugouts in conjunction with open emplacements. Those in right group not so good with exception of Metropolitan which has a tunnelled dugout & open emplacement	

T2134. Wt. W708–776. 500000. 4/15. Sir J. C. & S.

Army Form C. 2118.

WAR DIARY
or
~~INTELLIGENCE SUMMARY.~~
(Erase heading not required.)

Instructions regarding War Diaries and Intelligence Summaries are contained in F. S. Regs., Part II. and the Staff Manual respectively. Title pages will be prepared in manuscript.

Page 42

Map Reference BELGIUM 28 N.W. 1:20000

Place	Date	Hour	Summary of Events and Information	Remarks and references to Appendices
TRENCHES near				
ZILLEBEKE.	24th & 25th		Nothing to report from trenches. All quiet on our front.	29th Lt H. G. Smith to Hospital sick
	26th		Heavy shelling on front line about 8. am. near MOUNT SORREL & OBSERVATORY RIDGE (from about I 30 b 4.5 to about I 24 d 6 3)	
	27th		No 3 section relieved three guns No1 section in Left Group.	
			Five positions now occupied by 4 guns No 3 section & 1 gun No1.	
	28th		No 4 section relieved No. 2 section in Right Group.	
			Three reserve guns No1 section brought up into Brigade reserve at ZILLEBEKE BUND about I 21 b 2.3.	
	29th		O.C. 1st Australian M.G. Coy & 3 officers arrived at 9 a.m. to reconnoitre the line. Heavy rain late in the day.	
	30th		Very heavy rain all day. All quiet on our front.	
	31st		Company relieved from line by 1st Australian M.G. Coy.	

T2134. Wt. W708–776. 500000. 4/15. Sir J. C. & S.

10th Brigade.

4th Division.

10th BRIGADE

MACHINE GUN COMPANY

SEPTEMBER 1 9 1 6

No 10 Company. Machine Gun Corps.

WAR DIARY

ORIGINAL COPY.

From September 1st 1916

to September 30th 1916.

4/10/16

A. Lowe
Major
Comdg 10th Coy. M.G.C.

Vol 8

4

page 43

Instructions regarding War Diaries and Intelligence Summaries are contained in F. S. Regs., Part II. and the Staff Manual respectively. Title pages will be prepared in manuscript.

WAR DIARY
or
~~INTELLIGENCE~~ SUMMARY.
(Erase heading not required.)

Army Form C. 2118.

Map Reference
BELGIUM Sheet 28 NW 1:20000 + Sheet 27 1:40,000

Place	Date	Hour	Summary of Events and Information	Remarks and references to Appendices
	SEPTEMBER			
ERIE CAMP	1.		Company arrived into Camp by sections, last section	Arrivals.
G. 11. C			arriving at 4.45 am from the trenches before	1/ 2 o.r. from Base
			ZILLEBEKE	6/ 2 o.r. (N.C.O's) from
	2		Day spent in care & cleaning of guns & ammunition	Base
	3.		Sunday. Church parades & inspections.	8/ 2/Lt R. Stock from
L CAMP	4.		Company moved to billets in L Camp.	115th Company M.G.C.
	5		Company training in following subjects.	(Transport officer)
	6		Gun drill. Advanced drill. Indication of targets.	
	7		Mechanism. Stoppages.	Departures
	8		Training is much needed at present.	3/ 1 o.r. to 11th Company CQMS Whiting (promoted CSM)
	9		Tactical schemes for officers & N.C.O.s in afternoon	8/ Lt Smith to U.K. struck
	10		Sunday. Church parades & inspections.	off strength.
	11.		Training continued on lines of previous	9/ 1 o.r. to Hptl.
	12		work. Very decided improvement visible	
	13		almost at once. Training of last drafts from	
	14		base is very incomplete	

T2134. Wt. W708—776. 500000. 4/15. Sir J. C. & S.

Army Form C. 2118.

Instructions regarding War Diaries and Intelligence Summaries are contained in F. S. Regs., Part II. and the Staff Manual respectively. Title pages will be prepared in manuscript.

WAR DIARY
or
~~INTELLIGENCE SUMMARY.~~

(Erase heading not required.)

Maps BELGIUM 27 1:40000 FRANCE AMIENS 17 1:100,000

Place	Date	Hour	Summary of Events and Information	Remarks and references to Appendices
	SEPTEMBER			
L CAMP	15		Training continued	
"	16		Orders received to entrain at PROVEN.	
			Parade 8 pm. marched to PROVEN. Entrained 10.54 pm	19th Cor. L Hqr
Dittemove	17		Detrained at LONGEAU near AMIENS at 12.30 pm.	2nd
			Marched to billets in RAINNEVILLE.	2Lt. Lt H.C.
RAINNEVILLE	18		Training at RAINNEVILLE	Denson from Base
	19		Company practised in training for offensive operations	19th Cor. from Hpl.
	20		Weather fine & very suitable for training	
	21		Country admirable for training	
	22			
Dittemove	23.		Brigade moved at 8 am. from RAINNEVILLE to CORBIE.	
			Route CARDONETTE - ALLONVILLE - QUERRIEUX - PONT NOYELLES - LA NEUVILLE - CORBIE.	
			Brigade carried out a tactical exercise between ALLONVILLE & ~~CORBIE~~ QUERRIEUX. Company took part in this.	

Army Form C. 2118.

WAR DIARY
or
~~INTELLIGENCE SUMMARY.~~
(Erase heading not required.)

Instructions regarding War Diaries and Intelligence Summaries are contained in F. S. Regs., Part II. and the Staff Manual respectively. Title pages will be prepared in manuscript.

Page 45

Map. AMIENS. 17. 1:100000

Place	Date	Hour	Summary of Events and Information	Remarks and references to Appendices
	Sept			
On the move	24		Moved to SAILLY-LE-SEC. Route CORBIE - Road to MERICOURT - SAILLY.	28th 1 O.R. to Hospl
			Brigade carried out a tactical exercise on ground South of MERICOURT.	28th Lt G. N. A. Galt from Base.
SAILLY - LE-SEC.	25th 26th 27th 28th		Tactical training continued. Especial attention paid to consolidation of positions & to range-firing.	
			Physical training also had attention.	
To DAOURS.	29th		Route - VAUX - CORBIE - LANEUVILLE - DAOURS	
DAOURS	30th		Weather bad No training possible.	

T2134. Wt. W708-776. 500000. 4/15. Sir J. C. & S.

10th Brigade.

4th Division.

10th BRIGADE.

MACHINE GUN COMPANY

OCTOBER 1 9 1 6

Vol 9

Oct

WAR DIARY

No 10 Company, Machine Gun Corps.

Original Copy

From October 1st

– October 31st 1916.

A. Low
Major
Comdg No 10 Coy
M. G. C.

3/11/16

WAR DIARY
or
~~INTELLIGENCE SUMMARY.~~
(*Erase heading not required.*)

Army Form C. 2118.

Instructions regarding War Diaries and Intelligence Summaries are contained in F. S. Regs., Part II. and the Staff Manual respectively. Title pages will be prepared in manuscript.

Page 46

Map AMIENS 17 1:100000 & ALBERT Combined Sheet 1:40000 57D SE 57C SW. 62D NE 62C NW.

Place	Date	Hour	Summary of Events and Information	Remarks and references to Appendices
OCTOBER.				
DAOURS.	1. 2	}	Weather very bad. Very little training possible. Consolidation only practised.	1st 10r & 1Kptl
	3.		Weather again very bad. Brigade tactical in afternoon on ground N. of DAOURS & East of DAOURS - PONT NOYELLES Road.	5th 20r. & Kptl 6th
	4.		Weather extremely wet. Nothing done.	10r & Kptl.
	5.		Brigade Tactical Exercise at FRANVILLERS. Company marched off at 7 a.m. & returned to billets at 6 p.m. Attack on trenches flagged to represent LE TRANSLOY.	
	6.		Gentle training carried out.	
	7.		Company moved to billets in MÉAOLTE — Route AUBIGNY - FOUILLOY - CORBIE - MERICOURT - TREUX - VILLE-sur-ANCRE — MÉAOLTE.	
	8.		Moved to MANSEL CAMP South of MAMETZ above F 17 b	

T2134. Wt. W708–776. 500000. 4/15. Sir J. C. & S.

Page 47.

Instructions regarding War Diaries and Intelligence Summaries are contained in F. S. Regs., Part II. and the Staff Manual respectively. Title pages will be prepared in manuscript.

Maps ALBERT Combined sheet. 57C SW. 1:20,000.

WAR DIARY
or
~~INTELLIGENCE SUMMARY~~.
(Erase heading not required.)

Army Form C. 2118.

Place	Date	Hour	Summary of Events and Information	Remarks and references to Appendices
Moved to Line	9th		The Company moved into the line to relieve the 168th M. G. Company. in line E. of LESBOEUFS. Company disposed as under. 11th L.or. wounded	
			Coy. H.Q. & Nos 1 & 2 sections near the QUARRY GUILLEMONT about S 24 d 8.2.	
			No 3 Section 2 guns & 2/Lt. T. A. LAUDER in dugouts North of LESBOEUFS about N 34 c 4.1.	
			1 gun in THISTLE TR. about N 34 d 1.1.	
			1 gun in BURNABY TR about T. 4 b. 5.8.	
			No 4 Section 2 guns & 2/Lt R. W. A. Painter about T. 9 b. 6.1.	
			2 guns in GERMAN TR about T. 5 b 5.2.	
			Transport at F. 17 d 9.2.	
	10th 11th		Line Comparatively quiet. Nothing to report.	

Army Form C. 2118.

WAR DIARY
or
~~INTELLIGENCE~~ SUMMARY.
(Erase heading not required.)

Instructions regarding War Diaries and Intelligence Summaries are contained in F. S. Regs., Part II. and the Staff Manual respectively. Title pages will be prepared in manuscript.

Maps ALBERT Combined Sheet 57 c SW.

Place	Date	Hour	Summary of Events and Information	Remarks and references to Appendices
TRENCHES near LESBOEUFS	12th		Brigade attacked German line on the front N 34 d central to T 5 central. 1/R. Irish Fus & 1/R. Warwick Regt. attacked. Machine Guns in line were detailed to proceed forward to strong points as required. & to fire on appearance of suitable targets. No action was taken by the company as the attacks did not succeed.	12th 1 o.r. wounded.
			Gun withdrawn from BORNABY TRENCH to the Embankment about N 34 c 5.0	13th 1 o.r. wounded
	13th		Nos 1 & 2 sections relieved Nos 3 & 4 sections in the line. Relief complete by 11.30 pm.	12th 1 o.r. from Hptl.
			Nos 3 & 4 returned to Company H.Q.	
	14th		Brigade made a night attack on DEWDROP TRENCH (N.34 d 8.6. – T 5 a 38) & GUNPITS strong point (T 5 a 3.5) 2nd Seaforths attacked. To support this attack Lt POTTER with two gun teams & one gun proceeded to BORNABY TR.	

T2134. Wt. W708–776. 500000. 4/15. Sir J. C. & S.

Page 49

Instructions regarding War Diaries and Intelligence Summaries are contained in F. S. Regs., Part II. and the Staff Manual respectively. Title pages will be prepared in manuscript.

Maps ALBERT Combined sheet

WAR DIARY
or
~~INTELLIGENCE~~ SUMMARY.

(*Erase heading not required.*)

57c S.W. 1:20000.

Army Form C. 2118.

Place	Date	Hour	Summary of Events and Information	Remarks and references to Appendices
TRENCHES. E of LESBOEUFS.	14th		before ZERO (Zero 6pm.) with a view to crossing to GUNPITS when captured, to consolidate & use any German machine guns.	14th 2Lt G.N.A. Catto to M.G. School.
			Lt Malson with two guns proceeded to the Northern End of the new trench WARWICKSHIRE TRENCH (later re-named ANTELOPE TR). about T 5 c 87. with a view to establishing a horizontal barrage behind Gun pits to prevent counter attack from trench about T 5 a 98.	15th 2Lt T.A. Landen to Hospital (Sick).
			The attack was not successful.	16th 1 o.r. killed in action.
	15th 16th		Line comparatively restful. Except for heavy shelling on both sides.	17th 4 o.r. wounded
	17th		Company relieved by 11th M.G. Company at dusk. Relief complete by 1 am 18th.	14th 1 or from Hptl.
			Company went into reserve dugouts about A 3 d central	17th 3 o.r. from Base
			Total casualties for week 1 o.r. killed 8 o.r. wounded (1 o.r. died of wounds)	

T2134. Wt. W708—776. 500000. 4/15. Sir J. C. & S.

Army Form C. 2118.

WAR DIARY
or
~~INTELLIGENCE SUMMARY.~~
(Erase heading not required.)

Instructions regarding War Diaries and Intelligence Summaries are contained in F. S. Regs., Part II. and the Staff Manual respectively. Title pages will be prepared in manuscript.

Page 50 Maps. 57 C. S.W.

Place	Date	Hour	Summary of Events and Information	Remarks and references to Appendices
Dugouts about A 30	18th		Company arrived in dugouts by 4 a.m.	
	19th		Nothing to report	
	20th		Nothing to report. A working party of 50 men found by company	20th 1 o.r. wounded
	21		In reserve	26th 1 o.r. to Hptl sick
	22		Nothing to report	
	23		Company moved at 7 am. to a point just N. W. of GUILLEMONT QUARRY. in reserve to attack by 11th & 12th Brigades. No guns or teams were required to move forward, & the company bivouacked in this place for the night.	23rd 3 o.r. reinforcements 25th 5 o.r. reinforcements
	24th		Moved off at 9.45 a.m. to SANDPITS CAMP, just South of LE CARCAILLOT Xroads. E of MÉAULTE.	
	25		In rest at SANDPITS Camp. Weather very cold & rainy.	
	26			
	27			

page 51

Army Form C. 2118.

WAR DIARY
or
~~INTELLIGENCE SUMMARY~~

(*Erase heading not required.*)

Instructions regarding War Diaries and Intelligence Summaries are contained in F. S. Regs., Part II. and the Staff Manual respectively. Title pages will be prepared in manuscript.

Reference Maps. (a) ALBERT Combined sheet (c) ABBEVILLE – 1:100000. (b) AMIENS. 17. 1:100.000.

Place	Date	Hour	Summary of Events and Information	Remarks and references to Appendices
	OCTOBER			
SANDPITS – CORBIE	27th		Moved to CORBIE at 11 am. via MÉAULTE – VILLE – TREUX – MERICOURT. arrived in billets 5 pm	28th 1 or. promoted C.Q.M.S. of 11th Coy. (Sergt Pollock)
CORBIE	28th, 29th		Billets in CORBIE.	29th 1 or. from Base reinforcement
	30th		Entrained at CORBIE at 4 pm. detrained at AIRAINES (see DIEPPE sheet. 1:100,000). at 8.45 pm & marched via WANEL – SOREL – LIERCOURT to billets at BELLIFONTAINE. arrived in billets at 12.30 am	
BELLIFONTAINE	31.		Billets.	

T2134. Wt. W708–776. 500000. 4/15. Sir J. C. & S.

10th Brigade.

4th Division.

10th BRIGADE.

MACHINE GUN COMPANY

NOVEMBER 1 9 1 6

Army Form C. 2118.

6

WAR DIARY
or
~~INTELLIGENCE SUMMARY.~~
(*Erase heading not required.*)

Instructions regarding War Diaries and Intelligence Summaries are contained in F. S. Regs., Part II. and the Staff Manual respectively. Title pages will be prepared in manuscript.

Page 52

Reference Map. ABBEVILLE 1:100000

18th Mly Coy

Place	Date	Hour	Summary of Events and Information	Remarks and references to Appendices
	NOVEMBER.			
BELLIFONTAINE	1		Billets. Sections fired on 25x range	
ONICOURT.	2		Moved at 9.45 am via BAILLEUL - LIMEUX - HUPPY & billets in ONICOURT.	
	3.		Training around ONICOURT.	
	4.			
	5.		Church parades & inspections.	
	6.			
	7.		Training. Programme as under.	
	8		1 or 2 sections on range daily.	8/ 3 o.r. on leave.
	9		2. hours gun drill. 1 hour mechanism	
	10		1 hour Company drill. Physical Exercises &	11/ 1 o.r. to Hospital.
	11		Games from 3 pm on.	
	12.		Usual Sunday programme.	

T2134. Wt. W708—776. 500000. 4/15. Sir J. C. & S.

Army Form C. 2118.

WAR DIARY
or
~~INTELLIGENCE SUMMARY.~~
(Erase heading not required.)

Instructions regarding War Diaries and Intelligence Summaries are contained in F. S. Regs., Part II. and the Staff Manual respectively. Title pages will be prepared in manuscript.

Page 53 ABBEVILLE Map 1:100,000.

Place	Date	Hour	Summary of Events and Information	Remarks and references to Appendices
	NOVEMBER.			
ONICOURT	13.		Training continued. on lines of last week's programme	
	14		1 hour advanced gun drill	14/ Lt. C. Malton & 2 o.r. on leave.
	15		Route march on 17th.	
	16		Practice for gunners at night twice a week.	22/ 6 o.r. on leave.
	17			
	18			
	19		Sunday programme.	
	20			
	21		Training programme as for last week.	21/ Lt. A. Lander struck off strength.
	22			
	23			26/ Lt. W. E. Boyle struck off strength
	24			
	25			25/ Lt. W. M. Palmer from Base.
	26		Sunday.	26/ 1 o.r. to Hptl.

T2134. Wt. W708-776. 500000. 4/15. Sir J. C. & S.

Page 54

Instructions regarding War Diaries and Intelligence Summaries are contained in F. S. Regs., Part II. and the Staff Manual respectively. Title pages will be prepared in manuscript.

WAR DIARY

or

~~INTELLIGENCE SUMMARY.~~

(Erase heading not required.)

Army Form C. 2118.

ABBEVILLE 1:100 000

Place	Date	Hour	Summary of Events and Information	Remarks and references to Appendices
	NOVEMBER			
ONICOURT	27		Training Continued.	27/ Lt H. P. Barwood & 3 or on leave
	28			28/ 1 or. to H'pt
	29		29th Route March.	28/ Lt A. C. Neale from Base.
	30			
	1			

T2134. Wt. W708–776. 500000. 4/15. Sir J. C. & S.

10th Brigade.

4th Division.

10th BRIGADE.

MACHINE GUN COMPANY

DECEMBER 1 9 1 6

Vol XI War Diary

10th M. G. Company.

Original War Diary for the month of December 1916.

2/1/17.

[signature] Major
Cmd^s 10th M. G. Coy.

Instructions regarding War Diaries and Intelligence Summaries are contained in F. S. Regs., Part II. and the Staff Manual respectively. Title pages will be prepared in manuscript.

WAR DIARY
or
INTELLIGENCE SUMMARY.
(Erase heading not required.)

Army Form C. 2118.

P 55

ABBEVILLE 1:100000 ALBERT Combined Sheet 1:40000

Place	Date	Hour	Summary of Events and Information	Remarks and references to Appendices
	DECEMBER			
ONICOURT	1		Transport moved from ONICOURT at 1 pm. for MERILESSART on the way to the line. Training therefore ceases.	
"	2.		Nothing to record.	
Line of March.	3.		Company moved off at 8am. for OISEMONT Entrained at OISEMONT at 6pm. Detrained at MERICOURT-L'ABBE at 12 mn.	
"	4.		Marched to SAILLY-LE-SEC arriving there at 3.30 am. Moved on at 11am. for Camp 112 North of BRAY sur SOMME.	
Camp 112.	5.		Major Low. Lt Matson & 2Lt Painter proceeded to line South of SAILLISEL to reconnoitre line held by 79th French Regiment. Major Low returned same night	
Camp 112.	6.		Company moved to Camp 107 (BILLON WOOD) S. of MARICOURT Lt Matson & 2Lt Painter returned from line.	K. R. Barnard Capt for O.C. 181 Tun Coy RE [?]

T2134. Wt. W708–776. 500000. 4/15. Sir J. C. & S.

Army Form C. 2118.

WAR DIARY
or
~~INTELLIGENCE SUMMARY.~~
(Erase heading not required.)

Instructions regarding War Diaries and Intelligence Summaries are contained in F. S. Regs., Part II. and the Staff Manual respectively. Title pages will be prepared in manuscript.

P. 56 Ref. Map. ALBERT. & COMBLES 1:10,000.

Place	Date	Hour	Summary of Events and Information	Remarks and references to Appendices
Camp 107	7		Company moved to MARICOURT WOOD Camp	
	8.		Company moved at 3 pm. for the line to relieve 79th French Regiment	10th/ 2 or killed in action 2 or wounded
			Sixteen guns in action. 8 in front line four in support line & four in reserve line	11th/ 1 or wounded 1 or to Hptl buried by shell
Trenches S of SAILLISEL	0		Coy. H.Q. at [illegible] U 20 a 0.5	
	9.		Very heavy rain. Nothing to record. Trenches in a bad way. No shelter available for the men. Line very quiet.	13th/ 8 or to Hptl 1 or from Hptl 14th/ 9 or to Hptl
	10.		Nos 2 & 4 sections moved out of line to dugouts. No 4 to dugouts S of FREGICOURT. No 2 to cellars in COMBLES	15th/ 1 or to Hptl
	11.		Nothing to record	
	12.		Nothing to record. Work on Rt. Section H.Q.	
	13.		O.C. No 11 M.G. Coy reconnoitred the line.	
	14		Nothing to record.	

K. B. Harwood Capt. for OC 10th M.G. Coy

T2134. Wt. W708—776. 500000. 4/15. Sir J. C. & S.

p57

Map COMBLES 1:10000

Instructions regarding War Diaries and Intelligence Summaries are contained in F. S. Regs., Part II. and the Staff Manual respectively. Title pages will be prepared in manuscript.

WAR DIARY
or
INTELLIGENCE SUMMARY.
(Erase heading not required.)

Army Form C. 2118.

Place	Date	Hour	Summary of Events and Information	Remarks and references to Appendices
Trenches.	15		Company relieved by No 11 M. G. Coy. Relief complete 11. 30 p.m.	15th 4 o.r. for Hptl.
Camp 16	16.		Company moved by lorry to Camp 16.	17th 2 o.r. for Hptl.
"	17		No training possible.	18th 4 o.r. for Base
"	18		Conditions very bad.	19th 2 o.r. for Base
"	19		Time devoted to cleaning up of persons	22nd 2 o.r. to Hptl.
"	20		guns ammunition & equipment.	
"	21		Major Lowe & officers reconnoitred line	
"	22		held by 12th Inf Bde	
	23		Company relieved 12th M. G. Coy.	
			(a) Six guns in front & support trenches	
			(b) four guns in positions of readiness U. 14 c 11	
			(c) 2 guns in dugouts near MOUCHOIR COPSE T. 24. b 55	
			(d) 2 guns in dugouts at T. 29 d 88	
			(e) 2 guns in cellars in COMBLES	
			Coy H.Q. near MOUCHOIR COPSE.	
			(a) four of No 2. two of No 3	
			(b) No 4 Section (c) No 3 (d & e) No 1 Section	

H. B. Barwood Capt
for O.C. 10 MG Coy

T2134. Wt. W708—776. 500000. 4/15. Sir J. C. & S.

Page 58

Army Form C. 2118.

WAR DIARY
or
~~INTELLIGENCE SUMMARY.~~
(Erase heading not required.)

Instructions regarding War Diaries and Intelligence Summaries are contained in F. S. Regs., Part II. and the Staff Manual respectively. Title pages will be prepared in manuscript.

Map reference see previous page

Place	Date	Hour	Summary of Events and Information	Remarks and references to Appendices
Trenches.	24		Nothing to report. Line quiet. No fire	29/ 2Lt H.C.
	25		opened by any guns except short bursts	Dennison to Hpl.
	26		to test firing of guns.	2Lt to Hptl.
	27			
	28			
	29		Officers of 25th M.G. Coy came up to reconnoitre	
	30		Company relieved by 25th M G Coy. Relief of	
			Company complete by 6.50 pm.	
			Company returned by lorries to Camp 111	
			N of BRAY	
Camp 111	31.		Day spent in cleaning up.	

H. P. Barnard Capt
for OC 16 MG Coy

T2134. Wt. W708—776. 500000. 4/15. Sir J. C. & S.

4th Division

10th Infantry Bde

10th M. G. C.

January to August

1917

Vol 12

WAR DIARY

10th Machine Gun Company

for the month of January 1917

Original Copy.

A. Low
Major
Comdg 10th M. G. Company

2/2/1917

Page 1

Instructions regarding War Diaries and Intelligence Summaries are contained in F. S. Regs., Part II. and the Staff Manual respectively. Title pages will be prepared in manuscript.

WAR DIARY
or
INTELLIGENCE SUMMARY.
(Erase heading not required.)

Army Form C. 2118.

Ref. ALBERT Combined Sheet 1/40,000
BOUCHAVESNES 1/10,000.

Place	Date	Hour	Summary of Events and Information	Remarks and references to Appendices
1917	Jan			
Camp 111 L2a	1st		Major A. Law to U.K. on leave – Company resting & cleaning up after the trenches.	1st Major Law to leave to UK 1 or. from Base
	2nd } 3rd 4th 5th 6th		Training in & around Camp 111. Weather not very favourable for this.	3rd 1 or. to Hospital 4th 1 or. to Div. Reserve Coy. 6th 1 or. to Hospital 1 or. to Sanitation Course 8th 2 ors to Hospital
	7th		Divisional Xmas Day. Company had their Xmas Dinner – a good meal was provided through the Company Comforts Fund & officers subscriptions	9th 2 ors from Hospital 10th 1 or. from Div. Reserve Coy. 12th 2/Lt. H.C. Denson struck off strength.
	8th to 13th }		Training continued.	14th 2 ors. to M.G. Course. 15th 1 off. (2/Lt. Painter) & 2 ors. to leave to UK. Lt. F.P. Cobden from base 1 or. to Corps Rest Station.
	14th		Ptes. KANE, FINNEGAN & FITZGERALD presented with Military Medal ribbons by the Corps Commander. The three awards date back to YPRES 1915.	
	15th		Line to be taken over from the French reconnoitred by Capt. H.? Barwood, Lt. A.C. Potter & 2/Lt. V.H. Willoughby.	A. Law Major.

T2134. Wt. W708–776. 500000. 4/15. Sir J. C. & S.

Page 2.

Instructions regarding War Diaries and Intelligence Summaries are contained in F. S. Regs., Part II. and the Staff Manual respectively. Title pages will be prepared in manuscript.

WAR DIARY
or
INTELLIGENCE SUMMARY.
(Erase heading not required.)

Army Form C. 2118.

Ref. ALBERT Combined Sheet 1/40000
BOUCHAVESNES - 1/10000

Place	Date	Hour	Summary of Events and Information	Remarks and references to Appendices
	January.			
Camp 111	16		Moved from Camp 111 to billets in SUZANNE. Snow fell during night 16/17	16th 1 or. from Hospital
SUZANNE	17		Took over line from C21 b 2 6 to C 26 b 0 7, relieving 18th	2 ORs. from base
Trenches			French Division. 8 Guns (Nos. 1 & 3 Sections) in front line	17th 1 or. to leave to U.K
C21 b 2 6			system - 8 guns & H.Qrs. in reserve in ROAD WOOD	19th Major A Law from leave.
to C 26 b 0 7			C 25 a. Guns and ammunition for front line were carried	Lt. G. A. Brooke from base.
Transport at			on 20 pack animals to C 20 a 6 3 - one horse only	21st Lt A.C. Potter to No 19
MOULIN DE FARGNY			breaking down	M.G. Coy to be 2-in-C.
A 29 a central	18th		Normal trench routine - heavy frost - very cold.	1 or. to No 19 Coy
	19th		" " " . Major A Law returned from leave	2/Lt R. Stock to U.K on
	20th		Nos 2 & 4 Sections relieved Nos 1 & 3 in the line	four months leave overseas.
	21st		Routine normal. Weather still very cold. Some snow.	
	22nd		O.C. 98th M.G. Coy & one officer visited Company H.Q. to reconnoitre the line. O.C. 11th M.G. Coy also visited Company H.Q.	
	23rd		Company relieved on the right by 8 guns & H.Qrs of No 98 Coy on the left by two guns of No 11 Company. Relief reported complete at 10.30 pm. To billets in SUZANNE	A Law Major.

T2134. Wt. W708—776. 500000. 4/15. Sir J. C. & S.

Army Form C. 2118.

WAR DIARY
or
~~INTELLIGENCE~~ SUMMARY

Instructions regarding War Diaries and Intelligence Summaries are contained in F. S. Regs., Part II. and the Staff Manual respectively. Title Pages will be prepared in manuscript.

Page 3.

(Erase heading not required.)

Map Reference ALBERT. Combined Sheet 1/40,000.

Place	Date	Hour	Summary of Events and Information	Remarks and references to Appendices
	JANUARY			
SUZANNE.	24		Moved from SUZANNE to billets in BRAY arriving there 2.30pm.	Arrivals & departures
BRAY.	25.		Resting in billets. Bombs dropped in BRAY about midnight 24-25th & at 8 pm 25th	
Camp 112.	26.		Resting in billets. Nothing to report.	
	27		Company moved to Camp 112. Weather still very hard. Huts very old.	
	28		Church parades & inspections.	
	29 30. 31		Training. Time devoted as follows ½ hour daily to Physical Training 3 hours " to Gun drill. Stoppages & Mechanism. 1 hour " to Company drill	

A. Ross.
Major.

2449 Wt. W14957/M90 750,000 1/16 J.B.C. & A. Forms/C.2118/12.

Vol 13

WAR DIARY of

10th M. G. Coy.

From 1 - 28 February 1917.

Original Copy

1/3/17

A. Low.
Major.
Comdg 10th M.G. Coy.

Army Form C. 2118.

WAR DIARY

or

~~INTELLIGENCE~~ SUMMARY.

(Erase heading not required.)

Instructions regarding War Diaries and Intelligence Summaries are contained in F. S. Regs., Part II. and the Staff Manual respectively. Title pages will be prepared in manuscript.

Page 5.

Map for Reference ALBERT Combined Sheet 1:40000.

Place	Date	Hour	Summary of Events and Information	Remarks and references to Appendices
	FEBRUARY 1917			Arrivals & Departures
Camp 112.	1		Training continued. ½ hour Physical Training. 2 hours Gun drill. 1 hour Stoppages and mechanism.	1st 16155. C.S.M. Wylie appointed to Commission 1/ Kings Own R. L. Regt proceeded to take up his duties.
	2.		Company moved to huts & billets in SUZANNE. Move off 2. p.m. Major Low. Lt Willoughby, & 2 selected N.C.Os. attended a demonstration at 52nd Squadron R.F.C.	2nd/ 1 o.r. to Hospl. 3rd/ 1 o.r. to Hospl.
SUZANNE	3		Training continued as on lines of Feby 1.	
	4.		Church Parades & Inspections.	
	5.		Training as for Feby 1. Major Low, Lt Willoughby, & 3 N.C.Os. attended for attachment to 'P' Battery (A.A.) for instruction in anti-aircraft work.	

2353 Wt. W2544/1454 700,000 5/15 D. D. & L. A.D.S.S./Forms/C. 2118.

Army Form C. 2118.

WAR DIARY
or
~~INTELLIGENCE SUMMARY.~~
(Erase heading not required.)

Page 6 Instructions regarding War Diaries and Intelligence Summaries are contained in F. S. Regs., Part II. and the Staff Manual respectively. Title pages will be prepared in manuscript.

Map for Reference ALBERT Combined Sheet 1:40000 & BOUCHAVESNES 1:10000.

Place	Date	Hour	Summary of Events and Information	Remarks and references to Appendices
	FEBRUARY			
SOZANNE	6		As for Feby 5. 2 officers & 3 NCOs were again attached to R.AA Bty	Arrivals & Departures 10th 2/Lt P. McKinnee M.L.I. & MGC from base.
"	7		As for preceding day.	
"	8		On 8th Major Down & 3 other officers proceeded to	
"	9		ANDOVER PLACE to reconnoitre line held by 24th MGC	
	10		Company proceeded by march route to relieve 24th M.G. Coy. Move off from SOZANNE 10 a.m. via MARICOURT CURLU CORNER & MAUREPAS. Coy. H.Q. at ANDOVER C.13.a 6.4. & rear HQ at ANGOSTURA B16 d 8.8. 4 guns of No 3 Section in action forward RUTH position C 15 a 8 9. RACHEL " C 8 d 6 3 ROSE 1 " C 8 b 7 0. " 2 " C 8 d 4 4.	

2353 Wt. W2544/1454 700,000 5/15 D. D. & L. A.D.S.S./Forms/C. 2118.

Instructions regarding War Diaries and Intelligence Summaries are contained in F. S. Regs., Part II. and the Staff Manual respectively. Title pages will be prepared in manuscript.

Page 7

WAR DIARY
or
~~INTELLIGENCE SUMMARY.~~
(Erase heading not required.)

Army Form C. 2118.

Maps for Reference ALBERT Combined Sheet 1:40000 + BOUCHAVESNES 1:10000 also COMBLES 1:10000

Place	Date	Hour	Summary of Events and Information	Remarks and references to Appendices
Trenches 1st Line Transport at Y Wood.	10th		No 1 Section 2 guns on BETHUNE Road ROGER & REBECCA. C 8 c 3½ 3 2 guns A.A. at C 7 c 4 7 No 4 Section 4 guns in Intermediate Line No 2 section 1 gun forward RUPERT C 2 d 5.1½ 3 guns at ANGOSTORA Relief complete at 6.45 pm.	Departures & Arrivals 11th Capt H.P. Barwood R. Irish Fus & M.G.C. to Base Depot on appointment. 13/ 1 or to Hpl 14/ 1 or to Hpl 14th/ 2 or from Base.
	11th 12th 13th 14th		Ordinary trench routine. Nothing to report Weather very hard & frosty.	

2353 Wt. W2544/1454 700,000 5/15 D. D. & L. A.D.S.S./Forms/C. 2118.

Army Form C. 2118.

WAR DIARY
or
INTELLIGENCE SUMMARY.
(Erase heading not required.)

Instructions regarding War Diaries and Intelligence Summaries are contained in F. S. Regs., Part II. and the Staff Manual respectively. Title pages will be prepared in manuscript.

Page 8.

Maps for Reference
ALBERT Combined sheet 1:40000
BOUCHAVESNES 1:10000
COMBLES - 10000.

Place	Date	Hour	Summary of Events and Information	Remarks and references to Appendices
Trenches	15.		Machine Guns cooperated with Artillery bombardment. 2 sections 11th M. G. Company were attached to assist 10th Coy. Fire was opened in bursts between 3.50 pm & 4.20 pm. Targets - trenches in U 26 d. (1 section) trenches in C 3 b & C 4 a (3 sections. 3,000 rounds of ammunition were fired per gun in this half-hour. It was noticed that immediately on machine gun fire opening the enemy barraged our front line East of RANCOURT, opposite of PIERRE VAAST WOOD	Departures & Arrivals
	16 17 18		Normal trench routine. Frost breaking & mud becoming very bad.	
	19		Two new guns added at C 9 b 2.5 for defence of spur in C 9 b. (RICHARD & REGINALD)	

#353 Wt. W2544/1454 700,000 5/15 D. D. & L. A.D.S.S./Forms/C. 2118.

Army Form C. 2118.

WAR DIARY
or
~~INTELLIGENCE~~ SUMMARY.
(Erase heading not required.)

Instructions regarding War Diaries and Intelligence Summaries are contained in F. S. Regs., Part II. and the Staff Manual respectively. Title pages will be prepared in manuscript.

Page 9

Maps for Reference ALBERT Combined Sheet 1:40000 BOUCHAVESNES 1:10000

Place	Date	Hour	Summary of Events and Information	Remarks and references to Appendices
Trenches	20.		Two Guns ROBERT & ROSE I relieved by No 119 M.G. Company. O.C. 23rd M.G. Coy came up to reconnoitre our line	Departures & Arrivals
	21.		Company relieved by 23rd M.G. Coy. Relief complete at 7.45 pm. Company moved by lorry to Camp 12 North of CHIPILLY. Bad roads rendered lorries very slow. Last section in	21st C.S.M. [illegible] transferred from 61st M.G. Coy joined on appointment
	22.		No 1 Section at 5.15 am.	26th 1 OR to Hptl
	23 24		} Time spent in cleaning new Equipment & Guns.	
	25		Church parades	
	26.		Training. Programme as under. 7.30 - 8 am Physical Drill 9 - 12.30 pm Gun Drill & Mechanism 2 - 3 pm Company Drill	

2353 Wt. W2544/1454 700,000 5/15 D. D. & L. A.D.S.S./Forms/C. 2118.

Army Form C. 2118.

Page 10

WAR DIARY
or
~~INTELLIGENCE~~ SUMMARY.

(*Erase heading not required.*)

Instructions regarding War Diaries and Intelligence Summaries are contained in F. S. Regs., Part II. and the Staff Manual respectively. Title pages will be prepared in manuscript.

Map for Reference AMIENS Sheet 17

Place	Date	Hour	Summary of Events and Information	Remarks and references to Appendices
Camp 12.	Feb 27.		Training – as for 26th	
	Feb 28		As for 26th – firing on range added to programme	
			Departures 28th 3 OR to Hospl. Arrivals 28th 4 OR from Base	

2353 Wt. W2544/1454 700,000 5/15 D. D. & L. A.D.S.S./Forms/C. 2118.

Vol 14

WAR DIARY

10th M. G Company

Original Copy.

March 1st - 31st 1917

2/4/17.

A. Low
Major
Comdg 10th M.G. Coy.

Page 12.

Instructions regarding War Diaries and Intelligence Summaries are contained in F. S. Regs., Part II. and the Staff Manual respectively. Title pages will be prepared in manuscript.

Maps for Reference
AMIENS Sheet 17 1:100000 LENS Sheet 11 1:100000

WAR DIARY
or
~~INTELLIGENCE SUMMARY.~~
(Erase heading not required.)

Army Form C. 2118.

Place	Date	Hour	Summary of Events and Information	Remarks and references to Appendices
	MARCH 1917			
Camp 12. CHIPILLY	1		Training continued 1 section on ranges. other sections Gun drill – advanced drill – mechanism. 2-3 pm. Company Drill.	3/1 OR to 14 H.p.H. 1 OR from 70th Fd Ambulance 3/ 2 OR to 14 H.p.H.
	2.		as for 1st.	
	3.		as for 1st.	
	4		Company moved to CORBIE via main BRAY-CORBIE road. Moved from Camp 12. 12 noon arrived CORBIE 3.30 pm.	
	5.		Company moved off at 10. am & proceeded via PONT-NOYELLES – QUERRIEU – MOLLIENS-au-BOIS – VILLERS-BOCAGE to billets in MONTONVILLERS	
	6.		Company moved via TALMAS to billets in BEAUVAL	[illegible] Major

A5834 Wt. W4973/M687 750,000 8/16 D. D. & L. Ltd. Forms/C.2118/13.

Army Form C. 2118.

WAR DIARY
or
~~INTELLIGENCE SUMMARY.~~
(*Erase heading not required.*)

Instructions regarding War Diaries and Intelligence Summaries are contained in F. S. Regs., Part II. and the Staff Manual respectively. Title pages will be prepared in manuscript.

Map for Reference LENS Sheet 11 1 : 100,000

Page 13,

Place	Date	Hour	Summary of Events and Information	Remarks and references to Appendices
MN	7		Moved from BEAUVAL via DOULLENS to billets in REMAISNIL	7/ 1 or to Hptl
REMAISNIL	8, 9, 10		These three days were spent mainly in improving billets & checking & completing deficiencies in Equipment & clothing	9/ 1 or from Hptl 2 or to C.C.S. 1 or transferred to 48th M.G. Coy.
	11		Church parades & inspections	11/ 1 or from base
	12, 13, 14, 15, 16, 17		Training – Programme as follows. 7.30–8. am. Physical training. 9am – 12.30 pm Shooting on range. Gun drill. Advanced drill. Mechanism. 2–3 pm Platoon & Company drill.	12/ 1 or from base 14/ 1 or to Hptl 17/ 1 or from Hptl
	18.		Church parades inspections.	
	19.		Training on lines of previous week.	
	20		Moved from billets at 2 hours notice. Company moved to Embussing point X roads ½ mile N.E of BOFFLES. Thence by bus to OURTON 8 miles N.E of St. POL. Transport moved to ECOIVRES via FLERS.	20/ 1 or from Hptl. 1 or to Cadet School G.H.Q.

[illegible signature]

Page 14

Instructions regarding War Diaries and Intelligence Summaries are contained in F. S. Regs., Part II. and the Staff Manual respectively. Title pages will be prepared in manuscript.

WAR DIARY
or
~~INTELLIGENCE~~ SUMMARY.
(Erase heading not required.)

Army Form C. 2118.

Map Reference LENS. No 11. 1:100 000

Place	Date	Hour	Summary of Events and Information	Remarks and references to Appendices
OURTON	21		Day spent in rest. Transport marched at 2 pm.	22/ 11 or. for Base. 1 or. from Hptl.
	22.		Training continued.	23/ 2 or. to C.C.S.
	23.		" "	24/ 2 or for Base
	24		" "	28/ C. S. M. T. White from 106 M. G. Coy
	25		Church parades & inspection	
	26–31		Training continued. Programme on Schedules as previous week.	
	28		Major ..., Lt Painter & Lt Willoughby proceeded to line N. E of ARRAS to reconnoitre.	

2353 Wt. W2544/1454 700,000 5/15 D. D. & L. A.D.S.S./Forms/C. 2118.

W.O. 95/1505

10th Company M.G.C.

ORIGINAL.

WAR DIARY

MONTH APRIL 1917

C. Matson Lt
for Major
Commanding,
10th M.G. Coy

18/5/17

Army Form C. 2118.

WAR DIARY
or
~~INTELLIGENCE SUMMARY.~~
(Erase heading not required.)

Instructions regarding War Diaries and Intelligence Summaries are contained in F. S. Regs., Part II. and the Staff Manual respectively. Title pages will be prepared in manuscript.

AGE 15

Maps for Reference
LENS sheet 11 1:100000
51 B.N.W. 1:20.000

Place	Date	Hour	Summary of Events and Information	Arrivals & Departures	Remarks and references to Appendices
OURTON	APRIL 1		Sunday. Church parades & Inspections	1st Lt G.S. ALLAN, 2nd Lt HAMMETT E, 2nd Lt BUTLER H.H.	Reinforcements from Base a.h.
	2		Training continued as throughout previous week		a.h.
	3		9-12.30. 2 hours advanced drill	1st 2. O.R. to C.C.S.	a.h.
	4		1 hours Gun drill	2nd 1. O.R. to C.C.S.	a.h.
	5		½ hour mechanism	4th 1. O.R. Transfer to R.E.	a.h.
	6		2-3 Company Drill or Judging distance	5th 1. O.R. to C.C.S.	a.h.
CHELERS	7		Company moved off at 10.30am via La COMTÉ – HOUVELIN – MAGNICOURT – HERLIN Le Vert – to CHELERS – where it billetted the night. Final preparations made to go into action.	6th Lt F.P. COBDEN to hospital	a.h.
	8/		Company moved at 5 pm. via TINQUES – SAVY Crossroads 1 mile E of HAUTE AVESNES to X Hulments, 1000 x S of Ecoivres arriving there at 10.30 pm. Rested there the night		a.h.

a.h. [illegible] major

Instructions regarding War Diaries and Intelligence Summaries are contained in F. S. Regs., Part II. and the Staff Manual respectively. Title pages will be prepared in manuscript.

page 16

WAR DIARY
or
INTELLIGENCE SUMMARY.
(Erase heading not required.)

Army Form C. 2118.

Maps LENS 11. 1:100000
51 B N W 1: 20000

Place	Date	Hour	Summary of Events and Information	Remarks and references to Appendices
Line E of ARRAS north of La Scarpe	9		Monday. Z day. Zero hour 5.30 am Reveillé 4.30 am No 4 Section moved off at 5.30 am to assembly area with 11th M.G. Coy at G 8 d 5 3 H.Q. & Nos 1, 2, & 3 Sections moved off at 6.30 am to 10th Bde Assembly area at G 8 a 2 4 arriving there at 9 am A hot dinner was served at assembly area H.Q. & three sections moved off at 12.10 pm. No 4 Section having already moved off at 10.30 am. For this operation the Company was organised in three gun sections the 4th gun with team being left with 1st Line Transport. The following officers proceeded into action Major A. Low. Lieut C. Ralston Lt Painter & Lt Butler (No 4 Section) 2/Lt Neale & 2/Lt Hammett (No 1 Section) 2/Lt Palmer (No 2 Section) & 2/Lt Brooke (No 3 Section) The following officers remained at transport Lt G.S. Allan 2/Lt Willoughby (on leave) & 2/Lt R. McKinnie (Transport Officer) The task of 10th Bde was to consolidate Brown line (German third system) the final objective of 9th Divn while 11th & 12th Brigades captured German 4th System from H 11 b 9 3 to river Scarpe.	Arrivals & departures 9th 2nd Lt H.H. BUTLER Wounded 11th 5 OR Casualties in Action

A. Low

A5834 Wt. W4973/M687 750,000 8/16 D. D. & L. Ltd. Forms/C.2118/13.

page 17.

Instructions regarding War Diaries and Intelligence Summaries are contained in F. S. Regs., Part II. and the Staff Manual respectively. Title pages will be prepared in manuscript.

WAR DIARY
or
~~INTELLIGENCE SUMMARY.~~
(Erase heading not required.)

Army Form C. 2118.

Maps for Reference
51 B N.W. 1:20,000.

Place	Date	Hour	Summary of Events and Information	Remarks and references to Appendices
Line			& then HYDERABAD Redoubt & FAMPOUX & establish a Green Line from A18 Central to E Corner of HYDERABAD Redoubt, thence to Point du Jour. No 4 Section under Lt R. W. A. Painter was ordered to push his Section forward of Brown Line to cover left flank of 11th Brigade. This section moved from assembly area with 11th Brigade as stated & after a halt at the Blue – (Railway) Line moved forward to position about H4 c 1515. Coming into action here, Lt Painter was able to engage a German 105 mm battery (range 1500x) in action S of Point du Jour – GAVRELLE Road. (Probable position of battery H4 b 93) & accounted for some of the gun crews as they retired to GAVRELLE. This section also obtained other targets ~~[illegible]~~ one party of Germans moving towards GAVRELLE from the South being forced to scatter. Later however No 4 sect was compelled to retire by our own artillery which firing short inflicted casualties. New position taken up at H9 b 89. Meanwhile the rest of the Company carried out programme as arranged, moving from assembly area at 12 noon, via S. Catherine, St Nicholas, S Laurent Blangy to Blue Line arriving	R Hornsby [?]

A5834 Wt. W4973/M687 750,000 8/16 D. D. & L. Ltd. Forms/C.2118/13.

p. 18.

Instructions regarding War Diaries and Intelligence Summaries are contained in F. S. Regs., Part II. and the Staff Manual respectively. Title pages will be prepared in manuscript.

WAR DIARY
or
~~INTELLIGENCE SUMMARY.~~
(Erase heading not required.)

Map 57 B N W 1:20000

Army Form C. 2118.

Place	Date	Hour	Summary of Events and Information	Remarks and references to Appendices
Line			here at 2.15 pm. Six pack animals per section moved guns etc at 3 pm forward of Blue line to ravine running N at H16 a 7 3. whence sections moved up to positions prearranged. Company H.Q. H8 d 15. No 2 Section HQ & 1 gun H9 a 3 6 No 3 Section HQ & 1 gun H8 d 95. No 1 section HQ & 1 gun at H14 b 84 other guns at H9 b 20. H9 b 25. H9 c 51 H15 a 59. H15 a 84 H15 c 63. Touch was established at 4 pm with No 4 Section A reserve of belt boxes & rations were brought to Coy H.Q. by pack animals. A quiet night was spent.	ah
	10th		Consolidation carried on until 3 pm when the Company was warned to be ready to move on to Green Line should patrols of 11th & 12th Brigades make progress of Cavalry possible. Patrols of these brigades were driven back. Night spent in same positions as previous day.	A Kow[illegible] Major

A5834 Wt. W4973/M687 750,000 8/16 D. D. & L. Ltd. Forms/C.2118/13.

page 19.

Instructions regarding War Diaries and Intelligence Summaries are contained in F. S. Regs., Part II. and the Staff Manual respectively. Title pages will be prepared in manuscript.

WAR DIARY
or
~~INTELLIGENCE SUMMARY~~.

(*Erase heading not required.*) Map. 51 B NW 1:20000

Army Form C. 2118.

Place	Date	Hour	Summary of Events and Information	Remarks and references to Appendices
Line	11th		Brigade ordered to attack & capture 1st objective road ROEUX - GAVRELLE from I7a43 - Chateau I13d21. attack on first objective to be carried out by 2nd Seaforths on left & 1 R. Irish Fus on right No 3 section ordered to advance with Irish Fus & fire on PLOUVAIN Zero 12 noon. Household Battn on left & 1 R. Warwick Regt on right to advance through leading Bns starting at 12.10 pm & establish line PLOUVAIN - GREENLAND HILL to road at I7b07. 11th Bde forming a flank thence through line at I7a28 to HYDERABAD Redoubt. No 4 section which had been relieved at Point du Jour by S.A. M.G. Coy. at 9 am to advance with 1 R. War. R & Nos 1 & 2 with Household Bn & consolidate on Greenland Hill when taken. Coy H.Q. established at H16d23.	[signature] Major

p. 20

Page 20.

Instructions regarding War Diaries and Intelligence Summaries are contained in F. S. Regs., Part II. and the Staff Manual respectively. Title pages will be prepared in manuscript.

Reference Map 51 B. N.W 1: 20000

Army Form C. 2118.

WAR DIARY
or
~~INTELLIGENCE SUMMARY.~~
(Erase heading not required.)

Place	Date	Hour	Summary of Events and Information	Arrivals & Departures	Remarks and references to Appendices
Line E of FAMPOUX.	11th		This attack was not successful & no more ground was gained. Touch was not established with all sections until midnight. Major Low visited No 3 section (about H 18 a 01) about 3pm & No 4 section later (about H 17 b 69).		
	12th		Orders received about 2am. to withdraw whole company to 4th System & to open fire from ridge N of FAMPOUX on ROEUX – GAVRELLE road where held by the enemy, to cooperate with attack by 9th Division in afternoon. Major Low & Lieut. Mason visited all sections between 3am & 5am (No 2 section about H 17 a 98 & No 1 about H 11 d 76) & gave necessary orders for withdrawal. Company concentrated in PARROT & PEBBLE trenches in H 16 d. No 2 section went into position at once & fired at intervals on road between Inn X roads in I 7 a & Station X roads in I 13 a	2 OR Casualties in Action	

A. Low Major

A5834 Wt. W4973/M687 750,000 8/16 D. D. & L. Ltd. Forms/C.2118/13.

Instructions regarding War Diaries and Intelligence Summaries are contained in F. S. Regs., Part II. and the Staff Manual respectively. Title pages will be prepared in manuscript.

page 21

Maps 57 B NW 1:20000

WAR DIARY
or
~~INTELLIGENCE SUMMARY.~~
(Erase heading not required.)

Army Form C. 2118.

Place	Date	Hour	Summary of Events and Information	Arrivals & Departures	Remarks and references to Appendices
Line	12.		Attack made by 9th Divn in evening unsuccessful		AL
	13.		Company remained in reserve. One section (No 1) placed at disposal of 11th Bde for harassing fire on Enemy trenches around INN & X roads in I 4 a. Guns in position in LEMON TRENCH. in H 10 d.		AL
	14		No 4 section relieved No 1 in LEMON TRENCH. Company still held in reserve.	1. OR. to C.C.S	AL
	15		As 14th		AL
	16		Company relieved 11th M. G. Coy this night. Dispersal as follows:—	1. OR. Transfer to R.E.	
			Coy H.Q. at H 11 c 19 LUCID TRENCH		
			No 4 section remained in same position in H 10 d.		
			No 2 – in HUDSON TR. H 11 a & b.		
			2 guns No 1 – – HYDERABAD Redoubt H 11 b		
			2 guns No 3 in gun pit H 10 b 8 4.		
			1 gun No 1 & 1 gun No 3 in gun pits H 5 a O 2.		AL

A5834 Wt. W4973 M687 750,000 8/16 D. D. & L. Ltd. Forms/C.2118/13.

page 22

Instructions regarding War Diaries and Intelligence Summaries are contained in F. S. Regs., Part II. and the Staff Manual respectively. Title pages will be prepared in manuscript.

WAR DIARY
or
~~INTELLIGENCE SUMMARY.~~
(*Erase heading not required.*)

Army Form C. 2118.

51 B NW 1:20000

Place	Date	Hour	Summary of Events and Information	Arrivals/Departures	Remarks and references to Appendices
Line N of FAMPOUX	16.		1 Section 12th M.G. Coy placed at disposal of 10th Bde placed in HERON TR. H. 11. a		A.H.
	17 18 19		Nothing of importance to record. Weather very severe. More or less heavy shelling daily on both sides. Few casualties. Continuous harassing fire maintained on hostile trenches.	1. OR. Wounded	A.H.
	20.		10th Brigade relieved by 63rd Bde this night. 10th M.G. Coy was not relieved but remained in line to support proposed attack by 37th Divn.	1. OR. Wounded	A.H.
	21 22		Nothing to record. Much increased artillery activity. Weather distinctly improved.	21st 1. OR. to C.C.S. 2 OR. Wounded	
	23.		37th Divn attacked line of ROEUX – GAVRELLE road objective Greenland Hill & W edge of PLOUVAIN in conjunction with 51st Divn on right & XIII Corps on left. 10th M.G. Coy assisted by its fire advance to ROEUX – GAVRELLE road.	22nd 2nd Lt ABEL C. J. – KINGSHAW. R. W. – WALKER H. W. } Reinforcements from Base; Sgt LAMONT – commissioned – to M.G.C. Base Depot.	A. Howling(?)

A5834 Wt. W4973/M687 750,000 8/16 D. D. & L. Ltd. Forms/C.2118/13.

Army Form C. 2118.

Instructions regarding War Diaries and Intelligence Summaries are contained in F. S. Regs., Part II. and the Staff Manual respectively. Title pages will be prepared in manuscript.

page 23 51B NW 1: 20000

WAR DIARY
or
~~INTELLIGENCE SUMMARY.~~
(Erase heading not required.)

LENS Sheet 11
1 : 100,000

Place	Date	Hour	Summary of Events and Information	Arrivals & departures	Remarks and references to Appendices
Line N of FAMPOUX	23		Zero 4.30 a.m. Fire ceased at Zero + 45 minutes. Company remained in positions in readiness to move forward or continue fire if required. Attack only partially successful. & line established along & just E of ROEUX GAVRELLE road.		AH.
	24		Company ordered to withdraw from line at 12 noon & move to 1st line transport W of St. Nicholas. Sections arrived in field at 6 p.m. & bivouacked for the night. In connection with attachment of 10th M.G. Coy to 37th Divn following most favourable report was later received from G.O.C. 37th Divn through XVII Corps & 4th Divn dated 27.4.17.		AH Major

A5834 Wt. W4973/M687 750,000 8/16 D. D. & L. Ltd. Forms/C.2118/13.

WAR DIARY
or
INTELLIGENCE SUMMARY.
(*Erase heading not required.*)

Army Form C. 2118.

Instructions regarding War Diaries and Intelligence Summaries are contained in F. S. Regs., Part II. and the Staff Manual respectively. Title pages will be prepared in manuscript.

page 24 LENS sheet 11 1:100000

Place	Date	Hour	Summary of Events and Information	Remarks and references to Appendices
S. Nicholas	24.		Addsd XVII Corps 1/ I should like to bring to notice the good work done by 10th M. G. Company during operations of 23rd & 24th April 1917. 2/ It rendered valuable assistance in forming the Divnl M. G. Barrage for the attack of the 37th Divn on 23rd inst. & cooperated in repelling the counter-attacks delivered by the enemy on the afternoon 23rd & morning of 24th April. 3/ The Company under the command of Major Low was placed at my disposal when 37th Divn took over from 4th Divn & actually completed a period of 16 days in the line before it was withdrawn on the evening of 24th instant. 4/ Officers & men were under constant shell fire & it speaks well for their courage & powers of endurance that they should have been so efficient after such a long & trying spell of duty in a heavily shelled area H.Q. 27.4.17. Sgd. H. B. Williams Major General Commanding 37th Divn	

A5834 Wt. W4973 M687 750,000 8/16 D. D. & L. Ltd. Forms/C.2118/13.

Army Form C. 2118.

WAR DIARY
or
~~INTELLIGENCE SUMMARY.~~
(*Erase heading not required.*)

Instructions regarding War Diaries and Intelligence Summaries are contained in F. S. Regs., Part II. and the Staff Manual respectively. Title pages will be prepared in manuscript.

page 25. Map. LENS. Sheet 11. 1:100,000

Place	Date	Hour	Summary of Events and Information	Arrivals & Departures	Remarks and references to Appendices
S. NICHOLAS.	25		Orders received at 2 a.m. to proceed by lorry to SARS-les-BOIS.		
DENIER.			6 Lorries at Town Major's Office S. NICHOLAS at 11.20 am (1 hour late) Company Embussed. Billeting area changed En route to DENIER. Transport moved off at 9 a.m.		
			Company arrived about 3.30 pm. & transport about ½ hour later. Billets very bad indeed. It was decided to move the company to AMBRINES on following day.		[signature]
DENIER - AMBRINES	26		Company move to AMBRINES.	2 OR from Hospital.	[signature] Town Major

A5834 Wt. W4973 M687 750,000 8/16 D. D. & L. Ltd. Forms/C.2118/13.

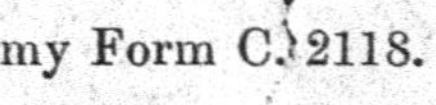

Army Form C.2118.

WAR DIARY
or
INTELLIGENCE SUMMARY.
(Erase heading not required.)

Instructions regarding War Diaries and Intelligence Summaries are contained in F. S. Regs., Part II. and the Staff Manual respectively. Title pages will be prepared in manuscript.

Page 26

Place	Date	Hour	Summary of Events and Information	Arrivals & departures	Remarks and references to Appendices
AMBRINES	27		Day devoted to overhauling & cleaning up of guns & equipment, & fitting belts etc. Orders received at mid-day to move to Y huts on following day.		
	28.		Company moved at 10 am. by march route to Y Huts N of ETRUN. via. VILLERS - SIR - SIMON. IZEL - les - HAMEAU - HERMAVILLE.		
	29		Company moved via S. POL - ARRAS road to billets in ARRAS. moving from Y. Huts at 11am & arriving in billets at 2 pm. Major Low! Lt Painter, & 2Lt Willoughby went on to reconnoitre line held by 101st Brigade E of FAMPOUX South of ARRAS - DOUAI railway. From I 13 d 55 - I 19 c 14.	1. O.R. to C.C.S.	

[illegible] Major

Instructions regarding War Diaries and Intelligence Summaries are contained in F. S. Regs., Part II. and the Staff Manual respectively. Title pages will be prepared in manuscript. 51 B N.W 1:20000

page 27

Army Form C. 2118.

WAR DIARY
or
~~INTELLIGENCE SUMMARY.~~
(Erase heading not required.)

Place	Date	Hour	Summary of Events and Information	Remarks and references to Appendices
ARRAS + trenches	30		Morning & early afternoon spent in rest. Company fell in & moved off at 5.30 pm via St. NICHOLAS – St. LAURENT-BLANGY – ATHIES – FEUCHY – thence along ARRAS - DOUAI railway to Coy. H.Q. arriving there at 9 pm. Sections at 5 minutes interval. Here guides were supposed to be waiting but considerable delay was caused by their being scattered. Company was finally disposed as under. H.Q. & 1 section in Sunken road (LANCER LANE) & Embankment in H 23 b. 3 sections in Sunken Road in H 24 b (CROUP TRENCH. The guns here were sited for no apparent purpose CROUP allowing a field of fire of ~~[illegible]~~ approximately 25°	

A. [illegible] Major

A5834 Wt. W4973/M687 750,000 8/16 D. D. & L. Ltd. Forms/C.2118/13.

Army Form C. 2118.

WAR DIARY
or
INTELLIGENCE SUMMARY.

(Erase heading not required.)

Instructions regarding War Diaries and Intelligence Summaries are contained in F. S. Regs., Part II. and the Staff Manual respectively. Title pages will be prepared in manuscript.

28. 57 B N W 1:20,000

Place	Date	Hour	Summary of Events and Information	Remarks and references to Appendices
Trenches	30		They were spaced at even intervals along this ~~trench~~ sunken road on taking over from 101st Coy., for no apparent reason & no gun was able to open direct fire on German trenches. Relief complete at 11.30 pm.	A. Lowe Major

A5834 Wt. W4973 M687 750,000 8/16 D. D. & L. Ltd. Forms/C.2118/13.

WAR DIARY.

10th M.G Company.

May 1917.

Original Copy

A. Low

Major

Comdg 10th M.G. Coy.

4/6/17

Instructions regarding War Diaries and Intelligence Summaries are contained in F. S. Regs., Part II. and the Staff Manual respectively. Title pages will be prepared in manuscript.

WAR DIARY
or
INTELLIGENCE SUMMARY.
(Erase heading not required.)

Army Form C. 2118.

Map Ref. 51. B. N.W.
FAMPOUX (51. B.N.W.4) 1:10,000
BIACHE (Special Sheet) 1:20,000

Place	Date	Hour	Summary of Events and Information	Reinforcements / Casualties	Remarks and references to Appendices
Line	1st		Major A. Low was sent for by the G.O.C. 4th Division to take up the duties of Actg Divisional R.E.O., & the command of the Company temporarily devolved upon Lieut G. Hatsin.	1. OR to Hospital	
	2nd		Brigade Operation orders were issued for attack on the enemy's positions. Objective 1 Black Line on Map attached 2 Blue Line on Map attached 3 Red Line on Map attached Brigade orders to the Company were: "(a) 2 sections are placed under orders of the Division. "Remaining two sections will move from embankment behind 2nd wave "of 1st Royal Warwickshire Regiment & take up positions on highest ground "East of Gavrelle – Roeux Road. "The two sections under the Division will report by wire to Brigade "H.Q. when their work under the Division is completed." Zero hour was fixed at 3.45 a.m. the 3rd		

A5834 Wt. W4973/M687 750,000 8/16 D. D. & L. Ltd. Forms/C.2118/13.

Scale 1 : 20,000. BIACHE
Detail and Trenches revised to 30-4-17. SPECIAL SHEET.
OPPY SUPPORT TRENCH
LINK TRENCH
FRESNES
ROUVROY
LINE
Neuvireuil
Oppy
Gavrelle
Fresnes les Montauban
Izel-les Equerchin
BRITISH
LINE
DIV. NORTHERN BOUNDARY
BRIGADE BOUNDARY
SOUTHERN BOUNDARY
Fampoux
Roeux
REGENT WORK
PARK WORK
Orange Hill
3rd Field Survey Co., R.E.

Instructions regarding War Diaries and Intelligence Summaries are contained in F. S. Regs., Part II. and the Staff Manual respectively. Title pages will be prepared in manuscript.

WAR DIARY
or
INTELLIGENCE SUMMARY.
(Erase heading not required.)

Army Form C. 2118.

Place	Date	Hour	Summary of Events and Information	[illegible]	Remarks and references to Appendices
Line.	2nd		No 2 Section (under Lt W. M. PALMER) + No 3 Section (under 2nd Lt V. H. Willoughby) assembled in CRUMP TRENCH.		
			No 2 Section was ordered to follow behind the 2nd wave of the 1st R. W. R, + No 3 behind the 2nd wave of the [illegible] Bn		
	3rd		No 2 Sect. left their Assembly positions at Zero + 10 minutes [illegible] our old front line at [illegible] B. c. 7. 1 [illegible] the [illegible]	2nd Lt ABEL G. J. wounded	
			No 3 Sect. left Assembly positions at Zero + 10 mins. [illegible] our old front line at its junction with [illegible] Trench.	2nd Lt WALKER H. W. wounded	
			By this time the attack had failed + most of the attacking troops were back in the old front line.	Sgt [illegible] wounded	
			2 Guns + Tripods were damaged by shell fire + 2 officers + [illegible] were wounded amongst these two sections.	7 O.R. wounded	
			1 team of No 3 Section sniped two Germans in the [illegible].	2 O.R. missing.	
			At about 1 p.m. these eight guns were withdrawn to CRETE Trench.		

Instructions regarding War Diaries and Intelligence Summaries are contained in F. S. Regs., Part II. and the Staff Manual respectively. Title pages will be prepared in manuscript.

WAR DIARY
or
INTELLIGENCE SUMMARY.
(Erase heading not required.)

Army Form C. 2118.

Place	Date	Hour	Summary of Events and Information	Remarks and references to Appendices
Line	3rd		No 1 Section (under 2nd Lt. E. H. C. NEALE) + No 4 Sect (under 2/Lt R. N. [illegible]BURTER) were dug in at about H 24 c 1 9 in some old German gun pits. These six guns were placed under Divisional Orders + received orders from the A/D M.G.O. as follows:– 'from Zero to Zero + 5 mins. to barrage from I 14 a 3.0 – I 14 c 4.0. 'from Zero + 5 mins. to Zero + 18 mins from I 14 b 2.0 – I 14 d 4.0. 'from Zero + 18 mins to Zero + 38 mins. from I 14 b 5.0 – I 14 d 9.0 'from Zero + 38 mins. to Zero + 45 mins. from I 15 a 0.1 – I 21 a 1.9. 'To cease fire at Zero + 45 mins. 'to search Eastwards to a depth of 300x from each successive 'barrage line. Rate of fire, 1 belt per 4 minutes. The above orders were carefully carried out, – the barrage lines given being divided between the two sections + again amongst the gun teams.	

A5834 Wt. W4973/M687 750,000 8/16 D. D. & L. Ltd. Forms/C.2118/13.

Instructions regarding War Diaries and Intelligence Summaries are contained in F. S. Regs., Part II. and the Staff Manual respectively. Title pages will be prepared in manuscript.

WAR DIARY
or
INTELLIGENCE SUMMARY.
(Erase heading not required.)

Army Form C. 2118.

Place	Date	Hour	Summary of Events and Information	Arrivals & Departures.	Remarks and references to Appendices
Line.	4th		The guns in the front line system were re-distributed, & the positions after the night 4/5th were: No 2 Sect. 2 guns in CRETE Trench, & 1 gun in [illegible] Trench. No 3 Sect. 3 guns in CEYLON Trench. The 1st Hampshire Regt relieved the 1st R. W. R. & part of the 1st Royal Irish Fusiliers. H. B. [illegible] [illegible] the [illegible] & relieved the 1st Somerset Light Infantry down to the River. 2nd Seaforth Highlanders relieved part of the R. I. F. [illegible] of CORONA Trench & the H. B. as far S. as COMET Trench		
	5th		The Heavy Artillery bombarded the CHATEAU & CHEMICAL WORKS [illegible]	1. O.R. wounded	
			Nos 2 & 3 sections were relieved in the line by the [illegible] [illegible] [illegible] Nos 2 & 3 went to the barrage positions at H. 24 c. 1. 9.		

A5834 Wt. W4973/M687 750,000 8/16 D. D. & L. Ltd. Forms/C.2118/13.

Instructions regarding War Diaries and Intelligence Summaries are contained in F. S. Regs., Part II. and the Staff Manual respectively. Title pages will be prepared in manuscript.

WAR DIARY
or
INTELLIGENCE SUMMARY.
(Erase heading not required.)

Army Form C. 2118.

Place	Date	Hour	Summary of Events and Information	Arrivals Infantry	Remarks and references to Appendices
Line	6th		Bombardment by our H.A. of Chateau, Chemical Works & Cemetery etc. Front line evacuated during the day re-occupied at dusk.		
	7th		1st R.I.F. relieved the H.B. in right sub. sector on night 7/8th	2 O.R. wounded 1 to Base for dental treatment	
	8th		A Chinese attack was delivered by us at 7 p.m. Garrison in front line trenches were thinned out. The enemy placed a heavy barrage on CEYLON & CRUMP trenches, along the Railway Embankment & on the ground on each side of the River SCARPE The 1st R.W.K. relieved the 2nd S.H. in Left sector, in front of Mount Pleasant Wood, in relief of the R.I.F.		

A5834 Wt. W4973/M687 750,000 8/16 D. D. & L. Ltd. Forms/C.2118/13.

SECRET.
2nd Objective
1st Objective
Barrage line
CASH
CROOK
CROW
50th Bde.
Cardigan
11th Bde.
Bde. Boundary
10th Bde.
Battn Boundary
ROEUX

Attached Map (2) to come in here.

Instructions regarding War Diaries and Intelligence Summaries are contained in F. S. Regs., Part II. and the Staff Manual respectively. Title pages will be prepared in manuscript.

WAR DIARY
or
INTELLIGENCE SUMMARY.

(*Erase heading not required.*)

Army Form C. 2118.

Place	Date	Hour	Summary of Events and Information	Remarks and references to Appendices
Line	9th		Preliminary Instruction No 1 were issued by the Brigade. 1. XVII Corps will resume the offensive with the object of gaining the line ROEUX CEMETERY – CORONA – CODIA northward. The attack will be carried out in 2 phases on Z & Z+1 day. 2(a) On Z day 4th Division will attack Black line (see Map attached) (b) On Z+1 day 4th Div (11th Bde) will attack Blue line (— do —). 3. 10th Bde will attack on the right. Boundaries are shown on attached map. HB will attack on L with Cemetery as objective. 2nd SH will follow close in rear as moppers up for the buildings. R.I.F. will form defensive flank on the right. 1st RWR will be in support in present front line. Preliminary Moves. On Z day troops will be formed up in assembly areas before 4 A.M. 10th H.G. Coy 2 Sect. (M.G.s) in Cox Trench behind the Pheasant Wood	

A5834 Wt. W4973/M687 750,000 8/16 D. D. & L. Ltd. Forms/C.2118/13.

Instructions regarding War Diaries and Intelligence Summaries are contained in F. S. Regs., Part II. and the Staff Manual respectively. Title pages will be prepared in manuscript.

WAR DIARY
or
INTELLIGENCE SUMMARY.
(Erase heading not required.)

Army Form C. 2118.

Place	Date	Hour	Summary of Events and Information	Arrivals / Departures	Remarks and references to Appendices
Line	9th		"1 sect (2 guns) in front line ([illegible]) with R. [illegible] "2 Sects 10th M.G. Coy (4 guns) will advance in rear of 2nd [illegible] & will at once take up positions to bring flanking fire in direction N & E. "1 Sect (2 guns) will advance in rear of R. [illegible] to bring flanking fire to bear in direction N.E. & S. "1 gun will be sent to S. front of 1st R. [illegible] about I.19.a.5.1 "1 Section 9th [illegible] M.G. will assemble in CEYLON Lane between its junction with CRANE and CREEK & will operate with 10th M.G. Coy to assist in [illegible] [illegible]. "1st R.W.K. will detail 15 men as a carrying party to report to H.Q. 10th M.G. Coy at 12 Midnight 10/11th. 2 guns were ordered to move up to the front line immediately after the attack started, to take up defensive positions, in that line with the R.W.K.		

A5834 Wt. W4973/M687 750,000 8/16 D. D. & L. Ltd. Forms/C.2118/13.

Instructions regarding War Diaries and Intelligence Summaries are contained in F. S. Regs., Part II. and the Staff Manual respectively. Title pages will be prepared in manuscript.

WAR DIARY
or
INTELLIGENCE SUMMARY.
(Erase heading not required.)

Army Form C. 2118.

Place	Date	Hour	Summary of Events and Information	Arrivals & Departures	Remarks and references to Appendices
Line	9th		Z day was to be 11th		
	10th		During the night 10/11th the Sections took up their positions of assembly according to the orders quoted above. 2 carriers were attached to each of the advancing teams, & plans were discussed & settled with the Officer i/c R.E. Section.	2nd [illegible] E.A.C. [illegible] to Hospital.	
			2 Sect (4 guns) were thus assembled in Ex. Trench	1 O.R. Killed	
			1 Sect (2 guns) in Cusp Trench	1 O.R. Wounded.	
			1 gun in CRETE Trench		
			1 gun in CRIMP Trench		
	11th		All these guns were in position by 2 AM		
			2 days' Rations were carried, water bottles filled, + 1 petrol tin of water per team was taken to the assembly positions for drinking during the day of the 11th.		
			1 Sect. (No 3, under 2nd Lieut F. H. Willoughby) was established at H. 23 b. 9. 1 — H. 24 c. 2. 8.		

A5834 Wt. W4973/M687 750,000 8/16 D. D. & L. Ltd. Forms/C.2118/13.

Instructions regarding War Diaries and Intelligence Summaries are contained in F. S. Regs., Part II. and the Staff Manual respectively. Title pages will be prepared in manuscript.

WAR DIARY
or
INTELLIGENCE SUMMARY.
(Erase heading not required.)

Army Form C. 2118.

Place	Date	Hour	Summary of Events and Information	Arrivals & Departures	Remarks and references to Appendices
Line	11th		Orders were issued by the O/C M.G.O. for this section as follows		
			Fire Action on Z Day		
			(i) from Zero to Zero + 4 mins:–		
			to barrage from X Rds I.19 d 6.6 to road junct. I.20 c 20.15		
			(ii) from Zero + 4 mins to Zero + 30 mins		
			from X Rds I.19 d 6.6 to rd junction I.20 c 20.15		
			Note. These lines will be [illegible] during the night of Y/Z		
			(iii) At Zero + 30 mins sustained fire will cease.		
			Group Commanders will arrange [illegible]		
			(iv) In addition, the area behind the enemy's line must be kept under constant fire by guns of barrage groups firing on barrage line.		
			Special attention must be paid to		
			River Valley E of ROEUX [illegible]		
			Fire Action on Z + 1 Day		
			(i) from Zero to Zero + 5 mins:–		

A5834 Wt. W4973/M687 750,000 8/16 D. D. & L. Ltd. Forms/C.2118/13.

9

Instructions regarding War Diaries and Intelligence Summaries are contained in F. S. Regs., Part II. and the Staff Manual respectively. Title pages will be prepared in manuscript.

WAR DIARY
or
INTELLIGENCE SUMMARY.
(Erase heading not required.)

Army Form C. 2118.

Place	Date	Hour	Summary of Events and Information	Arrivals & Departures	Remarks and references to Appendices
Line	11th		'fire on line I 20 a 8.5 – I 20 c.7.7 '(ii) from Zero +5 mins – Zero + 30 mins on line I 20 a 8 5 – I 20 c.7.7 ' These are S.W. lines from Zero + 30 mins on Z+1 s ayonwards. 'Rate of fire 1 rd per gun per 4 mins.		
	11th		The day was hot. Troops had orders to make as little movement in the trenches as possible & to remain concealed. Zero hour was fixed at 7.30 p.m. Watches were synchronised at 12 Noon. There was little shelling of our front line System by the enemy & there was not much hostile aerial activity. 3 minutes before Zero the enemy shelled our front line north of the Railway embankment heavily.		

A5834 Wt. W4973/M687 750,000 8/16 D. D. & L. Ltd. Forms/C.2118/13.

Instructions regarding War Diaries and Intelligence Summaries are contained in F. S. Regs., Part II. and the Staff Manual respectively. Title pages will be prepared in manuscript.

WAR DIARY
or
INTELLIGENCE SUMMARY.
(Erase heading not required.)

Army Form C. 2118.

Place	Date	Hour	Summary of Events and Information	Arrivals & Departures	Remarks and references to Appendices
Line	11th		The Section doing barrage fire carried out its orders, & all the guns maintained the fire laid down.		
			Major A. Low A/ [illegible] received a bullet wound in the right shoulder whilst walking over the open to visit this section at about Zero + 20 mins.	Major A. Low Wounded	
			Our Artillery barrage was particularly good. The reply by the enemy opened soon afterwards, was not very strong.		
			No 1 Sect. (2 guns) left the old front line at Zero + 45 mins & reached the line formed by the R.I.F. Positions were established at I 19 c 9. 8½ & I 19 c 8½ 6½. 1 Gun was damaged next morning, 12th, by shell fire & replaced.		
			No 2 Sect. (2 guns) left its assembly position at Zero + 0 mins & eventually reached position in the line of the [illegible] with the R.I.F. on the Right at about I. 19. b. 3. 3.	1 O.R. Killed	

A5834 Wt. W4973/M687 750,000 8/16 D. D. & L. Ltd. Forms/C.2118/13.

Instructions regarding War Diaries and Intelligence Summaries are contained in F. S. Regs., Part II. and the Staff Manual respectively. Title pages will be prepared in manuscript.

WAR DIARY
or
INTELLIGENCE SUMMARY.
(Erase heading not required.)

Army Form C. 2118.

Place	Date	Hour	Summary of Events and Information	Arrivals & Departures	Remarks and references to Appendices
Line	11th		(under Lt. Rawles) No 4 Section (2 guns) left Assembly positions at Zero + 3 mins, starting behind the S.H. The two teams reached the points gained by the A.B. & during the night 11/12th established & consolidated positions at about 19.b. central & 19.b.4.6. They were with the A.B. The nearest troops on the Left were the Hampshire Regt (11th Bde) in CORONA Trench. Lcpl Murphy's team on the Left captured 24 prisoners from the Northern buildings of the Chemical Works at about Midnight 11/12th. These were escorted by the Section Runner, & one of the carriers, & handed over to the Seaforth Highlanders. About 1 hour after Zero, while his Officer had gone forward on a reconnaissance Lcpl P. Murphy rallied a party of about 20 of the A.B., which included 2 Lewis Guns & their teams. He sited posts & personally placed these two Lewis Gun teams in position where there was a gap of 100 yds. between		

A5834 Wt. W4973 M687 750,000 8/16 D. D. & L. Ltd. Forms/C.2118/13.

Instructions regarding War Diaries and Intelligence Summaries are contained in F. S. Regs., Part II. and the Staff Manual respectively. Title pages will be prepared in manuscript.

WAR DIARY
or
INTELLIGENCE SUMMARY.
(Erase heading not required.)

Army Form C. 2118.

Place	Date	Hour	Summary of Events and Information	Arrivals & Departures	Remarks and references to Appendices
Line	11th		his (Lcpl Murphy) gun, & the mixed troops on his left, who were of the [illegible] in CORONA Trench. During the day of the 12th the team of this N.C.O. engaged & dispersed many small parties of the enemy, who were retiring along the N bank of the R. SCARPE. This N.C.O. has been recommended for the Military Medal. The other team (Pte [illegible]) found a German M.G. & ammunition, which they brought into action against the enemy. The carriers who went forward with the first teams did their work well, & the action of the R.E. was of great value in helping to consolidate. 3 of the carriers were wounded.		

A5834 Wt. W4973 M687 750,000 8/16 D. D. & L. Ltd. Forms/C.2118/13.

Instructions regarding War Diaries and Intelligence Summaries are contained in F. S. Regs., Part II. and the Staff Manual respectively. Title pages will be prepared in manuscript.

WAR DIARY
or
INTELLIGENCE SUMMARY.
(Erase heading not required.)

Army Form C. 2118.

Place	Date	Hour	Summary of Events and Information	Arrival & Departure	Remarks and references to Appendices
Line	11th		After the attacking troops had left our old front line, two guns were at once pushed up to take up defensive positions in it. One was established in C.U.S.P. Trench & the other in C.B.P. Trench. The gun previously established with post at I.19.c.5.1. remained there.		
	12th		The enemy shelled our old front line system at intervals. Prisoners continued to come in all day from the Cemetery buildings.		
			The Brigade Major (Capt A.G. Fellows M.C.) died of wounds received at about 6 a.m. from a sniper, shortly afterwards he had spoken to the Points of his gun teams.		
			The 11th Bde continued the attack at 6.30 a.m. They were successful & gained their objective.		

WAR DIARY
or
INTELLIGENCE SUMMARY.
(Erase heading not required.)

Army Form C. 2118.

Instructions regarding War Diaries and Intelligence Summaries are contained in F. S. Regs., Part II. and the Staff Manual respectively. Title pages will be prepared in manuscript.

Place	Date	Hour	Summary of Events and Information	Remarks and references to Appendices
Line	12th		The 12th Division carried out an attack [illegible] on DEVIL'S Reach in I. 32 a at 6 pm. No 3 Sect. assisted by placing barrage fire on the line I 26.c 1.4½ — I. 26 c. 0.7, from 6 pm – 8 pm	
			The Company was relieved in the line & in support by the 152nd M. G. Coy. The following positions were taken over by their teams from ours:—	
			(1) About I. 19.c 8½ 6½	
			(2) I 19.c 9.5½	
			(3) I 19. b 3.3	
			(4) I 19. b 3.2	
			(5) I 19. b central	

A5834 Wt. W4973/M687 750,000 8/16 D. D. & L. Ltd. Forms/C.2118/13.

Instructions regarding War Diaries and Intelligence Summaries are contained in F. S. Regs., Part II. and the Staff Manual respectively. Title pages will be prepared in manuscript.

WAR DIARY
or
INTELLIGENCE SUMMARY.
(Erase heading not required.)

Army Form C. 2118.

Place	Date	Hour	Summary of Events and Information	Remarks and references to Appendices
Line	12th		(6) I.19.b.4.6	
			(7) I.19.c.5.1	
			(8) Cusp. H. I.19.c.5.6½	
			(9) I.19.a.7.6	
			(10, 11 & 12) About H.23.b.9.1 – H.24.c.2.8	
	13th		The relief was complete at 2 a.m. & all the teams had passed by Coy H.Q. at 3 a.m.	
			Sections then marched to the Railway Bridge on [illegible] – Fampoux Rd, where the troops had tea, & bivouacked for 4 hours.	
			The Company paraded at 10.30 a.m. & marched to the OCTROI, ARRAS (G.21.b.5.7) where troops entrained & were taken to billets at HOUVIN HOUVIGNEUL.	
			The Company billets were at Houvigneul at the W. of village	

A5834 Wt. W4973/M687 750,000 8/16 D. D. & L. Ltd. Forms/C.2118/13.

Instructions regarding War Diaries and Intelligence Summaries are contained in F. S. Regs., Part II. and the Staff Manual respectively. Title pages will be prepared in manuscript.

WAR DIARY
or
INTELLIGENCE SUMMARY.

(Erase heading not required.)

Army Form C. 2118.

Place	Date	Hour	Summary of Events and Information	Arrivals & Departures	Remarks and references to Appendices
Billets	14th		Day of rest. Address to the Brigade by G.O.C. 4th Division. Major R. J. [illegible] temporarily attached to the [illegible]	1. O.R. to C.C.S. 20 O.R. Reinforcements from Base.	
	15th		Church Parade + Baths.	1 O.R. from C.R.S. 3. O.R. from Hospital 1. O.R. from leave. 1. O.R. to Hospital 1 O.R. (Sgt. [illegible] to Base)	
	16th		The Brigade was inspected at 10.30 a.m. by the Army Commander who afterwards addressed the troops. Clean clothing was issued to the men.		
	17th		Parade under Sect. Officers for cleaning of [illegible] & preparing lists of deficiencies.		

A5834 Wt. W4973 M687 750,000 8/16 D. D. & L. Ltd. Forms/C.2118/13.

Instructions regarding War Diaries and Intelligence Summaries are contained in F. S. Regs., Part II. and the Staff Manual respectively. Title pages will be prepared in manuscript.

WAR DIARY
or
INTELLIGENCE SUMMARY.
(Erase heading not required.)

Army Form C. 2118.

Place	Date	Hour	Summary of Events and Information	Arrivals & Departures	Remarks and references to Appendices
Billets	18th		Parade in the morning under Sect. Officer for P.T. & cleaning of all ammunition etc. & inspection of Box Respirators.		
			Baths.		
			Major A. Corr returned to the Company from C.C.S.	1 Officer (Lt A. [illegible])	
				12 OR from [illegible] Base	
	19th		Kit Inspection.	1 OR to Hospital	
			Inspection by the C.O. at 11 a.m.		
			The G.O.C. 4th Division came to see the Coy. on parade.	1 Offr. (Lt H.M. PALMER) Special Leave to U.K.	
	20th		Church Parade.		
			Inspection of billets by the O.C.		
	21st			1 Off (2nd Lt P. McKinnie) Special Leave to U.K.	
				1 OR To Hospital.	
				1 OR to Rest [illegible]	

A5834 Wt. W4973 M687 750,000 8/16 D. D. & L. Ltd. Forms/C.2118/13.

Army Form C. 2118.

WAR DIARY
or
INTELLIGENCE SUMMARY.

(Erase heading not required.)

Instructions regarding War Diaries and Intelligence Summaries are contained in F. S. Regs., Part II. and the Staff Manual respectively. Title pages will be prepared in manuscript.

Maps for Reference 51c 1:40000 LENS. Sheet 11 1:100000

Place	Date	Hour	Summary of Events and Information	Arrivals & Departures	Remarks and references to Appendices
Billets at HOUVIGNEUL	22nd		Training started – 1½ hours Gun drill. 1 hour Mechanism. 1 hour Stoppages. 1 hour Company drill Transport inspected by O.C. 4th Divnl Train.	nil.	
	23rd		Programme as for 22nd The company held athletic sports in the afternoon.	nil.	
	24th		Company route march SIBVILLE – BONEVILLE – MONCHEAUX – MONTS en TERNOIS – HOUVIN – HOUVIGNEUL.	nil.	
	25th		Programme as for 22nd.	nil.	
	26th		Programme for morning as for 22nd. Brigade sports held in afternoon at HOUVIGNEUL.	nil.	

A5834 Wt. W4973 M687 750,000 8/16 D. D. & L. Ltd. Forms/C.2118/13.

Instructions regarding War Diaries and Intelligence Summaries are contained in F. S. Regs., Part II. and the Staff Manual respectively. Title pages will be prepared in manuscript.

Maps 51 c 1:40000

WAR DIARY
or
INTELLIGENCE SUMMARY.

(*Erase heading not required.*)

LENS Sheet 11 1:100000.

Army Form C. 2118.

Place	Date	Hour	Summary of Events and Information	Remarks and references to Appendices
BILLETS in HOOVIGNEOL	27th		Inspections of billets etc. Church parades. Services R.C. in HOOVIN church, C of E. in Theatre HOOVIN	27 Lt MATSON on leave for 1 month. Lt ... on for 10 days.
	28th		Programme: 1 hour Elementary Drill. 2 hours advanced Drill. ½ hour mechanism. 1 hour Judging distance.	29 3 OR on LEAVE.
	29th		Programme as for 28th	
	30th		Programme as for 28th. No 3 Section on range.	
	31st		Company fired on range near PLAGNICOURT	

A5834 Wt. W4973/M687 750,000 8/16 D. D. & L. Ltd. Forms/C.2118/13.

WAR DIARY

10th MACHINE GUN COMPANY.

JUNE 1 - JUNE 30 1917

Original Copy

A. Low
Major
Comdg 10th M.G. Coy

1/7/17

9817

Army Form C. 2118.

WAR DIARY
or
~~INTELLIGENCE SUMMARY.~~
(Erase heading not required.)

Instructions regarding War Diaries and Intelligence Summaries are contained in F. S. Regs., Part II. and the Staff Manual respectively. Title pages will be prepared in manuscript. Maps 51c 1:40000

Place	Date	Hour	Summary of Events and Information		Remarks and references to Appendices
	JUNE.				
HOUVIN - HOUVIGNEUL	1		Extract from Company orders dated 31/5/17. "No 3 Section will relieve A.A. m. guns of 9th Divn at ROELLECOURT & LIGNY-St. FLOCHEL tomorrow. Parade to move off at 6.30 am." Relief was reported complete by 1 pm. Divisional Horse Show was held on GOUY-TERNAS road. The company entered teams for Team of four L.D horses in G.S. Limbered wagon & Pair of L.D. horses harnessed without vehicles, also a pack pony in Pack animal class; but no prizes were awarded.	3 O.R. Leave to U.K	a.h.
	2		Company route marched at 9 a.m. route CANETTEMONT - REBREUVE - SIBIVILLE - HOUVIGNEUL.	2nd Lt P. McKinnie from Leave to U.K.	a.h.
	3.		Church parades & inspections.		
	4.		No1 Section on range. Other sections 1. hour Gun drill 1½ hours Advanced drill 1 hour Mechanism. 2.3 Company drill	2 O.R. reinforcements from Base - 4 O.R. Leave to U.K.	a.h.
					a.h.

A5834 Wt. W4973/M687 750,000 8/16 D. D. & L. Ltd. Forms/C.2118/13.

Instructions regarding War Diaries and Intelligence Summaries are contained in F. S. Regs., Part II. and the Staff Manual respectively. Title pages will be prepared in manuscript. 57 C 1:40,000

WAR DIARY
or
~~INTELLIGENCE SUMMARY.~~
(Erase heading not required.)

Army Form C. 2118.

Place	Date	Hour	Summary of Events and Information		Remarks and references to Appendices
HOUVIN-HOUVIGNEUL	5		Training continued as on 4th.		
	[illegible]		No 4 section cooperated with Household Bn with flanking covering fire for a bombing attack.		a.h.
	6		Training as on 4th		a.h.
	7		The Company took part in a tactical scheme with 1/R Irish Fus on LIENCOURT training area. No 2 section supplied covering fire for the assault & No 1 section advanced to consolidate the position gained. No 4 section took up concealed positions to act as enemy. No 16646 Sgt J. Loydall was mentioned in despatches by G.O.C. 4th Divn.	5 O.R. from Rest Camp. 2 O.R. to Hospital.	a.h.
	8.		Training continued under Section Officers.	4 O.R. from Leave 1 O.R. from M.G. Course 4 O.R. to Rest Camp. 1 O.R. Leave to U.K. Lt. Brooks to Hospital. 3 O.R. Trans. to 12th M.G. Coy 10 " " 11 "	a.h.
	9.		Inter Section Competition was held on range. Competition was a test of unpacking limbers, running gun into action, firing on plates, coming out of action & repacking limbers. Major Low & Major Pettle acted as judges. No 2 section 1st. No 4 Section 2nd No 1 Section 3rd Great keenness was shown by all ranks.	1 O.R. from Leave. 1 O.R. to Hospital 6. 2M.-M.G. Course 1 O.R. ditto.	a.h.

A5834 Wt. W4973/M687 750,000 8/16 D. D. & L. Ltd. Forms/C.2118/13.

Instructions regarding War Diaries and Intelligence Summaries are contained in F. S. Regs., Part II. and the Staff Manual respectively. Title pages will be prepared in manuscript.

Maps 51 C 1 : 40000

WAR DIARY
or
INTELLIGENCE SUMMARY.
(Erase heading not required.)

Army Form C. 2118.

51 B NW 1/20000

Place	Date	Hour	Summary of Events and Information		Remarks and references to Appendices
HOUVIN HOUVIGNEUL	JUNE 10		Company attended Inspection & Medal presentation by G.O.C. 4th Division 10th Brigade paraded at 9.30 am. Dress fighting order. Corpl Murphy was presented with ~~the~~ ribbon of military medal for conspicuous gallantry near ROEUX on May 11th. Competitions for horsemanship & riding were held at Transport in afternoon.	Lt. Watson recalled from leave for evidence on F.G.C.M. 36 O.R. leave to U.K.	A.h.
	11		Training continued under Section officers. Major A. Low appointed a/D.R.E.O. & proceeded to line near ROEUX to visit trenches.		A.h.
	12.		Company moved by busses to billets in ARRAS. Embussing at 1.30 pm. Transport to ~~St.~~ Nicholas G.9.b by march route moving off at 6.45 am.	16 O.R. from leave	A.h.
ARRAS	13.		Sections marched out for training under Section officers in & about ROCLINCOURT ravine.		A.h.

Instructions regarding War Diaries and Intelligence Summaries are contained in F. S. Regs., Part II. and the Staff Manual respectively. Title pages will be prepared in manuscript. 57 B NW 1: 20000

WAR DIARY
or
INTELLIGENCE SUMMARY.
(Erase heading not required.)

~~[illegible]~~ PLOUVAIN 1: 10,000

Army Form C. 2118.

Place	Date	Hour	Summary of Events and Information		Remarks and references to Appendices
ARRAS.	JUNE			1 O.R. From Transport Course 1 O.R. to Hospital.	
	14 } 15 } 16 }		Routine as for 13th.	2 O.R. From Leave. 1 O.R. Leave 1 O.R. To Hospital.	A.H.
				10 O.R. Trans. to 27th M. G. Coy.	
	17		Company moved at 5 pm to FIRE CAMP. ~~No of St. NICHOLAS.~~		A.H.
	18		Company proceeded to line to relieve 12th M. G. Company in CHEMICAL WORKS Sector. Sections moved off in following order at 10 m. interval. H.Q. & No 2. 4 30 pm. No 1. No 3 No 4. Location as follows. H.Q. & No 2 Section in reserve at No 3. CUPID Trench 1 14 a 0 8 " 1 14 a 25.40 CINEMA 1 13 b 38 CORONA SUPPORT. 1 13 b 52. No 4 CROFT 1 14 c 56 " 1 14 c 63 CORONA 1 14 c 16 COLOMBO. 1 14 c 22	2 O.R. Leave to U.K.	A.H.

A5834 Wt. W4973 M687 750,000 8/16 D. D. & L. Ltd. Forms/C.2118/13.

Instructions regarding War Diaries and Intelligence Summaries are contained in F. S. Regs., Part II. and the Staff Manual respectively. Title pages will be prepared in manuscript.

Maps
51 B NW

WAR DIARY
or
INTELLIGENCE SUMMARY.
(*Erase heading not required.*)

PLOUVAIN 1:10000.

Army Form C. 2118.

Place	Date	Hour	Summary of Events and Information	Remarks and references to Appendices
Trenches.	18		No 1 Section in Reserve Line H 18 b 83. I 13 c 26. I 13 c 23. I 19 a 29. Relief Complete at 9 pm.	a.h.
	19.		Day quiet, nothing to report Harassing fire carried out by guns in Reserve Line onto Enemy approaches near HAOSA WOOD.	1 Offr. Wounded Lt. E. A. C. Neale. a.h.
	20.		Usual harassing fires carried out at night. 2/Lt E.A.C. NEALE wounded in Reserve Line. 2/Lt R. McKINNIE came up from Transport to take over No 1 Section.	1 O. R. to Hospital. a.h.
	21.		Nothing to report.	2 O. R. from to 12th M. G. Coy. 1 O. R. to Hospital. a.h.
	22.		No 2 Section relieved No 3 Section in left subsector. No 3 Section on relief by No 2 relieved No 1 Section. No 1 Section relieved No 4. No 4 returned to reserve at Coy H.Q. Relief Complete 7 pm.	1 O. R. to Hospital a.h.

A5834 Wt. W4973/M687 750,000 8/16 D. D. & L. Ltd. Forms/C.2118/13.

Instructions regarding War Diaries and Intelligence Summaries are contained in F. S. Regs., Part II. and the Staff Manual respectively. Title pages will be prepared in manuscript. Maps 51B NW 1:2000

WAR DIARY
or
INTELLIGENCE SUMMARY.
(Erase heading not required.)

PLOUVAIN 1:10000

Army Form C. 2118.

Place	Date	Hour	Summary of Events and Information		Remarks and references to Appendices
Trenches.	23.		Nothing unusual to report. Aeroplanes engaged by guns in reserve line, usual harassing fire at night.	1 O.R. Leave to U.K.	[illegible]
	24.		During day, aeroplanes engaged by M.G. fire.	1 O.R. Leave to U.K. 1 O.R. Struck off strength (Pte Mc Guffick)	
			At 10.15 pm. 1/R. Irish Fus carried out a raid on enemy's outpost line between 114 c 7510 114 c 9050.		
			10th M.G. Coy cooperated. 1 gun from CROFT (No1 Section) at 114 a 52 firing due E.		
			No. 3 Section cooperated from CORDITE C. ~~[illegible]~~ fired long range indirect fire onto HAOSA WOOD & neighbouring area.		
			1 gun from No 4 Section fired from Railway Bank about 113 c 13 & searched railway from 114 b07 to 18 d 86.		
			The raid was successful.		
			The following letter received by O.C. 10th M.G. Coy from O.C. 1/R.I.F.		
			"I write to thank you for the able assistance your Company afforded us last night. It was due to the help of other arms that we met with the success we did. I hope you will thank those concerned for their cooperation & thank them on my behalf		[illegible]

A5834 Wt. W4973/M687 750,000 8/16 D. D. & L. Ltd. Forms/C.2118/13.

Army Form C. 2118.

WAR DIARY
or
~~INTELLIGENCE~~ SUMMARY.
(*Erase heading not required.*)

Instructions regarding War Diaries and Intelligence Summaries are contained in F. S. Regs., Part II. and the Staff Manual respectively. Title pages will be prepared in manuscript.

Maps 57c NW 1:20000 PLOUVAIN 1:10000

Place	Date	Hour	Summary of Events and Information		Remarks and references to Appendices
	24		for their unselfish help" Sd A. B. I. Webber Lt Col Comdg 1/R. I. [illegible].		[illegible]
	25.		Nothing to report	36 R. from [illegible]	[illegible]
	26		Company H.Q. shelled extremely heavily & accurately all morning. Company was relieved in present sector by 52nd M.G. Coy in daylight. Relief complete by 5 pm. Nos 1 & 2 sections proceeded to STIRLING CAMP. Nos 3 & 4 sections prepared to relieve 11th M.G. Coy in line near ROEUX. Coy H.Q. moved at 6.30 pm to H23c79. Location as follows.	26 R. [illegible] O.R. 36 R. to Rest Camp	[illegible]

A5834 Wt. W4973/M687 750,000 8/16 D. D. & L. Ltd. Forms/C.2118/13.

Instructions regarding War Diaries and Intelligence Summaries are contained in F. S. Regs., Part II. and the Staff Manual respectively. Title pages will be prepared in manuscript.

Maps 57B NW

WAR DIARY
or
~~INTELLIGENCE SUMMARY.~~
(Erase heading not required.)

PLOOVAIN 1:10000

Army Form C. 21

Place	Date	Hour	Summary of Events and Information	Remarks and references to Appendices
Trenches			Locations:	
			No 3 section COLOMBO 120a54	
			〃 120a64	
			CEYLON 119b67	
			CRUMP (Reserve AA) 1[illegible]24 & 88	
			No 4 ROEUX 119d86	
			ROEUX Wood 125a59	
			〃 119c90	
			〃 119c65.	
			Relief complete 11pm.	a.l.
	27.		Nothing unusual to report. Harassing fire carried out by guns in ROEUX wood on enemy approaches especially along River bank	2nd Lt. Dalton - from Sary. 16 R. Irish Lancs. a.l.
	28		Nothing unusual.	a.l.

A5834 Wt. W4973/M687 750,000 8/16 D. D. & L. Ltd. Forms/C.2118/13.

Instructions regarding War Diaries and Intelligence Summaries are contained in F. S. Regs., Part II. and the Staff Manual respectively. Title pages will be prepared in manuscript.

WAR DIARY
or
INTELLIGENCE SUMMARY.
(Erase heading not required.)

Army Form C. 2118.

57 B NW 1:20000 ROOVAN 1:10000.

Place	Date	Hour	Summary of Events and Information	Remarks and references to Appendices
	29		Nothing to report during day. Guns in COLOMBO heavily ~~shell~~ rifle grenaded during night. Corporal Maguire was unfortunately badly wounded & died following day. This N.C.O. had been with the Company since its formation. He was formerly in the 1 Royal Irish Fusiliers; he came to France with the Battalion & had never been absent from duty with the Tenth Brigade throughout the whole war for a single day. Lt. Matson - Leave to U.K. 1 O.R. Hosp U.K. and struck off strength (Pte Walsh) 2 O.R. Wounded in Action	O.K.
	30.		Nothing to report. No 3 Section relieved at night by No 1. Relief Complete 11.30 pm. 3 O.R. From Leave 2 O.R. From Courses. Lt. J. A. Brooks from Hosp. 1 O.R. Reinforcement. 2 O.R. Leave to U.K. 1 O.R. Died of wounds.	O.K.

A5834 Wt. W4973 M687 750,000 8/16 D. D. & L. Ltd. Forms/C.2118/13.

10TH MACHINE GUN COY.

ORIGINAL – WAR DIARY – JULY 1917

[illegible] Lieut for Major

Commanding 10th Machine Gun Coy.

Instructions regarding War Diaries and Intelligence Summaries are contained in F. S. Regs., Part II. and the Staff Manual respectively. Title pages will be prepared in manuscript.

WAR DIARY

~~or~~

~~INTELLIGENCE SUMMARY.~~

(Erase heading not required.)

Army Form C. 2118.

Place	Date	Hour	Summary of Events and Information	Remarks and references to Appendices
ARRAS Sector	1/7/17		Two guns fired harassing fire during the night. Two O.R. reinforcements arrived from 28 M.G. Coy.	All map references on this sheet refer to FLOUVAIN parts of 51B. N.W. & S.W.
" "	2/7/17		Machine Guns only fired for A.A. purposes. Two O.R. returned from leave. Major Lowe posted to 4th Div. H.Q. One O.R. struck off strength. Major Pettle assumed command of the Coy. Bde. H.Q. moved from H23a. to H13d.	
" "	3/7/17		Several of the enemy were killed by M.G. fire while attempting to escape from artillery barrage. Two O.R. committed to prison. Five O.R. proceeded on leave.	
" "	4/7/17		A M.G. emp-nt was commenced at the CORONA gun position. At 2.30 a.m. four M.Gs. at I19c.6.4. fired 5,000 rounds in support of an Infantry raid	W.H.L.
" "	5/7/17		M.Gs. fired the usual harassing fire. One O.R. returned from leave. One O.R. wounded one O.R. evacuated to C.C.S. two O.R. admitted to hospital. Left half Coy. relieved by right half Coy. during the night.	W.H.L.
" "	6/7/17		Work on emp-nts in COLOMBO, CEYLON & CORONA Trenches was carried on. Two guns from I19c.6.1. fired during the night at SUNKEN RD. at I25d.8.9. Advanced Bde. H.Q. opened at H23a.	W.H.L.
" "	7/7/17		From 11 a.m to 1 p.m. three guns at I19c.9.3. fired on SUNKEN RD. GUN & ANGEL Trench. One O.R. returned from leave, one O.R. returned from hospital. Right half Coy relieved by left half Coy.	W.H.L.
" "	~~8/7/17~~			W.H.L.
" "	8/7/17		Two O.R. returned from leave — two O.R. proceeded to Rest Camp. One Sgt. transferred to 11th M.G. Coy.	W.H.L.
" "	9/7/17		Coy. Sgt. Major McAdams reported from 199th M.G. Coy. Right half Coy relieved left half Coy.	W.H.L.
" "	10/7/17		Two M.Gs. in ROEUX WOOD fired usual harassing fire. One O.R. returned from hospital. Four O.R. went on leave.	

A5834 Wt. W4973/M687 750,000 8/16 D. D. & L. Ltd. Forms/C.2118/13.

Instructions regarding War Diaries and Intelligence Summaries are contained in F. S. Regs., Part II. and the Staff Manual respectively. Title pages will be prepared in manuscript.

WAR DIARY

~~or~~

~~INTELLIGENCE SUMMARY.~~

(Erase heading not required.)

Army Form C. 2118.

Place	Date	Hour	Summary of Events and Information	Remarks and references to Appendices
ARRAS Sector	11/7/17		Four guns fired from 10.50 p.m. to 11 p.m. 250 rounds each from I 19 c. 5.4. in conjunction with an artillery barrage. Two guns in ROEUX WOOD fired the usual harassing fire. Lieut. Loch was posted to the Coy. One O.R. struck off strength and 2 O.R. proceeded on a month's leave.	All map references on this sheet refer to – PLOUVAIN parts of 51b N.W. & S.W.
" "	12/7/17		Two guns in ROEUX WOOD fired usual harassing fire. Three O.R. reinforcements arrived from 11th M.G. Coy. One O.R. returned from leave – one O.R. went to 4th Div. H.Q.	
" "	13/7/17		Guns fired from I 19 b. 7.7. H 24 a 7.8, I 19 c. 65. 35. to I 20 b. 4.5., I 21 a 2.9. I 21 a. 0.4. respectively. Five O.R. proceeded on leave.	
" "	14/7/17		Guns in ROEUX WOOD carried out their usual harassing fire. ~~Two~~ One O.R. evacuated from hospital – three O.R. proceeded on leave. Left half Coy. relieved right half Coy.	[illegible]
" "	15/7/17		Usual harassing fire from ROEUX WOOD. Our guns in ROEUX WOOD assisted in a raid by the Household Batn. Lieut. Loch joined the Coy. One O.R. struck off the strength – two O.R. proceeded on a month's leave.	[illegible]
" "	16/7/17		Usual harassing fire from ROEUX WOOD. One O.R. wounded – one O.R. admitted to hospital.	[illegible]
" "	17/7/17		Three guns at I 19 c. 65. 35. assisted in 12th. Div. operations by means of barrage fire from 9.55 p.m. to 10.15 p.m. Slow rate of fire carried on throughout the night. One O.R. proceeded on Veterinary Course	[illegible]
" "	18/7/17		Guns in ROEUX WOOD carried out their usual harassing fire. Six O.R. returned from leave – five O.R. proceeded on leave. Right half Coy. relieved left half Coy.	[illegible]
" "	19/7/17		Three guns in ROEUX WOOD fired from 12.30 a.m. to 1.30 a.m. in pursuance of O.O. No. 5. In the afternoon one gun opened fire at enemy post I 25 b. 25. 15. Two O.R. evacuated from hospital – two O.R. killed in action.	[illegible]

A5834 Wt. W4973 M687 750,000 8/16 D. D. & L. Ltd. Forms/C.2118/13.

Instructions regarding War Diaries and Intelligence Summaries are contained in F. S. Regs., Part II. and the Staff Manual respectively. Title pages will be prepared in manuscript.

WAR DIARY
~~or~~
~~INTELLIGENCE SUMMARY.~~

(*Erase heading not required.*)

Army Form C. 2118.

Place	Date	Hour	Summary of Events and Information	Remarks and references to Appendices
ARRAS Sector	20/7/17		Two guns in ROEUX WOOD carried out their usual harassing fire. 2/Lt. Stevens reported from Base – Lt. Matson returned from leave. Lieut. Brooke proceeded on leave, also 2 O.R.	All map references on this sheet refer to PLOUVAIN parts of 51B. N.W. & S.W.
" "	21/7/17		Usual harassing fire from ROEUX WOOD. Lieut. Allan wounded – one O.R. wounded one O.R. killed.	
" "	22/7/17		Usual harassing fire by guns in ROEUX WOOD. Three O.R. returned from Rest Camp Four O.R. proceeded to Rest Camp. Left half Coy. relieved the right half Coy.	
" "	23/7/17		Usual harassing fire from ROEUX WOOD. Two O.R. returned from leave. Lt. Painter proceeded on leave.	
" "	24/7/17		Usual harassing fire from positions in ROEUX WOOD.	
" "	25/7/17		Usual harassing fire from ROEUX WOOD. Two O.R. returned from leave & four O.R. proceeded on leave. Lieut. Palmer struck off strength.	
" "	26/7/17		At 11.15 p.m. the enemy obtained a direct hit on our gun in CORONA Trench. Two guns in ROEUX WOOD fired on GUN Trench from 10.47 p.m – 11.15 p.m. – 5,000 rounds were fired. Two O.R. returned from leave – one O.R. admitted to hospital. Major Pebble admitted to No 8 C.C.S. Right half Coy. relieved the left half Coy.	
" "	27/7/17		Usual harassing fire from ROEUX WOOD. Five O.R. returned from leave – two O.R. returned from M.G. Course – 2/Lt. Kingsman & two O.R. proceeded to M.G. Course. Lieut. Matson admitted No 38 Officers' Rest Station.	
" "	28/7/17		Our guns in ROEUX WOOD carried out harassing fire. The M.G. position at H24 a.4.7. was taken over by 234th M.G. Coy. who also found an A.A. post at H24 d.9.7. Our gun team from H24 a.4.7. took up a position at I19 c 6.9. One O.R. returned from leave – one O.R. from Veterinary Course – four O.R. proceeded on leave.	

A5834 Wt. W4973 M687 750,000 8/16 D. D. & L. Ltd. Forms/C.2118/13.

Army Form C. 2118.

Instructions regarding War Diaries and Intelligence Summaries are contained in F. S. Regs., Part II. and the Staff Manual respectively. Title pages will be prepared in manuscript.

WAR DIARY

or

~~INTELLIGENCE SUMMARY.~~

(Erase heading not required.)

Place	Date	Hour	Summary of Events and Information	Remarks and references to Appendices
ARRAS Section	29/7/17		Between 1a.m. & 3.30a.m. three guns at I19a.6.6., two guns at I19a.6.1. two guns from I19c.5.2. fired bursts of 30-40 rounds every three minutes on targets at I15d.4.2, I21b.4.4., I15d.3.2. respectively. One O.R. reported from Base – one O.R. from leave. Two O.R. sent to Base as reinforcements. On this day, owing to shortage in personnel, leave was stopped.	All map references on this sheet refer to – PLOUVAIN parts of 51b N.W. & S.W.
" "	30/7/17		Our guns fired as yesterday, except ~~that~~ fire opened one hour earlier. One O.R. returned from leave – one O.R. admitted to hospital.	
" "	31/7/17		Usual harassing fire from ROEUX WOOD. Two guns at I19a.6.1. and two guns at I19c.5.0. fired at targets I20b.4.2 & I20a.5.8. respectively. 2/Lt. Orchard reported from Base – Lieut. Brooke & three O.R. returned from leave. The left half Coy. relieved the right half Coy.	

A5834 Wt. W4973/M687 750,000 8/16 D. D. & L. Ltd. Forms/C.2118/13.

10th Machine Gun Company.

Original

War Diary

– for –

the month of August 1917.

Instructions regarding War Diaries and Intelligence Summaries are contained in F. S. Regs., Part II. and the Staff Manual respectively. Title pages will be prepared in manuscript.

WAR DIARY
or
~~INTELLIGENCE SUMMARY.~~
(Erase heading not required.)

Army Form C. 2118.

10th Machine Gun Coy

Place	Date	~~Hour~~	Ref. PLOUVAIN parts of 51B N.W. and S.W. Summary of Events and Information	Arrivals and Departures	Remarks and references to Appendices
Field	1st	Augt.	On this date the Coy. had two Sectns. (Nos: 3 & 4) in the line, the eight guns having positions as follows:- Left Sector (No: 4 Section – 2/Lt. R. Stevens in charge):- Position — S.O.S. Line 1. COLOMBO TRENCH about I.20.a.35.50. M. bearing of 67° 2. CEYLON AVENUE " I.19.b.75.60. " " 120° 3. CORONA SUPPORT " I.19.b.55.40. " " 47° 4. CORDITE RESERVE " I.19.c.65.90. " " 122° Right Sector (No: 3 Section – 2/Lt. P. McKinnie in charge):- 5. ROEUX VILLAGE about I.19.d.70.65. M. bearing of 95° 6. Near GANTRY " I.19.c.70.45 " " 33° 7. ROEUX WOOD " I.19.c.65.05. On ANGEL TRENCH (S. of RIVER) 8. ROEUX WOOD " I.19.c.80.15 " SUNKEN ROAD at I.25.d.7.9. The other two Sections were in reserve in STIRLING CAMP. Coy. H.Q. were near the Railway cutting at about H.23.a.75.00. Four of our guns co-operated in a shoot with the artillery. Two guns were placed in CORDITE RESERVE about I.19.a.6.0. and searched JUNCTION COPSE from I.20.b.9.2 to I.21.c.8.9. Two other guns were placed about I.19.c.5.0. and searched the River bank from I.20.d.5.8.	nil	

(A7092). Wt. W12839/M1293. 750,000. 1/17. D. D. & L., Ltd. Forms/C.2118/14.

Army Form C. 2118.

Instructions regarding War Diaries and Intelligence Summaries are contained in F. S. Regs., Part II. and the Staff Manual respectively. Title pages will be prepared in manuscript.

WAR DIARY
or
~~INTELLIGENCE SUMMARY.~~
(Erase heading not required.)

Place	Date	~~Hour~~	Summary of Events and Information	Arrivals and Departures	Remarks and references to Appendices
Field	1st	Augt.	to I 20 d. 8. 7. All these guns fired 23 bursts of 50 rounds each between 9.50 pm. and 3.30 A.M. Movement was seen at dugout S. of River at I 25 b. 35. 05. Between 4 pm. and 6 pm. 3 men were seen and fired at by our M.G's. in ROEUX WOOD. Two were killed and the other hit.		
	2nd	..	Similar co-operation with artillery as for previous night. Four guns were placed in same positions, and fired as on previous night at same targets.	Lt. R.W.A. Painter – returned from leave. Lt. Brooke to Hospital	
	3rd	..	Our two M. guns in ROEUX WOOD fired bursts during the night on the SUNKEN ROAD and ANGEL TRENCH S. of River. Our gun in CORDITE RESERVE fired bursts into HAUSA WOOD. No: 1 Section (2/Lt. R. C. Orchard) relieved No: 4 Sectn. in the left sector. No 2 Sectn. (Lt. V.H. Willoughby) relieved No: 3 Sectn. in the right sector. Both reliefs were complete by 10.30 pm. Nos: 3 + 4 Sectns. went into reserve at STIRLING CAMP.	1 O.R. rejoined from Base Depot	
	4th	..	Usual harassing fire by guns in ROEUX WOOD and CORDITE RESERVE	1 O.R. to Hospital	
	5th		Usual harassing fire. A German seen near the dugout at		[initials]

(A7092). Wt. W12839/M1293. 750,000. 1/17. D. D. & L., Ltd. Forms/C.2118/14.

Instructions regarding War Diaries and Intelligence Summaries are contained in F. S. Regs., Part II. and the Staff Manual respectively. Title pages will be prepared in manuscript.

WAR DIARY

~~or~~

~~INTELLIGENCE~~ ~~SUMMARY.~~

(Erase heading not required.)

Page 3.

Army Form C. 2118.

Place	Date	~~Hour~~	Summary of Events and Information	Arrivals and Departures	Remarks and references to Appendices
Field	5th	Augt.	about I 25 d. 35.95. was fired on by our M. gun in ROEUX WOOD and killed.		
	6th	..	Usual harassing fire from ROEUX WOOD and CORDITE RES. guns.	1 O.R. wounded Major R. G. Pettle from hospital	
	7th	..	Ditto. No: 3 Sectn. (2/Lt. P. McKinnie) relieved No: 1 Section in the left Sector. No: 4 Sectn. (2/Lt. R. Stevens) relieved No: 2 Sectn. in the right sector. Both reliefs were complete by 10.30 pm. Nos. 1 & 2 Sectns. went in reserve at STIRLING CAMP.	Lt. V. H. Willoughby - to U.K. on leave.	
	8th	..	Our M gun in CORDITE RES. fired long bursts during the day and night into PLOUVAIN, traversing from the X roads at I 15 b 70.85 to I 15 d. 7.9. During the night the two ROEUX WOOD guns enfiladed enemy positions S. of River. As the result of very close observation of enemy positions in I 25 d. during the day, two Germans were accounted for. At 11.15 am one man was seen in enemy post at I 25 d. 2.9. was fired on and killed. At noon three of enemy were seen in same post for two or three seconds only. At 3 pm they again appeared and one gun opened fire. One man was killed. No further movement was seen in the post. The man killed was wearing a black cap with white band.	1 O.R. evac. to C.C.S.	
	9th	..	Commencing at 8.15 am our artillery bombarded the enemy trenches South	Lt. J. McLellan - reinforcement from base	[initials]

(A7092). Wt. W12839/M1293. 750,000. 1/17. D. D. & L., Ltd. Forms/C.2118/14.

Army Form C. 2118.

Page 4.

Instructions regarding War Diaries and Intelligence Summaries are contained in F. S. Regs., Part II. and the Staff Manual respectively. Title pages will be prepared in manuscript.

WAR DIARY
or
~~INTELLIGENCE SUMMARY.~~

(Erase heading not required.)

Place	Date	~~Hour~~	Summary of Events and Information	Arrivals and Departures	Remarks and references to Appendices
Field	9th	Augt.	of the River for 13 hours, at the conclusion of which the 12th Bde. on our right raided the enemy trenches in conjunction with the 12th Division. Many prisoners were taken. These testified to the effectiveness of our machine gun harassing fire on PLOUVAIN and positions S. of RIVER, stating the working parties and ration parties had been caught. Two of our M. guns were placed in ROEUX WOOD about I.19.c.50.35 and co-operated with artillery by firing long bursts on enemy positions S. of RIVER, particularly GUN TRENCH. These guns continued a covering fire from ZERO onwards. The gun in CORDITE RES. continued its harassing fire into PLOUVAIN. Two M. guns in ROEUX WOOD firing from usual positions, were successful during the morning. At 10.20 am. a man was seen in enemy post in I.25.d., was fired on and killed. At 11.15 am. another man was fired on in same spot. He fell, and a minute or two later two more appeared, presumably to help the former away. These were both hit and killed. At 11.30 am. three men were seen crawling across ridge at top of SUNKEN ROAD in I.25.d. Fire was opened and all three were hit, two being killed.		
	10th	"	The M. guns in ROEUX WOOD and CORDITE RES. carried out usual harassing fire	1 O.R. to hospital 10 O.R. reinforcements from base	
	11th	"	Ditto No: 1 Section (Lt. J. McLellan) relieved No: 3 Sectn. in the		

(A7092). Wt. W12839/M1293. 750,000. 1/17. D. D. & L., Ltd. Forms/C.2118/14.

Army Form C. 2118.

Instructions regarding War Diaries and Intelligence Summaries are contained in F. S. Regs., Part II. and the Staff Manual respectively. Title pages will be prepared in manuscript.

WAR DIARY
~~or~~
~~INTELLIGENCE~~ SUMMARY.

(*Erase heading not required.*)

Place	Date	~~Hour~~	Summary of Events and Information	arrivals and departures.	Remarks and references to Appendices
Field	11th	Augt.	Left Sector. No: 2 Sectn. (Lt. H.I. Lock) relieved No: 4 Sectn. in the right Sector. Both reliefs were complete by 10.30 pm. Nos: 3 & 4 Sectns. went into reserve at STIRLING CAMP.	2/Lt. R.L. Orchard evac: C.C.S. 1 O.R. to hospital	
	12th	"	Usual harassing fire was carried out	2 O.R's. to hosp:	
	13th	"	Ditto. At 3.15 pm. one German ~~was~~ seen near post at I 25 d. 8 4. He was fired on by our M. gun in ROEUX WOOD and killed. He was wearing a light coloured forage cap.	Lt. G. A. Brooke evacuated.	
	14th	"	The artillery, assisted by one heavy Trench mortar, heavily bombarded the enemy positions in I 25 d. from 3 pm. to 4.40 pm. Three machine guns were placed in ROEUX WOOD to watch for enemy movement. During the day 14 Germans were observed in and about ANGEL TRENCH. Ten were killed by ~~our~~ M. guns. During the night 14/15th the gun in CORDITE RES. fired 3,000 rounds into PLOUVAIN.		
	15th	"	Four guns of No: 3 Sectn. (2/Lt. P. McKinnie) were placed in CORDITE RES. and fired in co-operation with artillery as follows:- Three guns fired on HAT TRENCH from I 27 b. 45.85 to I 27 b. 50.35. The fourth	2 O.R. from hosp.	

(A7092). Wt. W12839/M1293. 750,000. 1/17. D. D. & L., Ltd. Forms/C.2118/14.

Instructions regarding War Diaries and Intelligence Summaries are contained in F. S. Regs., Part II. and the Staff Manual respectively. Title pages will be prepared in manuscript.

WAR DIARY

~~or~~

~~INTELLIGENCE SUMMARY.~~

(*Erase heading not required.*)

Page 6

Army Form C. 2118.

Place	Date	~~Hour~~	Summary of Events and Information	Arrivals and Departures	Remarks and references to Appendices
Field	15th	Augt.	gun searched HAMBLAIN ROAD from I 27 b. 45. 85. to I 27 b. 70. 90. All four guns fired bursts of 4 minutes at 3 pm. and 7 pm. After this shoot No: 3 Sectn. proceeded to relieve No: 1 Sectn. in the left Sector. Relief was complete by 8. 30 pm. and No: 1 Sectn. went into reserve at STIRLING CAMP. No: 4 Sectn. (2/Lt. Stevens) relieved No. 2 Sectn. in the right Sector. Relief was complete by 10. 30 pm. No: 2 Sectn. went into reserve at STIRLING CAMP. The guns in CORDITE RESERVE fired the usual harassing fire into P. OUVAIN, its fire being intensified at dusk & dawn, in order to catch ration & working parties		
	16th	"	Usual harassing fire	Lt. C. Matson from hospital. 1 O.R. evacuated.	
	17th	"	During the day the two guns in ROEUX WOOD kept very close watch on enemy positions S. of RIVER. At about 10 am. a man was seen in post approx: I 25 b 3. 0. He was immediately fired on and killed. Two guns were placed in CORDITE RES. at I 19 c. 5. 4 and I 19 c 5. 5 respectively, and co-operated with artillery by firing on the road East of JUNCTION COPSE at I 21 a. 9. 0. Both guns fired eight bursts	1 O.R. evacuated. 5 O.R. reinf: from base.	

(A7092). Wt. W12839/M1293. 750,000. 1/17. D. D. & L., Ltd. Forms/C.2118/14.

Instructions regarding War Diaries and Intelligence Summaries are contained in F. S. Regs., Part II. and the Staff Manual respectively. Title pages will be prepared in manuscript.

WAR DIARY

or

~~INTELLIGENCE SUMMARY.~~

(Erase heading not required.)

Page 7

Army Form C. 2118.

Place	Date	~~Hour~~	Summary of Events and Information	Arrivals and departures	Remarks and references to Appendices
Field	17th	Augt.	of 50 rounds each between 11.31 pm and 1.56 am. The gun in CORDITE RES. fired 3000 rds. into PLOUVAIN during the night		
	18th	..	Usual harassing fire from guns in ROEUX WOOD and CORDITE RES.	Lt. V.H. Willoughby from leave. 16 R. evacuated	
	19th	..	No: ~~1~~ 2 Sectn. (Lt. H.I. Lock) relieved No: 3 Sectn in the left Sector. No: 1 Sectn (2/Lt. McKinnie) relieved No. 4 Sectn in the right Sector. Both reliefs were complete by 9.30 pm. Nos: 3 & 4 Sectns. went into reserve at STIRLING CAMP. Two guns were placed in CORDITE RES. and fired on HAUSA WOOD in co-operation with artillery. Both guns fired from 1~~0~~1.30 pm to 11.45 pm at the rate of one belt every 3 mins. Two guns in ROEUX WOOD kept up harassing fire during the night	NIL	
	20th	..	Usual harassing fire.	Major R.G. Pettle leave to U.K.	
	21st	..	Ditto. Our right gun in ROEUX WOOD silenced a hostile M.G. firing from approx. I 25. d. 65. 80., at 9.45 pm.		
	22nd	..	Usual harassing fire. Two guns in ROEUX WOOD fired on hostile		

(A7092). Wt. W12839/M1293. 750,000. 1/17. D. D. & L., Ltd. Forms/C.2118/14.

Instructions regarding War Diaries and Intelligence Summaries are contained in F. S. Regs., Part II. and the Staff Manual respectively. Title pages will be prepared in manuscript.

WAR DIARY
~~or~~
~~INTELLIGENCE~~ SUMMARY.
(Erase heading not required.)

Page 8.

Army Form C. 2118.

Place	Date	~~Hour~~	Summary of Events and Information	Arrivals and Departures	Remarks and references to Appendices
Field	22nd	Augt.	post at I 25 d. 20 80 at 3 pm. in conjunction with trench mortars. A man was seen to come out of a dugout in SUNKEN ROAD at I 25 d, at 6.45 am. He was fired on by own gun in ROEUX WOOD and killed, his body remaining there till dark. At 3 pm when the T.M's. fired, a man climbed over the parapet. He was fired on and killed.		
	23rd	..	Usual harassing fire. No: 4 Sectn. (2/Lt. Stevens) relieved No: 2 Sectn. in left Sector. No: 3 Sectn. (Lt. V.H. Willoughby) relieved no 1 Sectn. in right Sectr. Both reliefs complete by 9.30 pm. Nos: 1 & 2 Sectns. went into reserve at STIRLING CASTLE.	3 O.R. from base depot	
	24th	..	Usual harassing fire. One of our guns in ROEUX WOOD neutralised an enemy M.G. firing S. of the River at 9.30 pm.	2/Lt. A. Roger from base depot	
	25th	..	Ditto. During the day the guns in ROEUX WOOD fired bursts on enemy observed in ANGEL TRENCH. One man, observed climbing over the parados, was fired on and killed.		
	26th	..	Usual harassing fire by guns in ROEUX WOOD and CORDITE RES. Very	1 O.R. from hosp.	

(A7092). Wt. W12839/M1293. 750,000. 1/17. D. D. & L., Ltd. Forms/C.2118/14.

Page 9

Instructions regarding War Diaries and Intelligence Summaries are contained in F. S. Regs., Part II. and the Staff Manual respectively. Title pages will be prepared in manuscript.

WAR DIARY

~~or~~

~~INTELLIGENCE SUMMARY.~~

(*Erase heading not required.*)

Army Form C. 2118.

Place	Date	~~Hour~~	Summary of Events and Information	Arrivals and Departures	Remarks and references to Appendices
Field	26th	Augt.	Little movement was observed in ANGEL TRENCH during the day. One man only was seen. He was fired at and fell into the bottom of the trench. Two guns in CORDITE RES. co-operated with an artillery gas-shell bombardment. Right gun fired on dugouts at I 15 d. 1.2. Left gun fired on dugouts at I 15 d. 4.3. Both guns fired from 11.45 pm. to 12 mn. at rate of one belt every three minutes.		
	27th	..	Usual harassing fire by guns in ROEUX WOOD and CORDITE RES. No. 1 Sectn. (2/Lt. P. McKinnie) relieved No. 4 Sectn. in the left Sector. No. 2 Sectn. (Lt. J. McLellan) relieved No. 3 Sectn. in the right Sector. Both reliefs were complete by 9.30 pm. Nos: 3 & 4 Sectns. went into reserve at STIRLING CAMP.	—	
	28th	..	Usual harassing fire. The two guns in ROEUX WOOD prevented movement by day in the enemy lines S. of River and continued their harassing fire by night. Gun in CORDITE RES. fired 2500 rounds into PLOUVAIN. The fire was intensified at dusk and dawn with a view to harassing ration and working parties.	—	
	29th	..	Ditto. Usual harassing fire	—	

(A7092). Wt. W12839/M1293. 750,000. 1/17. D. D. & L., Ltd. Forms/C.2118/14.

Army Form C. 2118.

Instructions regarding War Diaries and Intelligence Summaries are contained in F. S. Regs., Part II. and the Staff Manual respectively. Title pages will be prepared in manuscript.

WAR DIARY
~~or~~
~~INTELLIGENCE SUMMARY.~~

(*Erase heading not required.*)

Place	Date	~~Hour~~	Summary of Events and Information	Arrivals and Departures	Remarks and references to Appendices
Field	30th	Augt:	The gun in CORDITE RES fired usual harassing fire into PLOUVAIN. The two guns in ROEUX WOOD harassed the enemy positions S. of River.		
	31st	"	Two of our guns co-operated with the artillery during a gas-shell bombardment. One gun of No: 1 Sectn. in CEYLON TRENCH fired on and enfiladed the trench in I 26 b. 9. 4. at a range of 1600x. One gun of No. 2 Sectn. in ROEUX WOOD at I 19 c. 50·35 fired on CARTRIDGE TRENCH at I 32 b. 2. 5. at range of 2000x. Both guns fired from 5·30 am. to 5·40 am. at the rate of one belt every three minutes. In the afternoon between 2 pm. and 3·30 pm. our heavy T. M. in CORDITE RES. fired on to ARCHIE and APE trenches and enemy positions S. of River. Our GANTRY position machine gun was placed in the trench in ROEUX WOOD to the right of our other two guns and a careful watch was kept. Only one German appeared and he was fired on by our guns & killed. After the shoot our guns resumed their normal positions and carried out the usual harassing fire, as also did the gun in CORDITE RES. No: 4 Sectn. (2/Lt. R.W. Kingsman) relieved No: 1 Sectn. in the left	Major R. G. Pettle returned from leave.	

(A7092). Wt. W12839/M1293. 750,000. 1/17. D. D. & L., Ltd. Forms/C.2118/14.

Instructions regarding War Diaries and Intelligence Summaries are contained in F. S. Regs., Part II. and the Staff Manual respectively. Title pages will be prepared in manuscript.

WAR DIARY

~~or~~

~~INTELLIGENCE SUMMARY.~~

(Erase heading not required.)

Page 11

Army Form C. 2118.

Place	Date	~~Hour~~	Summary of Events and Information	Arrivals and Departures	Remarks and references to Appendices
Field	31st	Augt.	Sector. No. 3 Sectn. (Lt. V. H. Willoughby) relieved No: 2 Sectn. in the right Sector. Both reliefs were complete by 9.30 pm. Nos: 1 & 2 Sections went into reserve at STIRLING CAMP.		
	1st to 31st	..	During the month, training was carried out at STIRLING CAMP as follows:- On the day following each relief, each Sectn. spent the morning in cleaning and overhauling guns, tripods, spare parts, clothing and equipment. The next two days - in gun drill, mechanism, stoppages and immediate action, and lectures by Sectn. Officers on Indirect and barrage fire. Also drill with gas appliances, physical training and practice with Yukon packs. The morning of fourth day was spent in preparing for trenches. Each afternoon bathing & swimming parades were held in the River SCARPE.		

R.C. Pettle. Major
O.C. 10th M. G. Coy

1st Sept. 1917.

(A7092). Wt. W12839/M1293. 750,000. 1/17. D. D. & L., Ltd. Forms/C.2118/14.

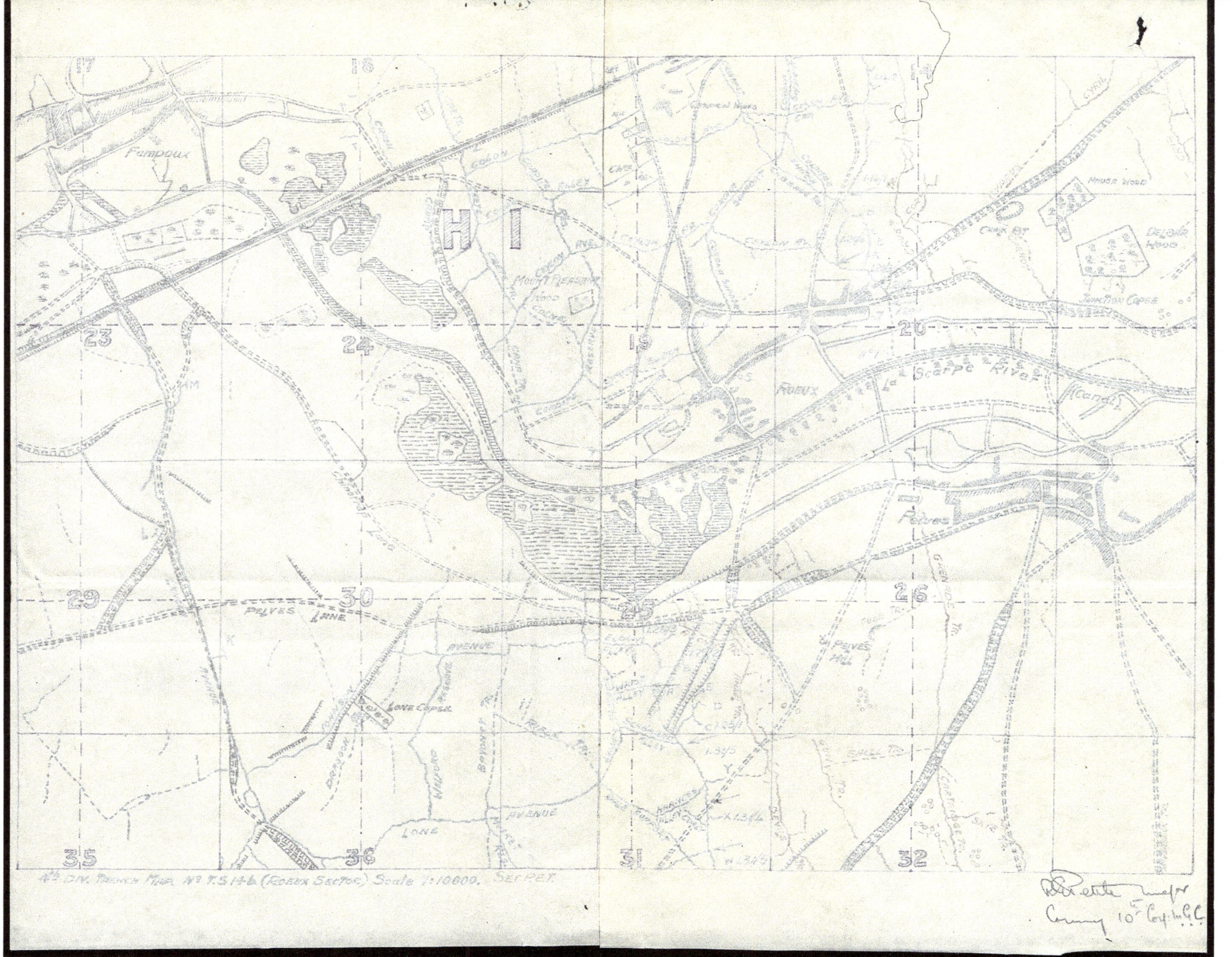

Fampoux
H
I
Mount Pleasant Wood
Mayor Wood
Delbar Wood
Junction Copse
Roeux
Scarpe River
(Canal)
Pelves
Pelves Lane
Pelves Hill
Lone Copse
Avenue
Bayonet
Walford
Lone
Chinstrap Lane
Greenland Tr.
Cartridge Tr.
Shell Tr.
17
18
19
20
23
24
25
26
29
30
31
32
35
36
4th DIV. TRENCH MAP No T.S.14.b (ROEUX SECTOR) Scale 1:10000. SECRET.

4th Division

10th Infantry Bde

10th M. G. C.

September – December

1917

T

10TH INFANTRY BRIGADE.

ORIGINAL WAR DIARY

for September 1917

10 M.G. Coy Vol 20

FIELD.

8-10-17

R.L. Pettit. MAJOR.

COMMANDING 10TH MACHINE GUN COY.

Instructions regarding War Diaries and Intelligence Summaries are contained in F. S. Regs., Part II. and the Staff Manual respectively. Title pages will be prepared in manuscript.

WAR DIARY 10th M. G. Coy.

or

~~INTELLIGENCE SUMMARY.~~

(Erase heading not required.)

Army Form C. 2118.

Place	Date	~~Hour~~	Ref: PLOUVAIN parts of 51B N.W. and S.W. Summary of Events and Information	Arrivals + Departures	Remarks and references to Appendices
Field.	Sept:	1.	On this date the Coy. had two Sections (Nos: 3 + 4) in the line, the eight guns having positions as follows:-	Sergeant Tompkins from leave.	Privates Ashby + Tomalin leave to U.K.
			Left Sector (No: 4 Sectn. – 2/Lt. R.W. Kingsman):-		
			Position. — S. O. S. Line		
			1. COLOMBO TRENCH about I. 20. a. 35. 50. — M. bearing of 67°		
			2. CEYLON AVENUE " I 19 b. 75·60. — " " 120°		
			3. CORONA SUPPORT " I 19 b. 55·40 — " " 47°		
			4. CORDITE RESERVE " I 19 d. 65. 90. — " " 122°		
			Right Sector (No: 3 Sectn. – Lt. O.H. Willoughby):-		
			5. ROEUX VILLAGE about I 19. d. 70·65. — M. bearing of 95°		
			6. near GANTRY " I 19. c. 70·45 — " " 33°		
			7. ROEUX WOOD " I 19. c. 65.05. — On ANGEL TRENCH. (S. of River.)		
			8. ROEUX WOOD " I 19. c. 80. 15. — On SUNKEN ROAD at I. 25 d. 7. 9.		
			The other two Sections were in reserve in STIRLING CAMP.		
			Coy. H. Q. were near the Railway Cutting at about H. 23. a. 75.00.		

2353 Wt. W2544/1454 700,000 5/15 D. D. & L. A.D.S.S./Forms/C. 2118.

2

WAR DIARY

or

~~INTELLIGENCE SUMMARY.~~

(Erase heading not required.)

Army Form C. 2118.

Instructions regarding War Diaries and Intelligence Summaries are contained in F. S. Regs., Part II. and the Staff Manual respectively. Title pages will be prepared in manuscript.

Place	Date	~~Hour~~	Summary of Events and Information	Arrivals & Departures	Remarks and references to Appendices
Field.	Sept:	1.	Our gun in CORDITE RES. fired bursts of harassing fire into PLOUVAIN during the day and night. The fire was intensified at dusk and dawn with a view to catching ration and working parties. Two guns in ROEUX WOOD fired during the night on enemy positions S. of River.		
	"	2.	Usual harassing fire by above three guns. At 12·30 pm our gun in CEYLON fired on CHALK-PIT and CYPRUS and dispersed an enemy party working there.	Lance Corporal Wharton from Rest Camp. 4 O.Rs from leave.	1.O.R to hospital
	"	3.	A party of about 40 Germans were observed working in front of HAUSA WOOD at 3 am. A screen was put up and COLOMBO gun opened fire. The enemy immediately dispersed. Two of our guns co-operated in a shoot with the artillery. Gun in CEYLON traversed CYPRUS TRENCH at a range of 1100x. Gun in CORDITE RES. traversed CARROT TRENCH at a range of 1550x. Each gun fired five belts between 6 pm and 6·18 pm. Two guns in ROEUX WOOD co-operated with a shoot by the Stokes Mortars S. of River on ANGEL and ARCHIE trenches. Only one of the	2 O.Rs. from leave.	1 O.R. to hospital

£353 Wt. W2544/1454 700,000 5/15 D. D. & L. A.D.S.S./Forms/C. 2118.

3

Instructions regarding War Diaries and Intelligence Summaries are contained in F. S. Regs., Part II. and the Staff Manual respectively. Title pages will be prepared in manuscript.

WAR DIARY

or

~~INTELLIGENCE SUMMARY.~~

(Erase heading not required.)

Army Form C. 2118.

Place	Date	Hour	Summary of Events and Information	Arrivals + Departures	Remarks and references to Appendices
Field	Sept.	3.	enemy was disturbed. he was fired on and killed, the body remaining in the trench. This occurred at 4.45 p.m. During the night, the usual harassing fire was carried out.		
		4.	Three guns in ROEUX WOOD co-operated with heavy T.M. shoot on ARCHIE and APE from 2 pm. - 3 pm. During this shoot two of the enemy left the trench at I. 25 b. 3.0. One was killed by our gun, the other jumped into a shell-hole at the same time a shell landed and he was not seen again. The body of the other man remained in the open until dusk. Both wore great-coats (apparently quite new) and soft caps. After this shoot, our three guns resumed their normal positions and kept up harassing fire during the night		
		5.	Usual harassing fire by guns in CORPITE RESERVE and ROEUX WOOD. This was a particularly quiet day. It was noticed that the German killed the day before was still lying out, no attempt having been made to remove the body.	1 O.R. from hospital	

2353 Wt. W2544/1454 700,000 5/15 D. D. & L. A.D.S.S./Forms/C. 2118.

4.

Instructions regarding War Diaries and Intelligence Summaries are contained in F. S. Regs., Part II. and the Staff Manual respectively. Title pages will be prepared in manuscript.

WAR DIARY

~~or~~

~~INTELLIGENCE SUMMARY.~~

(*Erase heading not required.*)

Army Form C. 2118.

Place	Date	~~Hour~~	Summary of Events and Information	Arrivals &	Remarks and references to Appendices Departures
Field	Sept.	6.	On this day the Coy. was relieved by the 45th Coy. 15th Divn. Seven guns in the line were relieved by day, the relief being complete by 4.30 pm. The gun in ROEUX VILLAGE was relieved after dusk, the relief being complete by 10 pm. The whole Coy. moved into billets in ARRAS.	1. O.R. from leave	3. O.Rs. leave to U.K. 1. O.R. to hospital. 1. O.R. transferred to stationary hospital
	"	1st to 6th	During this period, training was carried out at STIRLING CAMP by Nos. 1 & 2 Sectns. – gun drill, mechanism, stoppages & immediate action, lectures by Sectn. Officers on Indirect and Barrage fire. Also drill with gas appliances, physical training and practice with Yukon packs.		
		4th	From 9 – 11 am. the Coy. paraded for cleaning guns & equipment and packing of limbers, and from 11 am. – 12 noon attended to personal cleanliness. The Coy. moved to a new area in the afternoon. Leaving ARRAS	1 O.R. from Base Depot.	

2353 Wt. W2544/1454 700,000 5/15 D. D. & L. A.D.S.S./Forms/C. 2118.

5

Instructions regarding War Diaries and Intelligence Summaries are contained in F. S. Regs., Part II. and the Staff Manual respectively. Title pages will be prepared in manuscript.

WAR DIARY

~~or~~

~~INTELLIGENCE SUMMARY.~~

(*Erase heading not required.*)

Army Form C. 2118.

Place	Date	~~Hour~~	Summary of Events and Information	Arrivals &	Departures Remarks and references to Appendices
Field	Sept.	7th	at 2.15 pm, Coy. marched to BAILLEULMONT, arrived there at 6 pm. The men were billetted there in a large hut.		
		8th	9 am - 12 noon. - cleaning of guns and equipment. Checking deficiencies of equipment and gear.		1 O.R. to C.C.S.
		9th	The Coy. attended Church Parades. Inspection of billets by C.O.	1 O.R. from Leave	2 O.Rs to Hospital
		10th	9 - 9.30 am. Physical training. 9.45 - 10.20 am. Company drill. 10 - 30 am - 12.30 pm. The Sections when not at baths carried out gas respirator drill, instruction in German M. guns, stoppages and I. A. 2 - 4 pm. Coy. marched out to training area, and practised attack over old British & German trenches, guns, tripods & belt-boxes being carried on pack animals.		

2353 Wt. W2544/1454 700,000 5/15 D. D. & L. A.D.S.S./Forms/C. 2118.

6/

Instructions regarding War Diaries and Intelligence Summaries are contained in F. S. Regs., Part II. and the Staff Manual respectively. Title pages will be prepared in manuscript.

WAR DIARY
~~or~~
~~INTELLIGENCE SUMMARY.~~
(*Erase heading not required.*)

Army Form C. 2118.

Place	Date	~~Hour~~	Summary of Events and Information	Arrivals & Departures	Remarks and references to Appendices
Viela	Sept	11th	9 AM to 9-3 AM Physical training. 9-45 AM to 10-45 AM Company Drill 11 AM to 12-30 PM Parades under Section Officers;- Instruction in German Gun, Gun Drill, & Mechanism. 2 PM to 4 PM. Section Officers marched their Sections to Training Area, Explained "Barrage" Drill. Pack animals were taken.		
"		12th	The Company Marched off at 6-30 AM to the training area, & on the field firing range, put down a barrage on a hidden target.	1. OR. from leave.	2 ORs leave to U.K. 1 OR. to hospital
"		13th	9 AM to 10 AM Physical Training. 10 AM to 11-30 AM. The company had Baths. 11-3 AM to 12-30 PM. The Sections under Section Officers were instructed in Gun Drill & Mechanism. 2 PM to 5-30 PM. The company in fighting order, without guns, did an exercise in topography.	3 O.Rs. from leave	3. ORs Evacuated.
"		14th	9 AM to 10 AM Physical Training 10-15 to 11-15 AM. Company Drill. 11-15 AM to 12-30 PM. Gun Drill under Section Officers. 2 PM to 3 PM. The Company paraded for practise in German Machine Guns. 3-30 PM. The Company paraded in walking out order marched to Bailleul to watch football match between the Company, & No 2 Company, 4th Division Train, the Company winning 2 — nil	1 O.R. from hospital	1 O.R. to Rest Camp 2 O.R. leave to U.K.

A5834 Wt. W4973/M687 750,000 8/16 D. D. & L. Ltd. Forms/C.2118/13.

7

Instructions regarding War Diaries and Intelligence Summaries are contained in F. S. Regs., Part II. and the Staff Manual respectively. Title pages will be prepared in manuscript.

WAR DIARY
~~or~~
~~INTELLIGENCE SUMMARY.~~
(Erase heading not required.)

Army Form C. 2118.

Place	Date	~~Hour~~	Summary of Events and Information	Arrivals	Remarks and references to Appendices / Departures
Fils	Sept	15th	Church parades under Brigade arrangements.	2 ORs from Gas School	1 O.R. to hospital
	"	16th	9 AM to 10 AM. Physical Training. 10-15 AM to 11-15 AM. Company Drill. 11-15 AM to 12-30 PM. Box respirator drill. Instructions under Section Officers. 2 PM. to 4 PM. Gun Drill company parade to see football match Company versus 3/10th Middlesex Battalion Result; 4 – nil in the company's favour.		
	"	17th	9 AM to 12-30 PM. Parades as for the 16th 2 PM to 4 PM. – Baths.	1 O.R. from leave	
	"	18th	The Company entrained at SAULTY LABRETTE at 9 AM & detrained at PROVEN at 6 PM.	1 OR from U.K. 1 OR from hospital	1 OR to hospital 1 OR transferred to 107 Company
	"	19th	9 AM to 10 AM. Physical Training. 10-15 AM to 11 AM. Company Drill 11 AM to 12-30 PM. Gun Drill & Mechanism. 2 PM to 4 PM. Stoppages & Immediate action.		2 ORs leave to U.K.
	"	20th	9 AM to 10 AM. Physical training. 10-15 AM to 2-30 PM. Route March.	1 OR. from hospital	

A5834 Wt. W4973 M687 750,000 8/16 D. D. & L. Ltd. Forms/C.2118/13.

8/

Instructions regarding War Diaries and Intelligence Summaries are contained in F. S. Regs., Part II. and the Staff Manual respectively. Title pages will be prepared in manuscript.

WAR DIARY

or

~~INTELLIGENCE SUMMARY.~~

(Erase heading not required.)

Army Form C. 2118.

Place	Date	Hour	Summary of Events and Information	Arrivals & Dispatches	Remarks and references to Appendices
Fill	Sept	21st	9 AM to 10 AM. Physical Training. 10-15 AM to 11-15 AM. Company Drill. 11-30 AM to 12-30 PM. Mechanism & Stoppages. 2 PM to 3 PM. Gun Drill. 3 PM to 4 PM. Box Respirators Drill.		
	"	22nd	Corporal Bardett & Corporal Murphy, reported to 9th FIELD Coy. R.E., to instruct the men in the VICKERS & Lewis Machine Guns. Church parade under Brigade arrangements. Corporal Homer & Lance-Corporal Hopkins returned from Gas course, with a report "GOOD".		2 ORs to hospital 2 ORs leave to U.K.
	"	23rd	9 AM to 10 AM Physical Training. 10-15 AM to 2 PM. Route March.	Sergeant Platts from Base Depot	
	"	24th	9 AM to 10 AM. Physical Training. 10-15 AM to 11-15 AM Company Drill. 11-30 AM to 12-30 PM. Parade under Section Officers for Gun Drill & E.D. The Company was warned to be prepared to go into the line on night 26th/27th.	2 ORs from leave	2 ORs leave to UK. 2 ORs to hospital
	"	25th	9 AM to 10 AM. Physical Training. 10 AM to 12-30 PM. Numbers 1 & 2 Sections paraded under Section Officers. Numbers 3 & 4. the Baths. 2 PM to 4 PM. Numbers 3 & 4 Sections under Section Officers Numbers 1 & 2 the Baths.		4 ORs to hospital 1 OR [illegible] to C.C.S.

A5834 Wt. W4973/M687 750,000 8/16 D. D. & L. Ltd. Forms/C.2118/13.

9.

Instructions regarding War Diaries and Intelligence Summaries are contained in F. S. Regs., Part II. and the Staff Manual respectively. Title pages will be prepared in manuscript.

WAR DIARY

~~or~~

~~INTELLIGENCE SUMMARY.~~

(Erase heading not required.)

Army Form C. 2118.

Place	Date	~~Hour~~	Summary of Events and Information	Arrivals & Departures	Remarks and references to Appendices
Field	Sept	26th	9AM to 9-45AM Physical Training 10.15AM to 2PM. Route March.		1 O.R. Evacuated to C.C.S. accidentally injured 2 Lieut Kingham leave to U.K. 1 O.R. Hospital
"		27th	Parades as for 26th.	2 O.Rs. from hospital	1 O.R. leave to U.K.
"		28th	Parades as for 21st		2 O.Rs to Rest Camp
"		29th	The Company relieved the 61st Machine Gun Company in the support area at SOULT CAMP. Reserve details were sent to DRAGON CAMP.		
"		30th	Church parades under Brigade Arrangements.		1 O.R. leave to U.K.

A5834 Wt. W4973 M687 750,000 8/16 D. D. & L. Ltd. Forms/C.2118/13.

10TH MACHINE GUN COY

ORIGINAL

WAR

DIARY

107

FOR MONTH OF OCTOBER
1917.

FIELD.

W.H. Willoughby Lt. for MAJOR

3. 11. 17

COMMANDING 10TH M.G. COY

(6)

Instructions regarding War Diaries and Intelligence Summaries are contained in F. S. Regs., Part II. and the Staff Manual respectively. Title pages will be prepared in manuscript.

WAR DIARY
or
~~INTELLIGENCE SUMMARY~~.
(Erase heading not required.)

Army Form C. 2118.

Place	Date	Hour	Summary of Events and Information	Remarks and references to Appendices
In the Field	Oct-17.		Reference Maps.	
			Belgium & France, Sheet 26. N.W. } 1/20,000	
			" 27. N.E.	
			" 20. S.W.	
			" 19. S.E.	
			" 27 1/40,000	
			France " 51. B. 1:40,000	
			Lens. 11 " 1: 100,000	
			Special Maps { LANCEMARCK - BROEMBEEK, BROEMBEEK - WESTROOSEBEKE, BROEMBEEK, 1. Corps T.S. No 87(c). } Attached	

(A7092). Wt. W12839/M1293. 750,000. 1/17. D. D. & L., Ltd. Forms/C.2118/14.

(2)

Instructions regarding War Diaries and Intelligence Summaries are contained in F. S. Regs., Part II. and the Staff Manual respectively. Title pages will be prepared in manuscript.

WAR DIARY

or

~~INTELLIGENCE SUMMARY.~~

(Erase heading not required.)

Army Form C. 2118.

Place	Date	Hour	Summary of Events and Information	ARRIVALS	DEPARTURES	Remarks and references to Appendices
Field	Oct 1st /17		The Company was in SOULT CAMP, as mentioned in the Summary for 29th Ult. Transport was near BRIDGE JUNCTION B.20. C 3.7. Company parade for Physical Training from 9 AM to 10 AM. Guns and Gear were overhauled & prepared for Action.	2 ORs from Hosp 2 ORs from leave		
"	2nd		No 1 Section under the command of 2nd Lieut P. McKINNIE proceeded to the support line at EAGLE TRENCH, and was attached to O/C 2nd Seaforth Highlanders for orders in the forthcoming operations.	1 OR from leave 1 OR from Hosp 2 ORs reinforcements from Base Depot	1 OR Evacuated to C.C.S.	
	3rd		Nos 3 and 4 Sections under the command of Lt V. H. WILLOUGHBY moved up to barrage positions in front of LANGEMARK at U.23.c.8.7. Coy Headquarters and No 2 Section under the command of Lt H. I. LOCK moved up to Coy Headquarters at NORMAN JUNCTION at C.3.a.75-8. The following is a copy of Operations Orders No 63 issued by O.C. Company on 2/10/17.			[initials]

(A7092). Wt. W12839/M1293. 750,000. 5/17. D. D. & L., Ltd. Forms/C.2118/14.

(3)

Instructions regarding War Diaries and Intelligence Summaries are contained in F. S. Regs., Part II. and the Staff Manual respectively. Title pages will be prepared in manuscript.

WAR DIARY

or

~~INTELLIGENCE SUMMARY.~~

(Erase heading not required.)

Army Form C. 2118.

Place	Date	Hour	Summary of Events and Information	Remarks and references to Appendices
			Secret Operation Orders No: 63 Map Ref. – BROEMBEEK / LANGEMARCK } 1/10,000 1. No 1 Section will proceed into EAGLE TRENCH to relieve four guns of 12th M.G. Coy on night of 2/3rd inst. O.C. No: 1 Section will report to O.C. 2/Seaforth Highlrs relief complete. The guns of this Section will be at the disposal of O.C. 2/ Seaforth Highlanders. 2 No's 3 and 4 Sections will proceed to U. 23 c 8.7 for purposes of putting down a barrage on TRAGIQUE FARM and KANGAROO HUTS in U 13 c. These guns will be in position at ZERO minus 6 hours. Battery Commander will report to Coy H.Q. at NORMAN JUNCTION at C 3 a 70.95 by runner at this hour, using the code word "GOOD". 3. Instructions for barrage. The guns of the battery will work in pairs, using combined sights – (a) No: 1 pair (right hand) range of 2100x Q.A. 4° 48' (b) " 2 " " " 2000x " 4° 16' (c) " 3 " " " 1900x " 3° 48' (d) " 4 " (left hand) " " 1850x " 3° 36'	RR

(A7092). Wt. W12839/M1293. 750,000. 1/17. D. D. & L., Ltd. Forms/C.2118/14.

(8)

Instructions regarding War Diaries and Intelligence Summaries are contained in F. S. Regs., Part II. and the Staff Manual respectively. Title pages will be prepared in manuscript.

WAR DIARY
or
~~INTELLIGENCE SUMMARY.~~
(Erase heading not required.)

Army Form C. 2118.

Place	Date	Hour	Summary of Events and Information	Remarks and references to Appendices
			All guns of the battery will traverse between bearings of 75° M and 80° M	
			(e) Times & rates of fire, all guns. From Z to Z + 23 at rate of one belt per minute at Z + 23 - cease fire.	
			(4) Advance to S.O.S. lines. At Z + 23 the battery will move forward to a position on the right of the road U. 23 b. 35 20 and will lay guns on barrage lines from 70° M. to 80° M., i.e. difference of 1° 15' between guns. Combined sights will be used.	
			(a) No. 1 pair (right hand) range of 2350× Q.A. 6° 20'	
			(b) " 2 " " " 2250× " 5° 40'	
			(c) " 3 " " " 2150× " 5° 00'	
			(d) " 4 " (left hand) " " 2050× " 4° 30'	
			(e) This battery will open fire on the S.O.S. signal being sent up or written order from O.C. Coy. An intense fire for ten minutes, reduced to 25 rounds per minute, for further ten minutes.	
			(5) No. 2 Section will be in support at Coy H.Q. and will relieve No. 1 Section on Z + 1 night.	
			(6) Carrying party. The 1st R.W. Regt are supplying a carrying party of 16 men to be attached to No. 1 Section. This party will report to O.C. No 1 Section at 4 P.M. today. Rations for this party will arrive with rations of No. 1 Section.	RR

(A7092). Wt. W12839/M1293. 750,000. 1/17. D. D. & L., Ltd. Forms/C.2118/14.

(5)

Army Form C. 2118.

Instructions regarding War Diaries and Intelligence Summaries are contained in F. S. Regs., Part II. and the Staff Manual respectively. Title pages will be prepared in manuscript.

WAR DIARY
or
~~INTELLIGENCE SUMMARY.~~
(Erase heading not required.)

Place	Date	Hour	Summary of Events and Information	Remarks and references to Appendices
			(7) Rations — All men going into the line will carry two days rations, ie. cooked rations for the day after they arrive, and the iron ration for the day following. Two days rations for No. 1 Section will be delivered at AU. BON GITE on night of 2nd by the Coy Transport. The Q M Sergt will make arrangements with the Q.M. Sergt of 1st R W. Regt to draw rations for the party of 16 attached to No. 1 Section.	
			(8) O. C. Battery must arrange to warn all troops approaching the danger area in front of the battery barrage positions	
			(9) The S.O.S. signal will be one rifle rocket bursting into 4 red flares.	
			(Signed) R. G. Pitt[illegible] Major O.C. "DOME"	
			2-10-17 To:- all Section Officers Transport Officer.	

(A7092). Wt. W12839/M1293. 750,000. 1/17. D. D. & L., Ltd. Forms/C.2118/14.

Instructions regarding War Diaries and Intelligence Summaries are contained in F. S. Regs., Part II. and the Staff Manual respectively. Title pages will be prepared in manuscript.

WAR DIARY
or
~~INTELLIGENCE SUMMARY.~~
(Erase heading not required.)

Army Form C. 2118.

Place	Date	Hour	Summary of Events and Information	ARRIVALS	DEPARTURES	Remarks and references to Appendices
In the Field	4th		Lt J. McLELLAN was killed by shell fire at 11 PM 2nd Lt P. McKINNIE was killed. ZERO hour was at 6 A.M. 2nd Lt A ROGER then in command of No. 1 Section was wounded at ZERO. The barrage was carried out according to orders and with success. One gun was knocked out and 3 other ranks wounded. The battery then moved forward to EAGLE TRENCH and guns were laid on the S.O.S. lines. At this point Guns and men were buried and the teams suffered heavy casualties. The guns were dug out and again brought into action. No. 1 Section, 4 guns, followed behind the third wave of the Second Seaforth Highlanders Two of these guns were knocked out by shell fire during the advance, the teams became casualties, and the guns were lost. One gun took up a position on 19 METOR HILL but was put out of action by shrapnel and the gun was sent back. One gun reached V.18.c.9.5 with the leading Seaforths Highlanders and came into action when the left flank was checked by Machine Gun fire.			

(A7092). Wt. W12839/M1293. 750,000. 1/17. D. D. & L., Ltd. Forms/C.2118/14.

(7)

Instructions regarding War Diaries and Intelligence Summaries are contained in F. S. Regs., Part II. and the Staff Manual respectively. Title pages will be prepared in manuscript.

WAR DIARY
or
~~INTELLIGENCE SUMMARY.~~
(Erase heading not required.)

Army Form C. 2118.

Place	Date	Hour	Summary of Events and Information	DETAILS ARRIVALS	DETAILS DEPARTURES	Remarks and references to Appendices
In the field	4th	(Continued)	During the German Counter-Attack all the available ammunition was expended and the gun was then destroyed by the N.C.O. in charge. Corporal Howes was the N.C.O. in charge of this gun, and after having blown the gun up he came back and reported his action. Whereupon a fresh gun team was formed from eight other teams that was out of action and these with a carrying party were sent forward under Lieut I LOCK to take up position in the final objective which had by this time been reached. This team took up a position on 19 METRE HILL but was again put out of action by shell fire. Lieut I LOCK was wounded in the foot on the way up to EAGLE TRENCH. Lieut R.W.A. PAINTER was wounded during the afternoon at 5 P.M. No. 2 Section moved up to EAGLE TRENCH, and suffered many casualties on the way up.			RB

(A7092). Wt. W12839/M1293. 750,000. 1/17. D. D. & L., Ltd. Forms/C.2118/14.

(8)

Instructions regarding War Diaries and Intelligence Summaries are contained in F. S. Regs., Part II. and the Staff Manual respectively. Title pages will be prepared in manuscript.

WAR DIARY
or
~~INTELLIGENCE SUMMARY.~~
(Erase heading not required.)

Army Form C. 2118.

Place	Date	Hour	Summary of Events and Information	ARRIVALS	DEPARTURES	Remarks and references to Appendices
In the field	4th.	(Continued)	Two guns under LIEUT V. H. WILLOUGHBY went forward at 6. P.M and reached positions on 19 METRE HILL, where they came into action. LIEUT P. DALTON, ACTING Transport Officer, was detailed & sent up to EAGLE TRENCH to take command of the guns there owing to the severe Officer casualties. Six guns were collected there, teams were rapidly re-organized & the guns were laid on the S.O.S. lines & ready for Action.	1.O.R from Hospital.	Lt McLELLAN J. } 2nd Lt McKINNE P. } KILLED Lt PAINTER R.W.A. } Lt LOCK H. I. } 2nd Lt ROGERS. A } WOUNDED 26 O.Rs WOUNDED 2 O.Rs MISSING 4 O.Rs HOSPITAL 1 O.R Leave to U.K. 5. O.R KILLED	
"	5th		2nd LIEUT STEVENS relieved LIEUT V. H. WILLOUGHBY during the morning. All reserve details rejoined the Company in the line.	1. O.R. from Leave to U.K.		
"	6th		The Company, less one Section (which was placed under the orders of G.O.C. 11th Brigade) and commanded by 2nd Lt. STEVENS was relieved and withdrawn to SOULT CAMP	2 O.Rs from Leave to U.K.	2 ORs to Hosp 1 O.R. was to C.C.S.	
"	7th		The day was spent in re-organization 2nd Lt R. W. KINGSMAN returned from leave. The section in the line was withdrawn under orders of the 11th Brigade, and re-joined the Company.	2nd Lt KINGSMAN R.W. from leave 1. O.R. from Base Depot	~~2 ORs to Hosp~~ 1	[initials]

(A7092). Wt. W12839/M1293. 750,000. 1/17. D. D. & L., Ltd. Forms/C.2118/14.

(a)

Instructions regarding War Diaries and Intelligence Summaries are contained in F. S. Regs., Part II. and the Staff Manual respectively. Title pages will be prepared in manuscript.

WAR DIARY
or
~~INTELLIGENCE SUMMARY.~~
(*Erase heading not required.*)

Army Form C. 2118.

Place	Date	Hour	Summary of Events and Information	ARRIVALS	DEPARTURES	Remarks and references to Appendices
In The Field	8th		The Company, with a strength of 5 OFFICERS, and nine guns and teams, moved up to CANDLE TRENCH, as Brigade Support.	1.O.R from leave 1.O.R from Hosp.		
"	9th		The Company remained in support in CANDLE TRENCH	1.O.R from leave		
"	10th		The Company remained in support in CANDLE TRENCH.	2.O.Rs from Base Depot		
"	11th		The Company remained in support in CANDLE TRENCH Four Guns under 2ND LIEUT R.W. KINGSMAN moved off to be attached to battalions for forthcoming operations. Two of them were attached to the HOUSEHOLD BATTALION and the remaining two to the ROYAL WARICKSHIRE Regiment. These two battalions were placed under the command of the G.O.C. 12th Brigade for the next days operations. During this action the two guns attached to the ROYAL WARICKSHIRE Regiment suffered very few casualties and were eventually withdrawn when this regiment was relieved.	2ND LT. INSKIP } 2ND LT. LABES } from base depot 1.O.R from Hosp. 2ND LT R.W. KINGSMAN Missing & Believed Killed 2.O.Rs missing & believed Killed 3.O.Rs Wounded 2.O.Rs Missing	1.O.R. Evac to C.C.S	

(A7092). Wt. W12839/M1293. 750,000. 1/17. D. D. & L., Ltd. Forms/C.2118/14.

(10)

Instructions regarding War Diaries and Intelligence Summaries are contained in F. S. Regs., Part II. and the Staff Manual respectively. Title pages will be prepared in manuscript.

WAR DIARY
or
~~INTELLIGENCE SUMMARY.~~

(Erase heading not required.)

Army Form C. 2118.

Place	Date	Hour	Summary of Events and Information	Remarks and references to Appendices
In The Field	11th	(Continued)	The two guns attached to the HOUSEHOLD BATTALION however were lost, and 2nd Lt KINGSMAN was believed to be killed - the reason for these heavy casualties was the failure of the DIVISION on our right to take POEL-CAPALE, thus leaving the right flank unprotected, when the objective was taken	
"	12th		The Company less four guns was withdrawn from the line and moved to SOLFORINO CAMP, for the night.	ARRIVALS: 2nd Lt LAW.A.E., 2nd Lt MOOR.W.B. from Base Depot; 1.O.R. from leave; 1.O.R. " Course. DEPARTURES: 3.O.Rs leave to U.K.; 2 O.Rs to Hosp.
"	13th		The Company paraded at 11-45 P.M and marched to ELVERDINGE SIDING where it entrained. The Company detrained at PROVEN and marched to PEGWELL Camp PROVEN AREA (P.4). The Transport moved under separate orders, and marched to the above camp, starting at 8-30 AM. and arriving at 12 noon.	ARRIVALS: 22 O.Rs from Base Depot; 1.O.R. from Hospital. DEPARTURES: 2 O.Rs Evac to C.C.S.; 1.O.R. leave to U.K.
"	14th		The Company paraded in clean fatigue dress to overhaul guns and gear.	

(A7092). Wt. W12839/M1293. 750,000. 1/17. D. D. & L., Ltd. Forms/C.2118/14.

(11)

Instructions regarding War Diaries and Intelligence Summaries are contained in F. S. Regs., Part II. and the Staff Manual respectively. Title pages will be prepared in manuscript.

WAR DIARY
or
~~INTELLIGENCE SUMMARY.~~
(Erase heading not required.)

Army Form C. 2118.

Place	Date	Hour	Summary of Events and Information	ARRIVALS	DEPARTURES	Remarks and references to Appendices
In The Field	15th		The Company with transport, paraded at 9-45 A.M and marched to "L" camp. St JAN-TER-BIEZEN AREA			
"	16th		The O.C inspected the Company in Marching order. Billeting party of 1. OFFICER and 1 O.R. entrained at POPERINGE STATION to go in advance to the new AREA.	2 O.Rs from C.C.S		
"	17th		The morning was spent in the packing of limbers etc. The Company paraded at 1 P.M. and marched to HOUPOUTRE - SIDING L.17 d.5.6, where it entrained			
"	18th		The Company detrained at AUBIGNY at 3-30 A.M, and marched to "Y" Hutments on the ARRAS - St POL ROAD near ETRUN.			
"	19th		Sections paraded under Section Officers for inspection.	1 OR from C.C.S 1 OR from Hosp		
"	20th		9 ~~to~~ 10 A.M Box Respirators were inspected by the Brigade Gas N.C.O. 10 AM to 12-30 P.M. Baths at DUISANS		Cpl GARROW to Base Depot	

(A7092). Wt. W12839/M1293. 750,000. 1/17. D. D. & L., Ltd. Forms/C.2118/14.

(12)

Instructions regarding War Diaries and Intelligence Summaries are contained in F. S. Regs., Part II. and the Staff Manual respectively. Title pages will be prepared in manuscript.

WAR DIARY

or

~~INTELLIGENCE SUMMARY.~~

(Erase heading not required.)

Army Form C. 2118.

Place	Date	Hour	Summary of Events and Information	ARRIVALS	DEPARTURES	Remarks and references to Appendices
In the Field	21st		Church Services. The Company was warned to be prepared to proceed into the line on the 23rd inst. O.C. and 1 OFFICER embussed at Brigade Headquarters, & debussed at MAISON ROOGE N.34 and proceeded to interview O.C. 37th Machine Gun Company and to view the trench system prior to relief.	Coy S.M. STACY from 18th M.G. Coy.	1 O.R. leave to UK.	
"	22nd		The Company paraded in Marching order, and with Transport at 9.AM and marched to SCHRAMM BARRACKS, ARRAS. The transport marched on to the lines S of the town on the W. side of the BURQUOY ROAD.		Lt P. DALTON leave to U.K. 2 O.Rs leave to UK.	
"	23rd		The morning was spent in filling belts, preparing guns for the trenches, and packing limbers. The company paraded at 12.45 P.M and marched off at 1 P.M to relieve the 37th Machine Gun Company. After the relief the Company was in position as follows:- Company Headquarters at N.10.a.8.7 (Sheet 51b) No 1 Section at SPADE RESERVE. " 2 " " B' STONG POINT " 3 " " SHAMROCK CORNER " 4 " " ARRAS	1 O.R. from C.C.S.	1 O.R. whilst on Short leave admitted to Hosp (Doctors Certificate)	

(A7092). Wt. W12839/M1293. 750,000. 1/17. D. D. & L., Ltd. Forms/C.2118/14.

(13)

Instructions regarding War Diaries and Intelligence Summaries are contained in F. S. Regs., Part II. and the Staff Manual respectively. Title pages will be prepared in manuscript.

WAR DIARY

or

~~INTELLIGENCE SUMMARY.~~

(Erase heading not required.)

Army Form C. 2118.

Place	Date	Hour	Summary of Events and Information	ARRIVALS	DEPARTURES	Remarks and references to Appendices
In The Field	23rd	(Continued)	Relief was reported complete at 7-30 PM			
"	24th		The day was spent by Officers & teams in study the trench system & M. G. Positions. Usual trench routine	1. O.R. from Hosp.	1. O.R. whilst on Short Leave admitted to Hosp (Doctors certificate)	
"	25th		Harrassing fire was carried out at 6-5 P.M. until 1 AM by two guns of No. 1 Section and two guns of No. 2 Section on Tracks in O. 3. b. and strong point O. 9. b. 80. 75. this was in co-operation with the Artillery who bombarded with Gas Shell.	1. O.R. from C.C.S.		
"	26th		Harrassing fire was carried out at 5-15 P.M. until 7-30 P.M in conjunction with Artillery programme by two Guns of No. 1 Section in STIRRUP LANE.	22 O.R.s from Base Depot.	1. O.R. leave to U.K.	
"	27th		Nos. 1 and 2 Sections, two guns each, fired 4000 rounds on the NEW entrenching work at O. 9. a. 6. 9. and vicinity.	1. O.R. from leave	1. O.R. to Hosp	
"	28th		Two guns in SPADE RESERVE fired 2000 rounds on STIRRUP LANE in O. 9. b. and d. from 6.0 P.M. to 12-30 P.M. in co-operation with the Artillery	1. O.R. from leave		[initials]

(A7092). Wt. W12839/M1293. 750,000. 1/17. D. D. & L., Ltd. Forms/C.2118/14.

(14)

Instructions regarding War Diaries and Intelligence Summaries are contained in F. S. Regs., Part II. and the Staff Manual respectively. Title pages will be prepared in manuscript.

WAR DIARY

or

~~INTELLIGENCE SUMMARY.~~

(*Erase heading not required.*)

Army Form C. 2118.

Place	Date	Hour	Summary of Events and Information	ARRIVALS	DEPARTURES	Remarks and references to Appendices
In the Field	29th		No 1 Section was relieved by No 2 Section	1 O.R from Hosp		
			" 2 " " " " " 3 "			
			" 3 " " " " " 4 "			
			" 1 " returned to ARRAS.			
			EXTRACT from ROUTINE ORDERS BY MAJOR GENERAL T. G. MATTHEISON, Commanding 4th DIVISION:-			
			"2605 HONOURS AND AWARDS:- The Divisional Commander has much pleasure in announcing the following awards:-			
			"THE MILITARY MEDAL			
			"16141 Cpl H. HOMER 10th M.G. Coy. M.G.C			
			"16505 Pte B.B. OWENS —— " ——			
			"16161 " W. BLAIKIE —— " ——			
			"These awards were made for gallantry in Action during the period 4th to 12th Oct 17			
"	30th		Two Guns of No 3 Section in co-operation with Artillery searched STIRRUP LANE from 10 P.M until 11-30 P.M.	2nd Lt R.F. FRAYLING from Base Depot		
			2nd Lt R.F. FRAYLING M.G.C. joined this Company from M.G.C Base Depot.	2 O.Rs from Leave.		

(A7092). Wt. W12839/M1293. 750,000. 1/17. D. D. & L., Ltd. Forms/C.2118/14.

(15)

Instructions regarding War Diaries and Intelligence Summaries are contained in F. S. Regs., Part II. and the Staff Manual respectively. Title pages will be prepared in manuscript.

WAR DIARY
or
~~INTELLIGENCE SUMMARY.~~
(Erase heading not required.)

Army Form C. 2118.

Place	Date	Hour	Summary of Events and Information	ARRIVALS	DEPARTURES	Remarks and references to Appendices
In The Field	31st		Two Guns from No. 3 Section, in Conjunction with Artillery fired on the TRACKS and DUG-OUTS about O.9.b.8.9.			
			[signature] MAJOR COMMANDING 10TH MACHINE GUN COY			

(A7092). Wt. W12839/M1293. 750,000. 1/17. D. D. & L., Ltd. Forms/C.2118/14.

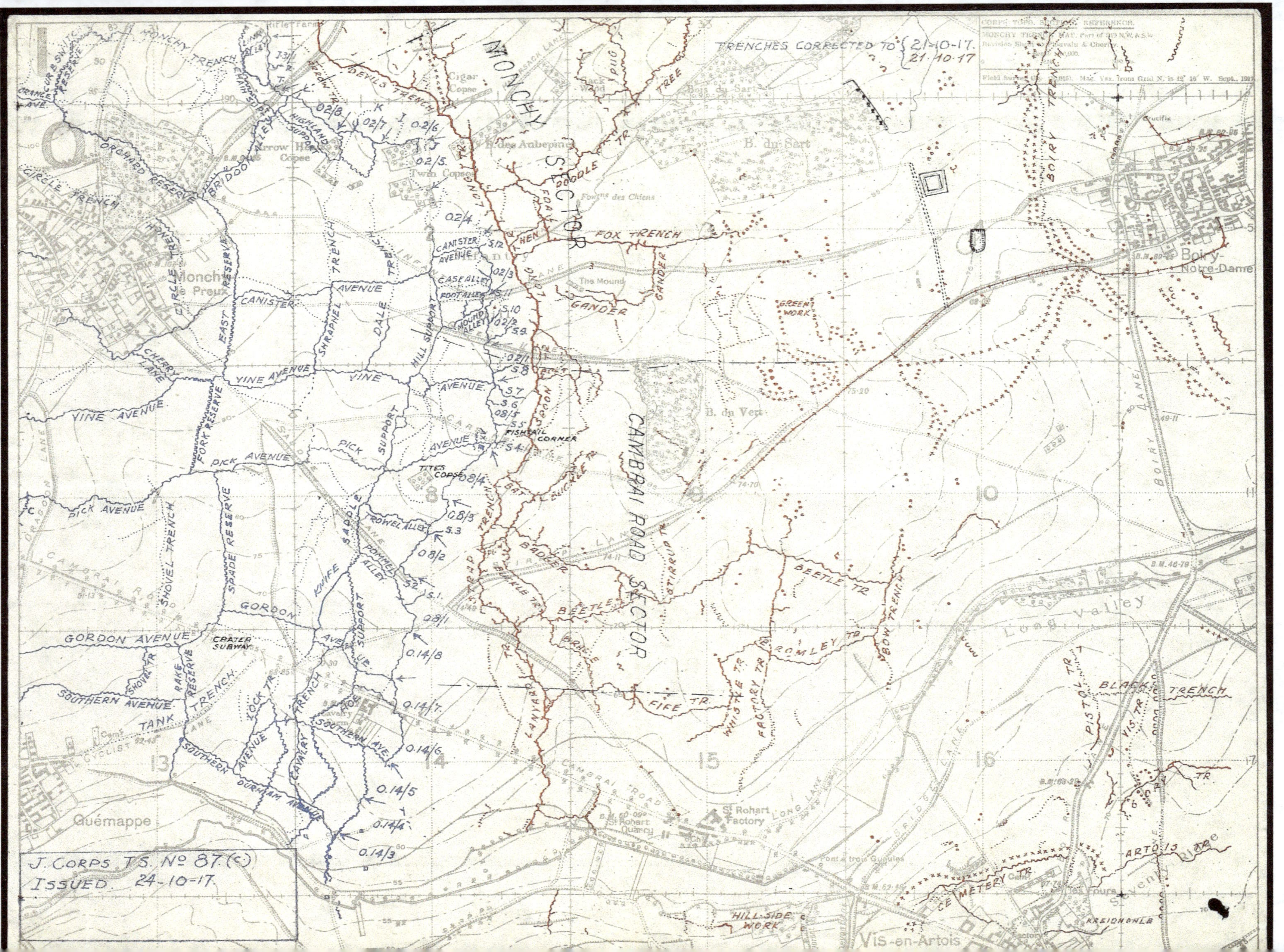

TRENCHES CORRECTED TO 21-10-17. 21-10-17
J. CORPS T.S. No 87(c)
ISSUED 24-10-17.
CAMBRAI ROAD SECTOR
MONCHY SECTOR
Boiry-Notre-Dame
Vis-en-Artois
Guémappe
Monchy le Preux
B. du Sart
B. du Vert
The Mound
St Rohart Factory
Long Valley
BOIRY TRENCH
FOX TRENCH
GANDER
GREEN WORK
BEETLE TR
BOW TRENCH
ROMLEY TR
FACTORY TR
WHISTLE TR
FIFE TR.
PISTOL TR
BLACK TRENCH
LANYARD TR
CE METERY TR.
HILL SIDE WORK
DEVILS TRENCH
MONCHY TRENCH
ORCHARD RESERVE
CIRCLE TRENCH
BRIDOON ALLEY
CHERRY LANE
VINE AVENUE
FORK RESERVE
PICK AVENUE
SPADE RESERVE
SHOVEL TRENCH
GORDON AVENUE
SOUTHERN AVENUE
TANK TRENCH
DURHAM AVENUE
CAVALRY TRENCH
HILL SUPPORT
SHRAPNEL TRENCH
CANISTER
CRATER SUBWAY
FISHTAIL CORNER
TITES COPSE

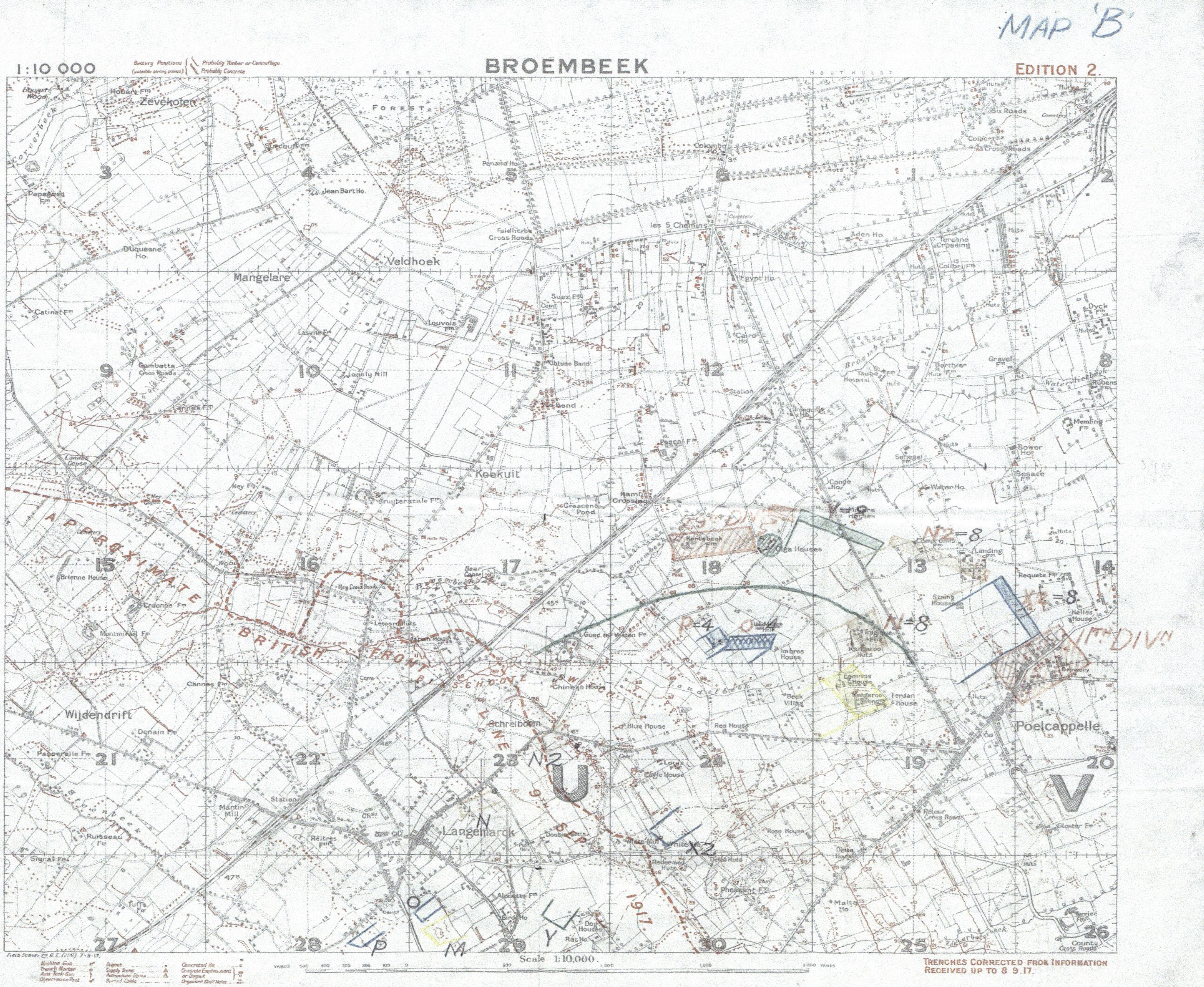

MAP 'B'

1:10 000

BROEMBEEK

EDITION 2.

FOREST OF HOUTHULST

Zevekoten
Hobart Fm
Papegoed Fm
Duquesne Ho.
Catinat Fm
Mangelare
Veldhoek
Jean Bart Ho.
Panama Ho.
Faidherbe Cross Roads
les 5 Chemins
Colombo
Six Roads
Colbert Cross Roads
Aden Ho.
Egypt Ho.
Suez Fm
Louvois Fm
Lauwe Fm
Lonely Mill
Gambetta Cross Roads
Lannes Fm
Vacher
Cairo Ho.
Station
Taube Hospital
Berthyer
Gravel Fm
Dyck
Mesaline Fm
Bower Ho.
Besace
Water Ho.
Pascal Fm
Koekuit
Crescent Pond
Gruuterzaale Fm
Ney Fm
Brienne House
Craonne Fm
Montmirail Fm
Wijdendrift
Cannes Fm
Donain Fm
Papegaaie Fm
Ruisseau Fm
Signal Fm
Tuffs Fm
Martin Mill
Reitres Fm
Langemarck
Schreiboom
Chinese House
Blue House
Red House
Louis Fm
Beck Villas
Eagle House
Rose House
Pheasant Fm
Malta Ho.
Poelcappelle
Gloster Fm
Retour Cross Roads
Requete Fm
Helles House
Landing Fm
Compromise Fm
Kempbeek Fm
Stoke Houses
Meunier House
Ferdan House
Kangaroo Huts
Limbros House
County Cross Roads

APPROXIMATE BRITISH FRONT LINE 9th SEP 1917.

11th DIVn

U
V
N2
N
X2
Y
M
P
N=8
N2=8
R-4
Y=9

TRENCHES CORRECTED FROM INFORMATION RECEIVED UP TO 8.9.17.

Scale 1:10,000

File.

Broembeek

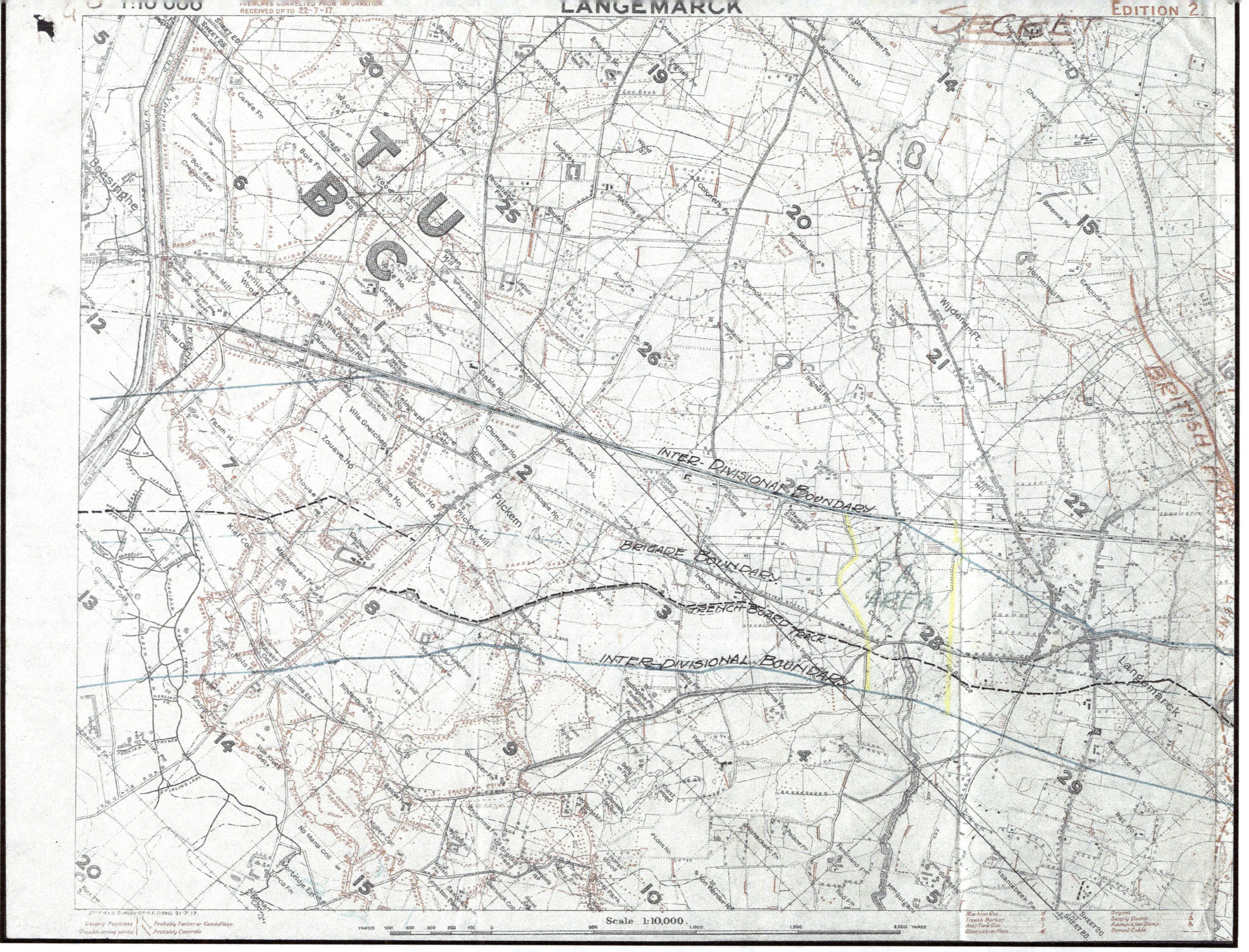

LANGEMARCK
TRENCHES CORRECTED FROM INFORMATION RECEIVED UP TO 22-7-17.
EDITION 2.
SECRET
BRITISH FRONT
Langemarck
Wijdendrift
Pilckem
Boesinghe
INTER-DIVISIONAL BOUNDARY
BRIGADE BOUNDARY
TRENCH BOARD TRACK
INTER-DIVISIONAL BOUNDARY
R.A. AREA
Scale 1:10,000.

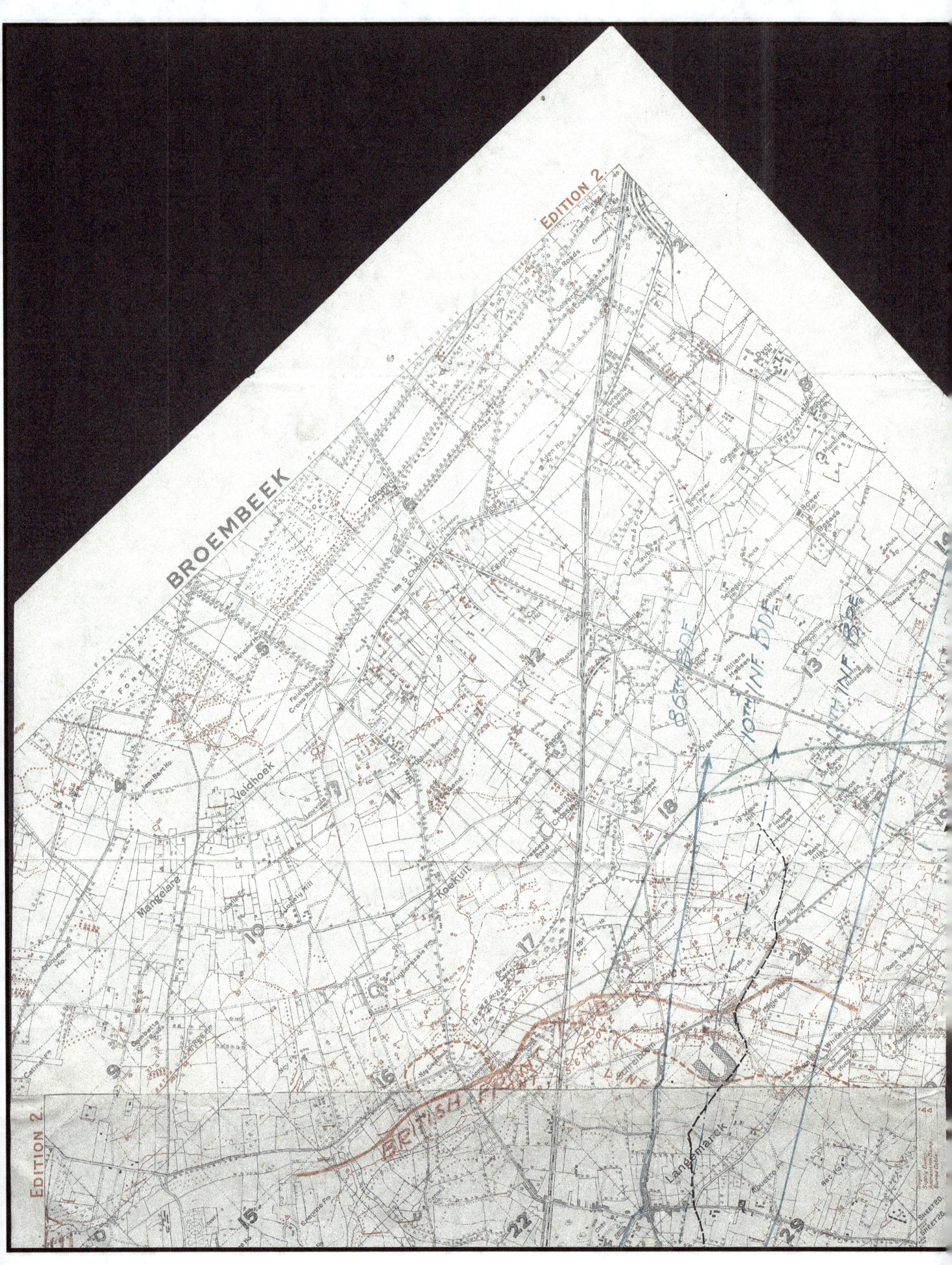

EDITION 2.
BROEMBEEK
Veldhoek
Mangelare
Koekuit
Langemarck
80TH BDE
10TH INF. BDE
11TH INF BDE
BRITISH FRONT LINE
EDITION 2.

Langemarck

Broombeek

File
WD

1:10 000
BROEMBEEK
Zevekoten
Hobart Fm
Mangelare
Veldhoek
Catinat Fm
Gambetta Cross Roads
Jean Bart Ho.
Duquesne Ho.
Louvois
Koekuit
les 5 Chemins
Brickfield
Egypt Ho.
Station
Vee Bend
Chinese Bend
Crescent Pond
Namur Crossing
Wijdendrift
Schreiboom
Langemarck
Chinese House
Blue House
Red House
Eagle House
Martin Mill
Station
Cannes Fm
Denain Fm
Passerelle Fm
Ruisseau Fm
Signal Fm
White House
Double Cotts
Alouette Fm
Pheasant Fm
APPROXIMATE BRITISH FRONT
U
3
4
5
6
9
10
11
12
15
16
17
18
21
22
23
24
27
28
29
30
Scale 1:10,000

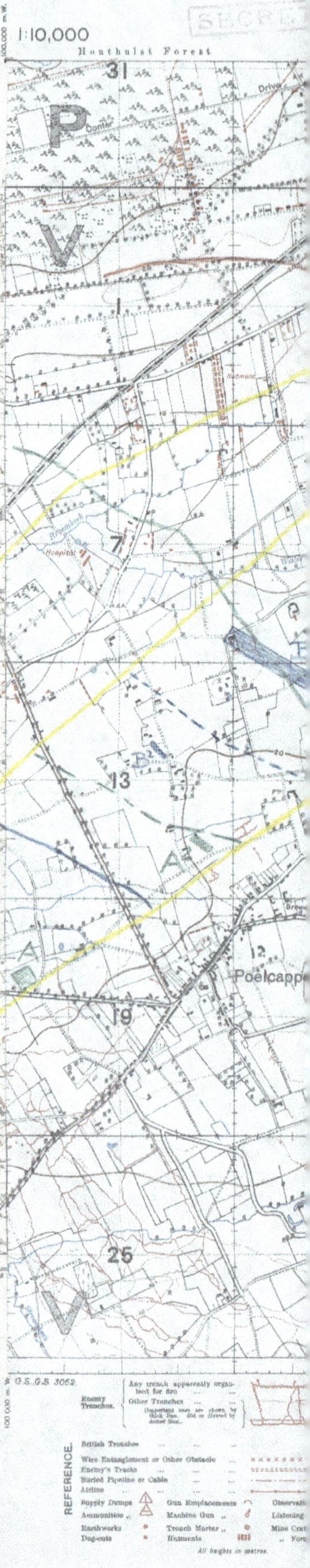
SECRE
1:10,000
Houthulst Forest
31
P
V
7
13
19
25
Poelcapp
V
G.S.G.S. 3062.
Enemy Trenches.
Any trench apparently organized for fire
Other Trenches
REFERENCE.
British Trenches
Wire Entanglement or Other Obstacle
Enemy's Tracks
Buried Pipeline or Cable
Airline
Supply Dumps
Ammunition
Earthworks
Dug-outs
Gun Emplacements
Machine Gun
Trench Mortar
Hutments
All heights in metres.

WESTROOSEBEKE.

SECRET

1:10,000

Houthulst Forest

To Thourout

STADEN

31 32 33 34 35

Vijfwegen

Stadendreef

Shaw Wood

Schaap-Balie

Polders Wood

Cabt

Koekuitberg Fm

Tiendenberg

Puzzle Wood

Spriet Copse

Spriet

Olga Haus

Imbros House

Beek Villas

Brewery

Poelcappelle

West Wood

Middle Copse

Mallet Wood

Double Copse

Rose House

Shaft

Goudberg Copse

Goudberg

2 3 4 5

7 8 9 10 11 12

13 14 15 16 17

19 20 21 22 23 24

25 26 27 28 29 30

G.S.G.S. 3062.

REFERENCE.

Enemy Trenches. Any trench apparently organised for fire ... ... Other Trenches ... ... (Important ones are shown by thick line. Old or disused by dotted line).

British Trenches ... ...

Wire Entanglement or Other Obstacle ...

Enemy's Tracks ... ...

Buried Pipeline or Cable ... ...

Airline ... ...

Supply Dumps | Gun Emplacements | Observation Posts

Ammunition „ | Machine Gun „ | Listening Posts

Earthworks | Trench Mortar „ | Mine Craters

Dug-outs | Emplacements | „ Fortified

All heights in metres.

Hedge, Fence or Ditch ... ...

Ditch with Permanent Water ... ...

Conspicuous Points ... ... Church. Wind Mill. Any trig. point. (Position of point is centre of circle. Dot shows that point is trigonometrically fixed).

Houses ... ... Standing. Ruined. Shrine +

Railways: Permanent — Normal Gauge, Double ... ; „ „ Single ... ; Light ... ... — Temporary — Trench Tramways ; Metre Gauge Railways

NOTE.—The fact that an obstacle is not represented on the map does not necessarily mean that there is none there. It is often impossible to distinguish obstacles or to identify their character. It may be assumed that there are obstacles in front of all fire trenches (shown by thick line).

Scale 1:10,000

Broenbeek

— Westroosbeke

10th M. G. Coy

10th MACHINE GUN COY.

ORIGINAL

WAR

DIARY

FOR MONTH OF NOVEMBER.

(1)

Instructions regarding War Diaries and Intelligence Summaries are contained in F. S. Regs., Part II. and the Staff Manual respectively. Title pages will be prepared in manuscript.

WAR DIARY FOR MONTH OF NOVEMBER

or

~~INTELLIGENCE SUMMARY.~~

(*Erase heading not required.*)

Army Form C. 2118.

Place	Date	Hour	Summary of Events and Information	ARRIVALS.	DEPARTURES	Remarks and references to Appendices
			Maps Reference			
			FRANCE Sheet 51B S.W. 1/20,000.			
			"J" Corps T.S. 87(b) issued 23-10-17 1/10,000			
			AIRY CORNER Trench Map. 1/10,000			
			"J" Corps T.S. No 88(c) issued 27-10-17 1/10,000			
Field	1-11-17		On this date the Company was in position as follows:-			
			Company Headquarters at N 10 a 8.7.			
			No 2 Section (under 2nd Lieut LABES) in SPADE RESERVE.			
			No 3 Section (under Lieut WILLOUGHBY) in "B" STRONG POINT			
			No 4 Section (under 2nd Lieut MOOR) at SHAMROCK CORNER.			
			No 1 Section (under 2nd Lieut STEVENS) in ARRAS.			

(A7092). Wt. W12839/M1293. 750,000. 1/17. D. D. & L., Ltd. Forms/C.2118/14.

(2)

Instructions regarding War Diaries and Intelligence Summaries are contained in F. S. Regs., Part II. and the Staff Manual respectively. Title pages will be prepared in manuscript.

WAR DIARY

or

~~INTELLIGENCE SUMMARY.~~

(Erase heading not required.)

Army Form C. 2118.

Place	Date	Hour	Summary of Events and Information	ARRIVALS.	DEPARTURES.	Remarks and references to Appendices
Field	1-11-17		Two guns of No 2 Section in SPADE RESERVE + two guns of No 3 Section in "B" Strong Point carried out harrassing fire from 5-45 PM to 3-30 AM on STIRRUP LANE + tracks in the vicinity in conjunction with artillery.	Lt Emmitt from leave.		
"	2-11-17		LIEUT C. MATSON proceeded to England. Two guns in SPADE RESERVE fired on tracks + shell holes at O.30.69. from 5-30 AM — 6 AM.		Lt C MATSON to U.K.	
"	3-11-17		Two guns in SPADE RESERVE fired 4000 rounds on BOW TRENCH + tracks around between 5 PM + 9 PM. and 11-30 PM to 1 AM. 2nd LIEUT HILLMAN from base depot.	2nd Lt HILLMAN from base depot. 1. OR. From leave		

(A7092). Wt. W12839/M1293. 750,000. 1/17. D. D. & L., Ltd. Forms/C.2118/14.

(3)

Instructions regarding War Diaries and Intelligence Summaries are contained in F. S. Regs., Part II. and the Staff Manual respectively. Title pages will be prepared in manuscript.

WAR DIARY
or
~~INTELLIGENCE SUMMARY.~~
(Erase heading not required.)

Army Form C. 2118.

Place	Date	Hour	Summary of Events and Information	ARRIVALS	DEPARTURES	Remarks and references to Appendices
Field	4-11-17		No 2 Section relieved by No 3 Section No 3 " " " No 4 " No 4 " " " No 1 " No 2 Section to ARRAS 4000 rounds fired in S.O.S lines in response to S.O.S. signal at 1-45 AM.	1.O.R. from leave	1.O.R. leave to U.K. 1.O.R Evac to C.C.S. L/Cpl PUNT Evac to Base Depot.	
"	5-11-17		Reference D. Routine Orders dated 5th November. (2623) The G.O.C has much pleasure in announcing the following awards - <u>THE MILITARY CROSS.</u> 2ND LT (TEMP LT) R.W.A. PAINTER 8th MIDDLESEX REGIMENT attached 10TH COMPANY MACHINE GUN CORPS. 4000 rounds fired on Strong Points in O.g.b.S.9 during night	1.O.R. from leave	Pte Scott whilst on short leave [illegible] to Hosp.	
"	6/11/17		Three Guns of No 3 Section fired 12.000 rounds during night on Works at O3d 65.30 and O4c 05.15 and X roads at O9b 85.65.		1.OR. Evac to C.C.S. L/Cpl Woods to Hosp. Cpl. HOPKINS TO M.G. Course Base	[initials]

(A7092). Wt. W12839/M1293. 750,000. 1/17. D. D. & L., Ltd. Forms/C.2118/14.

(4)

Instructions regarding War Diaries and Intelligence Summaries are contained in F. S. Regs., Part II. and the Staff Manual respectively. Title pages will be prepared in manuscript.

WAR DIARY
or
~~INTELLIGENCE SUMMARY.~~
(Erase heading not required.)

Army Form C. 2118.

Place	Date	Hour	Summary of Events and Information	ARRIVALS	DEPARTURES	Remarks and references to Appendices
Field	7-11-17		Two Guns in SPADE RESERVE fired 2000 rounds on BOIS de SART.		Uphill [illegible] Evac to C.C.S. [illegible] a [illegible] on Short leave to UK admitted to Hosp. Sgt MADDAMS trans to 12th M G Coy	
"	8-11-17		Two Guns in SPADE RESERVE in co-operation with artillery, fired on tracks in O9c.		2Lt LABES to Hosp. 1. O.R to Hosp.	
"	9/11/17		Four Guns of the Company fired as per following copy of O.D No 8. in support of a raid by 15th Division. Zero hour was 1-40 A.M. Attached Map A. shows area covered. Two guns in SPADE RESERVE fired 2000 rounds each during night on STIRRUP LANE in O9b.	1. OR from leave 1. OR from base depot.		

(A7092). Wt. W12839/M1293. 750,000. 1/17. D. D. & L., Ltd. Forms/C.2118/14.

(5)

Instructions regarding War Diaries and Intelligence Summaries are contained in F. S. Regs., Part II. and the Staff Manual respectively. Title pages will be prepared in manuscript.

WAR DIARY
or
~~INTELLIGENCE SUMMARY.~~
(Erase heading not required.)

Army Form C. 2118.

Place	Date	Hour	Summary of Events and Information	ARRIVALS.	DEPARTURES.	Remarks and references to Appendices
Field	10-11-17		No 2 Section relieved No 1 Section at SHAMROCK CORNER No 1 " " No 4 " " "B" Strong Point No 4 " " No 3 " in SPADE RESERVE No 3 Section returned to ARRAS.	1. O.R. Recd from C.C.S.	1. O.R. leave to U.K. 1. O.R. to Hosp.	
"	11-11-17		Usual harassing fire throughout the night.		1. O.R. [illegible] C.C.S.	
"	12-11-17		Harassing fire carried out on Tracks around and on STIRRUP LANE.			
"	13-11-17		Co-operation with Artillery on ~~[illegible]~~ BEETLE TRENCH.		2 O.R's to Hosp. 1 O.R. [illegible] C.C.S.	

(A7092). Wt. W12839/M1293. 750,000. 1/17. D. D. & L., Ltd. Forms/C.2118/14.

(6)

Instructions regarding War Diaries and Intelligence Summaries are contained in F. S. Regs., Part II. and the Staff Manual respectively. Title pages will be prepared in manuscript.

WAR DIARY
or
~~INTELLIGENCE SUMMARY.~~
(Erase heading not required.)

Army Form C. 2118.

Place	Date	Hour	Summary of Events and Information	ARRIVALS.	DEPARTURES.	Remarks and references to Appendices
Field	14-11-17		Usual harassing fire	1. O.R from Hosp	1. O.R to Hosp.	
"	15-11-17		Usual harassing fire in the early morning.	2. O.R from Hosp 2nd Lt LABES from Hosp. 6. O.R. reinforcements from Base Depot	1. O.R to Hosp.	
"	16-11-17		Two guns in SPADE RESERVE fired 4 000 rounds on their S.O.S lines in support of a raid on the enemy trenches by the Brigade on our left at 2 A.M. During the afternoon No 3 Section relieved No 2 Section at SHAMROCK Comm No 2 " " No 1 " "B" Point No 1 " " No 4 " SPADE and SHOVEL Trenches No 4 Section returned to ARRAS.		1. O.R to Hosp 2. O.R Evac to C.C.S.	
"	17-11-17		At 7.15 P.M. two guns in SPADE RESERVE and two guns in "B" Strong Point fired 6000 rounds on their S.O.S lines, in support of a raid by the Brigade on our left.	1. O.R from C.R.S.	2. O.R.S. months leave to UK. 1. O.Rs leave to UK Cpl Crangle to M.G.C Training centre.	

(A7092). Wt. W12839/M1293. 750,000. 1/17. D. D. & L., Ltd. Forms/C.2118/14.

(7)

Instructions regarding War Diaries and Intelligence Summaries are contained in F. S. Regs., Part II. and the Staff Manual respectively. Title pages will be prepared in manuscript.

WAR DIARY
or
~~INTELLIGENCE SUMMARY.~~
(Erase heading not required.)

Army Form C. 2118.

Place	Date	Hour	Summary of Events and Information	ARRIVALS	DEPARTURES	Remarks and references to Appendices
Field	18-11-17		Two guns in SPADE RESERVE fired 1000 rounds on POODLE TRENCH during the Smoke bombardment of the Enemys' lines at 3 PM. The four guns at SHAMROCK CORNER took up positions at O13c.9.0 at dusk in readiness for co-operation in a raid on 20-11-17			
"	19-11-17		Usual trench routine. No firing was done on account of guns being laid for co-operation in a raid. Guns at "B" Strong Point and guns in SHOVEL TRENCH took up positions in SPADE RESERVE at 12 noon for co-operation with a raid on the 20-11-17	1.OR from Hosp		
"	20-11-17		At 6-20 AM a party of the First Royal Warwickshire Regiment raided the enemys' lines. In support of this raid seven guns of the Company in SPADE RESERVE fired 14,000 rounds on POODLE and TREE Trenches, and four guns at O13c.9.0, south of the RIVER COTEUL fired 7000 rounds on BEETLE Trench. At dusk the four guns south of the COTEUL withdrew to SHAMROCK CORNER. Two guns from SPADE RESERVE withdrew to SHOVEL Trench, two to "B" Point and one to the BROWN LINE.			

RG

(A7092). Wt. W12839/M1293. 750,000. 1/17. D. D. & L., Ltd. Forms/C.2118/14.

(8)

Instructions regarding War Diaries and Intelligence Summaries are contained in F. S. Regs., Part II. and the Staff Manual respectively. Title pages will be prepared in manuscript.

WAR DIARY
or
~~INTELLIGENCE SUMMARY.~~
(Erase heading not required.)

Army Form C. 2118.

Place	Date	Hour	Summary of Events and Information	ARRIVALS	DEPARTURES	Remarks and references to Appendices
Field	21·11·17		Usual harassing fire.		1. OR to Hosp. 1. O.R to UK on leave. 2nd Lt STEVENS leave to U.K.	
"	22·11·17		During the afternoon:– No 4 Section relieved No 3 Section at SHAMROCK CORNER. No 3 " " No 2 " " "B" Point. No 2 " " No 1 " " SPADE RESERVE & SHOVEL Trenches. No 1 Section returned to ARRAS.	1. O.R from Hosp.	4. OR. leave to U.K. 1. O.R to Hosp.	
"	23·11·17		Usual harassing fire.	1. OR from leave	2. OR to Hosp.	

(A7092). Wt. W12839/M1293. 750,000. 1/17. D. D. & L., Ltd. Forms/C.2118/14.

(9)

Instructions regarding War Diaries and Intelligence Summaries are contained in F. S. Regs., Part II. and the Staff Manual respectively. Title pages will be prepared in manuscript.

WAR DIARY
or
~~INTELLIGENCE SUMMARY.~~
(*Erase heading not required.*)

Army Form C. 2118.

Place	Date	Hour	Summary of Events and Information	ARRIVALS	DEPARTURES	Remarks and references to Appendices
Field	24-10-17		Harassing fire was carried out in conjunction with the Artillery	Pte Kneas returned from Months leave	1 O.R to C.R.S.	
"	25-11-17		Two guns in SPADE RESERVE and two guns in "B" Strong Point fired on STIRRUP LANE from 4-30 PM to 7 AM 16,000 rounds were fired in all.	Pte Scott from Hospital England		
"	26-11-17		Usual harassing fire was carried out and four guns co operated with the gas projectors on our left at 11-50 P.M		2 O.Rs leave to UK 1 O.R to Base for Dentures	
"	27-11-17		Usual harassing fire & co-operation with the Artillery			

RP

(A7092). Wt. W12839/M1293. 750,000. 1/17. D. D. & L., Ltd. Forms/C.2118/14.

(10)

Instructions regarding War Diaries and Intelligence Summaries are contained in F. S. Regs., Part II. and the Staff Manual respectively. Title pages will be prepared in manuscript.

WAR DIARY
or
~~INTELLIGENCE SUMMARY.~~

(*Erase heading not required.*)

Army Form C. 2118.

Place	Date	Hour	Summary of Events and Information	ARRIVALS	DEPARTURES	Remarks and references to Appendices
Field	28-11-17		No 4 Section relieved one gun of No 3 Section at S1 position, + three guns of the 11th Machine Gun Company in S2, S3 and S4 positions. No 3 Section relieved No 2 Section in SPADE RESERVE and SHOVEL Trench. No 2 Section returned to ARRAS on completion of relief. No 1 Section relieved No 4 Section at SHAMROCK CORNER. The two guns at "B" Strong Point were relieved by two guns of the 234 Machine Gun Company.		2 O.Rs Evacuated to C.C.S.	
"	29-11-17		Our guns co-operated with Artillery and did usual harassing fire.	1 O.R from leave		
	30-11-17		No firing was carried out on this day this being the "SILENT" DAY.			

[signature] Major
Comdg 10th Coy M.G.C.

(A7092). Wt. W12839/M1293. 750,000. 1/17. D. D. & L., Ltd. Forms/C.2118/14.

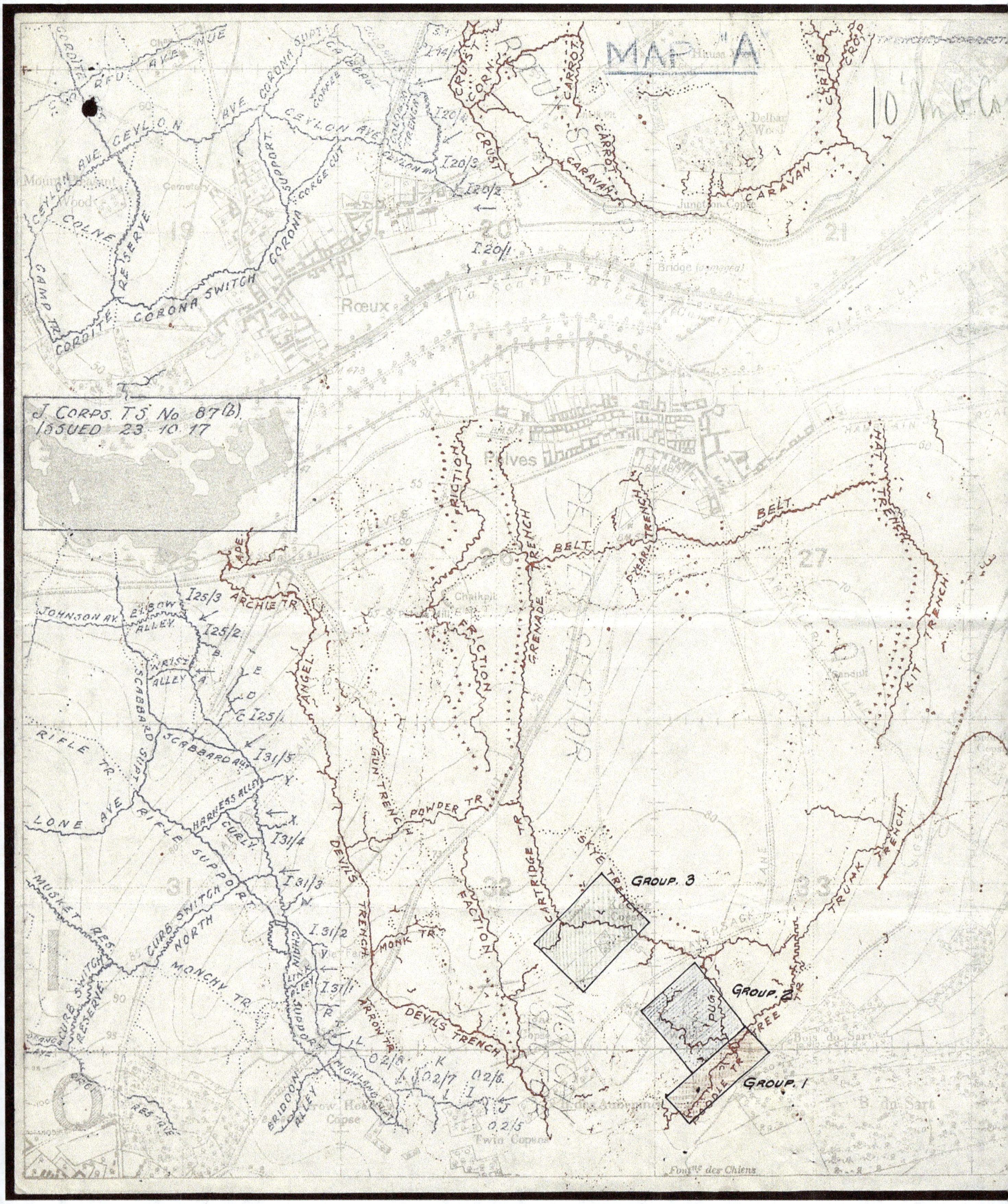

MAP "A"
10th M G C
J. CORPS. T.S. No. 87(B).
ISSUED 23. 10. 17
Rœux
Pelves
Mount Pleasant Wood
Cemetery
Delbar Wood
Junction Copse
Bridge (damaged)
Chalkpit
Sandpit
Bois du Sart
B. du Sart
Twin Copses
Fosse des Chiens
19
20
21
26
27
31
32
33
CEYLON AVE
CORONA SWITCH
CORONA SUPPORT
CORDITE
RESERVE
COLNE
CAMP TR
GORGE CUT
CRUST
CORN
CARROT
CARAVAN
CRIB
CROP
BELT
HAT TRENCH
KIT TRENCH
PEARL TRENCH
GRENADE TRENCH
FRICTION
FACTION
ANGEL
ARCHIE TR
DEVILS TRENCH
GUN TRENCH
POWDER TR
MONK TR
ARROW TR
CARTRIDGE TR
SKYE TRENCH
TRUNK TRENCH
HAVERSACK
PUG
POODLE TR
GROUP. 1
GROUP. 2
GROUP. 3
JOHNSON AV.
ELBOW ALLEY
WRIST ALLEY
SCABBARD ALLEY
SCABBARD SUPT
RIFLE TR
LONE AVE
RIFLE SUPPORT
HARNESS ALLEY
CURLY
CURB SWITCH NORTH
MONCHY TR
MUSKET RES
CURB SWITCH RESERVE
BRIDOON ALLEY
BRIDOON SUPPORT
HIGHLAND ALLEY
I.20/1
I.20/2
I.20/3
I.20/4
I25/1
I25/2
I25/3
I31/1
I.31/2
I31/3
I31/4
I31/5
O.2/5
O.2/6
O.2/7
O.2/8

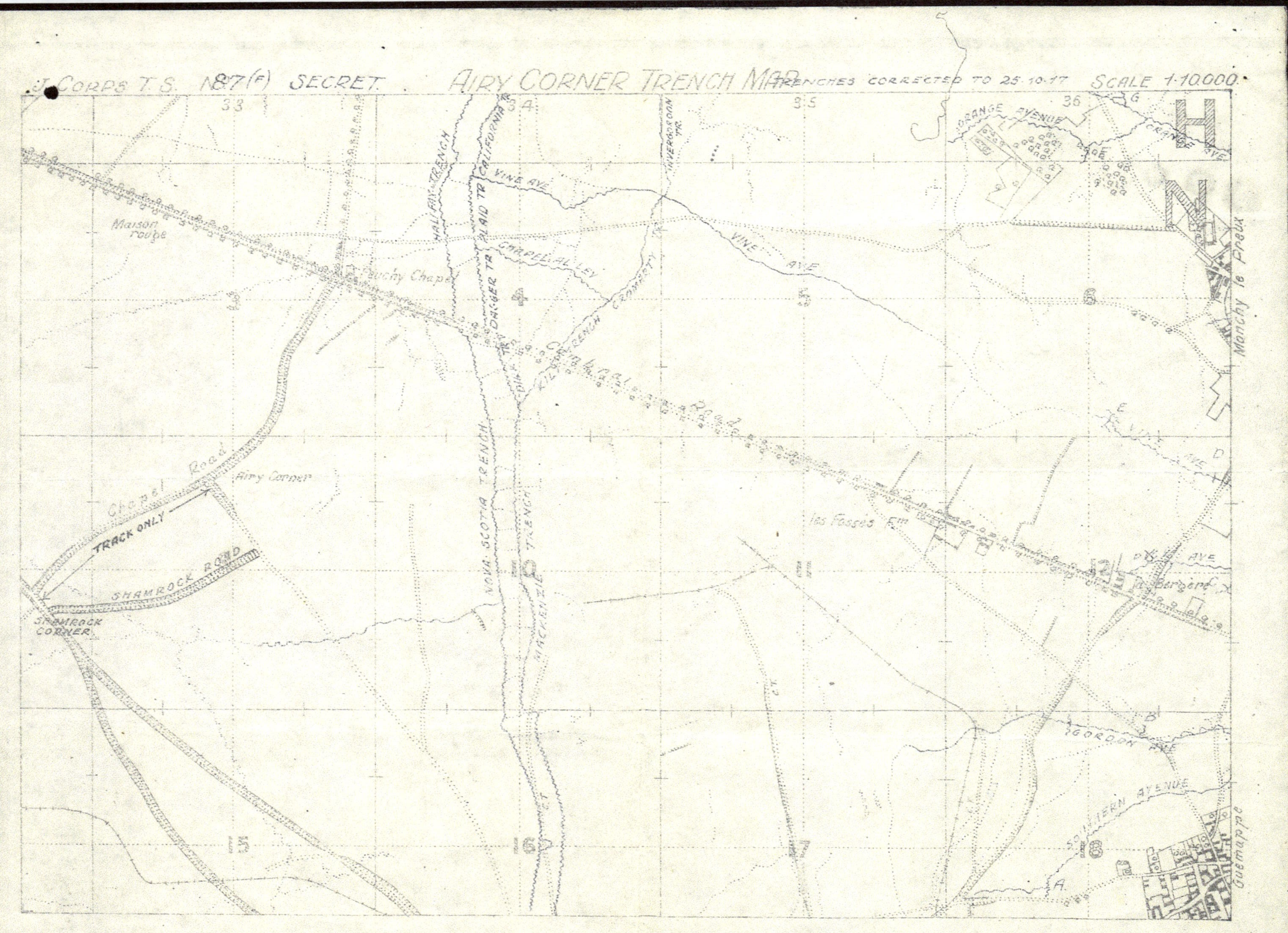
J. CORPS T.S. No 87 (F) SECRET.
AIRY CORNER TRENCH MAP
TRENCHES CORRECTED TO 25.10.17
SCALE 1:10.000
Maison rouge
Chapel Road
Airy Corner
TRACK ONLY
SHAMROCK ROAD
SHAMROCK CORNER
HALIFAX TRENCH
CALIFORNIA TR
PLAID TR
DAGGER TR
VINE AVE
CHAPEL ALLEY
INVERGORDON TR.
NOVA SCOTIA TRENCH
MACKENZIE TRENCH
KILT TRENCH
Cambrai Road
les Fosses Fm
Bergère
ORANGE AVENUE
ORANGE AVE
GORDON AVE
SOUTHERN AVENUE
Monchy le Preux
Guemappe

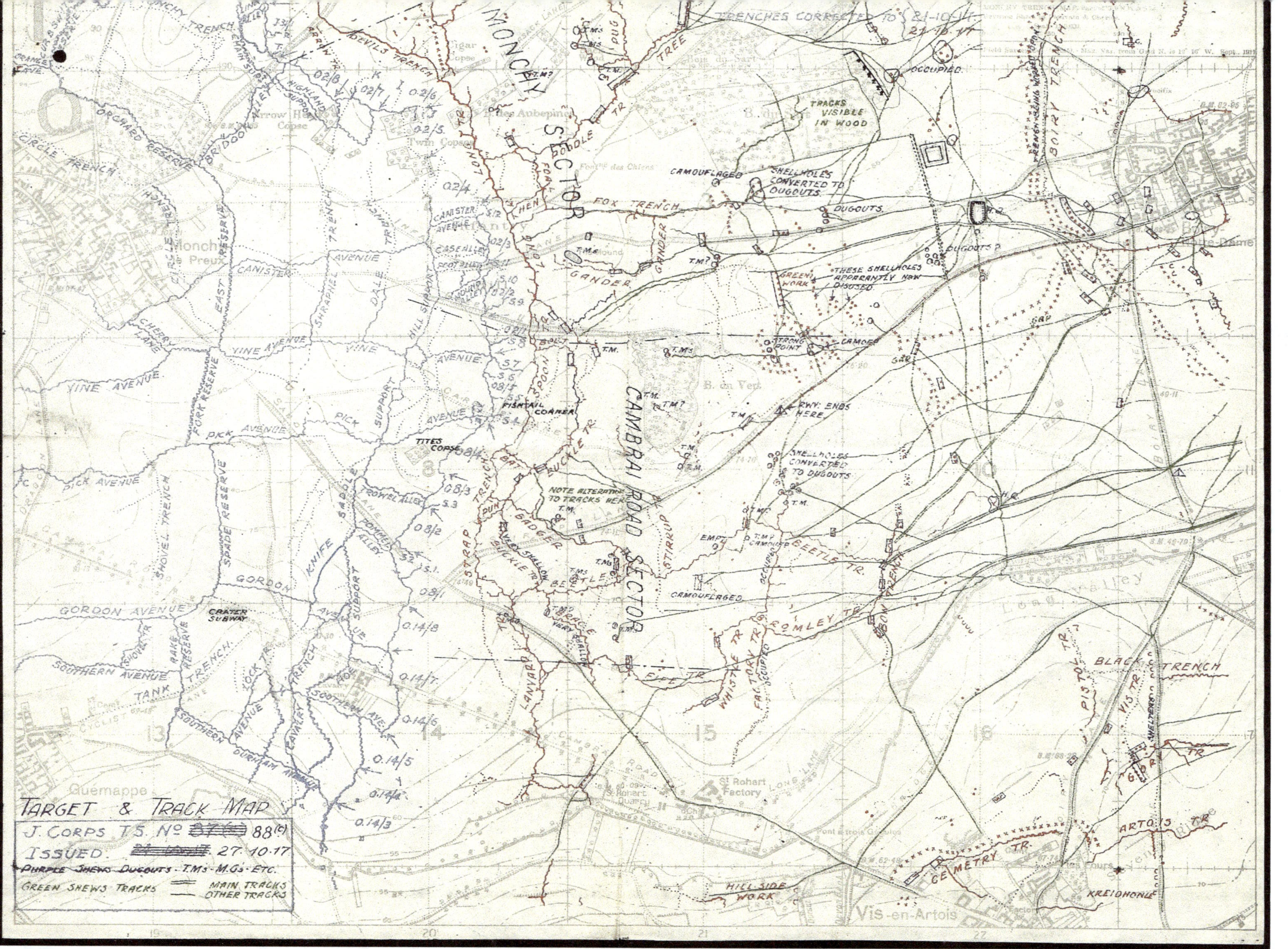
TARGET & TRACK MAP
J. CORPS T.S. Nº 88(c)
ISSUED. 27.10.17.
PURPLE SHEWS DUGOUTS. T.Ms. M.Gs. ETC.
GREEN SHEWS TRACKS
MAIN TRACKS
OTHER TRACKS
TRENCHES CORRECTED TO 21-10-17
MONCHY SECTOR
CAMBRAI ROAD SECTOR
TRACKS VISIBLE IN WOOD
SHELLHOLES CONVERTED TO DUGOUTS.
THESE SHELLHOLES APPARENTLY NOW DISUSED
NOTE ALTERNATIVE TO TRACKS HERE
RWY. ENDS HERE
FISHTAIL CORNER
TITES COPSE
CRATER SUBWAY
BOIRY TRENCH
FOX TRENCH
DEVILS TRENCH
STRAP TRENCH
BLACK TRENCH
HILL SIDE WORK
CEMETRY TR.
ARTOIS TR.
PISTOL TR.
BEETLE TR.
BROMLEY TR.
FACTORY TR.
WHISTLE TR.
LANYARD TR.
GORDON AVENUE
SOUTHERN AVENUE
SHOVEL TRENCH
SPADE RESERVE
FORK RESERVE
VINE AVENUE
PICK AVENUE
ORCHARD RESERVE
CIRCLE TRENCH
Guemappe
Vis-en-Artois

10TH MACHINE GUN COY.

ORIGINAL

WAR

DIARY

FOR MONTH OF DECEMBER

FIELD

R. [illegible] MAJOR

3-1-18

COMMANDING 10TH M.G. COY.

(1)

Instructions regarding War Diaries and Intelligence Summaries are contained in F. S. Regs., Part II. and the Staff Manual respectively. Title pages will be prepared in manuscript.

WAR DIARY

or

~~INTELLIGENCE SUMMARY.~~

(Erase heading not required.)

Army Form C. 2118.

Place	Date	Hour	Summary of Events and Information	Remarks and references to Appendices
			Map References:-	
			FRANCE. Sheet 51B. S.W. } 1/20,000	
			" 51B. N.W. } 1/20,000	
			HAMBLAIN - LES - PRES.	
			Edition 5E 1/20,000 attached	

(A7092). Wt. W12839/M1293. 750,000. 1/17. D. D. & L., Ltd. Forms/C.2118/14.

(2)

Instructions regarding War Diaries and Intelligence Summaries are contained in F. S. Regs., Part II. and the Staff Manual respectively. Title pages will be prepared in manuscript.

WAR DIARY
or
~~INTELLIGENCE SUMMARY.~~
(Erase heading not required.)

Army Form C. 2118.

Place	Date	Hour	Summary of Events and Information	ARRIVALS	DEPARTURES	Remarks and references to Appendices
In The Field	1/12/17		On this date the Company was in position as follows.- Coy. Headquarters at N.10.a.8.7 No 3 Section (2/Lt R. FRAYLING) in SPADE RESERVE and SHOVEL TRENCHES. No 4 Section (2/Lt D. B. MOOR) in HOE SUPPORT and SADDLE SUPPORT. No 1 Section (2/Lt H. A. HILLMAN) at SHAMROCK CORNER. No 2 Section (2/Lt A.E. LAW) in ARRAS. The guns of No 3 Section co-operated with gas bombardment, firing on STIRRUP LANE and BEETLE TRENCH. No 2 Section took part in tactical exercise on the Field Firing Range at ACHICOURT.		2. ORS [illegible] to C.C.S.	
"	2/12/17		Co-operation with artillery by the guns of No 3 Section		Lt DALTON H.P. to Hospital	
	3/12/17		On this date the Company was relieved by the 12th Machine Gun Company & on completion of relief returned to billets in ARRAS.			

(A7092). Wt. W12839/M1293. 750,000. 1/17. D. D. & L., Ltd. Forms/C.2118/14.

(3)

Instructions regarding War Diaries and Intelligence Summaries are contained in F. S. Regs., Part II. and the Staff Manual respectively. Title pages will be prepared in manuscript.

WAR DIARY
or
~~INTELLIGENCE SUMMARY.~~
(Erase heading not required.)

Army Form C. 2118.

Place	Date	Hour	Summary of Events and Information	ARRIVALS	DEPARTURES	Remarks and references to Appendices
In The Field	4/12/17		Company did the following parades:- 9 AM to 10 AM Physical Training under S.S.M. FIGG. 10-30 AM to 12-30 PM Cleaning guns and etc under Section Officers.	1 O.R. from Hosp. 1 O.R. from Leave	1 O.R. to Hosp.	
"	5/12/17		The following parades were carried out:- 9 AM to 10 AM Company drill under C.S.M. 10-15 AM to 11-30 AM [illegible] under Section Officers 12 NOON Inspection by C.O. 2 PM to 4 PM. Baths	Cpl [illegible] from M.G. Course	[illegible] to U.K. 2/Lt [illegible] and 2 ORs to [illegible] Inf. course	
"	6/12/17		Company paraded as follows:- 9 AM to 10 AM Physical Training under S.S.M. FIGG. 10-15 AM to 11-30 AM Preparing guns & etc for the Range at 12-30 PM the Company marched out of Billets to the Field Firing Range where they carried out a Tactical Exercise under the C.O.	1 O.R. from [illegible]	Cpl Rodgers to M.G. [illegible] Course	
"	7/12/17		No 2 Section under 2/Lt LAW co-operated with the 1st ROYAL WARWICKSHIRE REGIMENT in a Tactical Exercise on the Field Firing Range, leaving billets at 7 A.M.	2/Lt Stevens from Leave. 1 O.R. from Leave	1 O.R. to Hosp.	[initials]

(A7092). Wt. W12839/M1293. 750,000. 1/17. D. D. & L., Ltd. Forms/C.2118/14.

Instructions regarding War Diaries and Intelligence Summaries are contained in F. S. Regs., Part II. and the Staff Manual respectively. Title pages will be prepared in manuscript.

WAR DIARY
or
~~INTELLIGENCE SUMMARY.~~
(Erase heading not required.)

Army Form C. 2118.

Place	Date	Hour	Summary of Events and Information	ARRIVALS	DEPARTURES	Remarks and references to Appendices
In The Field	7/12/17 (Contd)	-	No 3 Section under 2/Lt FRAYLING left billets at 9-30 AM to take part in the Tactical Exercise by the HOUSEHOLD BATTALION. No's 1 & 4 Sections paraded as under:- 9 AM to 10 AM Physical Training under S.S.M FIGG. 10.15 AM to 11.30 AM Mechanism under Section Officers 11.30 AM to 12.30 P.M. Combined Drill.			
"	8/12/17		The Company paraded at 8-30 AM and spent the morning on the 30x Range	3 ORs from leave		
"	9/12/17		The Company paraded at 9-15 AM for testing of Box Respirators at the Divisional Gas School: the remainder of the morning was devoted to Church Parades. Four Officers of the Company reconnoitred the line in the new Brigade Area.	2 ORs from leave.		
"	10/12/17		Vide Divisional Orders the Company "Stood To" in ARRAS from 6-30 AM to 10 AM. Upon receiving orders to "Stand down" the Company Paraded under Section Officers until 12-30 P.M 2 PM to 4 PM. Preparations of Guns for Trenches			

(A7092). Wt. W12839/M1293. 750,000. 1/17. D. D. & L., Ltd. Forms/C.2118/14.

Instructions regarding War Diaries and Intelligence Summaries are contained in F. S. Regs., Part II. and the Staff Manual respectively. Title pages will be prepared in manuscript.

WAR DIARY
or
~~INTELLIGENCE SUMMARY.~~
(Erase heading not required.)

Army Form C. 2118.

Place	Date	Hour	Summary of Events and Information	ARRIVALS	DEPARTURES	Remarks and references to Appendices
In the Field	11/12/17		The Company again Stood To from 6-30 A.M until 10 A.M. On this date the Company relieved the 11th [illegible] Gun Company in the LEFT Brigade Sector. The relief commenced at 2 PM and was completed at 6 PM. The position of the Company was then as follows:- Company Headquarters at N.4 b 9.5. No 3 Section in the CORPS LINE. No 1 Section:- 1 Gun in LONE AVENUE H.36. b 35.40. 1 " " RIFLE TRENCH I.31 a 40.25. 2 " " BRIDOON ALLEY O.1. b 40.35. No 2 Section:- 1 Gun at H.36. d 6.5 1 " " I.31 c 8.4. 1 " in CURB SWITCH NORTH I.31.d 1.9 1 " " RIFLE SUPPORT I.31. b 40.05. No 4 Section:- 2 Guns in EAST RES. O.1.d 60.35. 2 " " SHRAPNEL TRENCH O.2 c 35.50. Two guns in No 4 Section & 1 gun in No 1 Section fired 6000 rounds on Tracks in O.9.C.		Major PETTES leave to U.K.	

(A7092). Wt. W12839/M1293. 750,000. 1/17. D. D. & L., Ltd. Forms/C.2118/14.

(6)

Instructions regarding War Diaries and Intelligence Summaries are contained in F. S. Regs., Part II. and the Staff Manual respectively. Title pages will be prepared in manuscript.

WAR DIARY
or
~~INTELLIGENCE SUMMARY.~~
(Erase heading not required.)

Army Form C. 2118.

Place	Date	Hour	Summary of Events and Information	ARRIVALS	DEPARTURES	Remarks and references to Appendices
In The Field	12/12/17		Two guns of No 1 Section and Two guns of No 4 Section fired 12,000 rounds between 3 AM. and 6-30 A.M. on Tracks in O.3.c. And O.3.d.			
"	13/12/17		Four guns fired 11,000 rounds in cooperation with Artillery between 3 AM + 6 A.M. One Gun in RIFLE SUPPORT fired 1,000 rounds on POODLE TRENCH in co-operation with a raid by the HOUSEHOLD BATTALION: ZERO hour was 4 A.M.			
"	14-12-17		Four guns fired 12,000 rounds on Tracks in O,3,c, + d. between 3 AM + 6-30 A.M.	2. ORs from Base Depot 2. O.Rs from leave	1 N.C.O. to Cadet School	
"	15-12-17		Three guns fired 6,000 rounds on BIT LANE and Tracks in I,33,d, during the early morning. During the afternoon:- No 3 Section relieved No 1 Section " 1 " " " 2 " " 2 " " " 4 " " 4 " returned to the CORPS LINE.	2/Lt T.S. PATON from Base Depot	1 N.C.O. to [illegible] School.	

(A7092). Wt. W12839/M1293. 750,000. 1/17. D. D. & L., Ltd. Forms/C.2118/14.

(7.)

Instructions regarding War Diaries and Intelligence Summaries are contained in F. S. Regs., Part II. and the Staff Manual respectively. Title pages will be prepared in manuscript.

WAR DIARY
or
~~INTELLIGENCE SUMMARY.~~
(Erase heading not required.)

Army Form C. 2118.

Place	Date	Hour	Summary of Events and Information	ARRIVALS	DEPARTURES.	Remarks and references to Appendices
In The Field	16/12/17		Four guns fired 4,000 rounds on Tracks in I, 32, b. & d, during the night.		1 N.C.O. Leave to U.K. 1 O.R. [illegible] to C.C.S.	
"	17-12-17		Four guns fired 8,000 rounds in co-operation with the Artillery on Tracks in I, 32, b. & d. during the early morning.			
"	18-12-17		8000 rounds were expended in harassing fire on Tracks in O.3. c. & d.	Sgt Anson D. H. from Base Depot.		
"	19-12-17		Between 3 AM & 6.30 A.M. harassing fire was carried out on the BOIS DU VERT, 10,000 rounds being expended. During the afternoon:- No 4 Section relieved No 3 Section " 3 " " " 1 " " 1 " " " 2 " " 2 " returned to the CORPS LINE.			
"	20-12-17		During the early morning two guns fired 10,000 rounds on Tracks in O.3, c. & d.			

(A7092). Wt. W12839/M1293. 750,000. 1/17. D. D. & L., Ltd. Forms/C.2118/14.

(8)

Instructions regarding War Diaries and Intelligence Summaries are contained in F. S. Regs., Part II. and the Staff Manual respectively. Title pages will be prepared in manuscript.

WAR DIARY
or
~~INTELLIGENCE SUMMARY.~~
(*Erase heading not required.*)

Army Form C. 2118.

Place	Date	Hour	Summary of Events and Information	ARRIVALS	DEPARTURES	Remarks and references to Appendices
In the Field	21-12-17		At 5.20 PM our guns opened fire on their S.O.S. lines in response to an S.O.S. signal. During the night two guns fired 4000 rounds on FOX TRENCH			
"	22-12-17		The usual harassing fire was carried out during the night, in conjunction with the artillery.		1. O.R. to Hosp.	
"	23-12-17		During the afternoon the following relief took place:- No 2 Section relieved No 4 Section; " 4 " " " 3 "; " 3 " " " 1 ". No 1 Section returned to positions in the Corps Lines.		2nd Lt [illegible] Cpl [illegible] Cpl [illegible] 2/Lt [illegible] Wounded.	to [illegible] [illegible]
"	24-12-17		At 6-20 P.M. the enemy raided "Y" sap, and our guns fired until 7 P.M. on S.O.S lines; 24,000 rounds were expended.			
"	26-12-17		10.000 rounds were fired on enemy tracks in I32b + c during the night.	C.Q.M.S. [illegible] from leave.	1. O.R. Evac to C.C.S.	

(A7092). Wt. W12839/M1293. 750,000. 1/17. D. D. & L., Ltd. Forms/C.2118/14.

(9)

Instructions regarding War Diaries and Intelligence Summaries are contained in F. S. Regs., Part II. and the Staff Manual respectively. Title pages will be prepared in manuscript.

WAR DIARY
or
~~INTELLIGENCE SUMMARY.~~
(Erase heading not required.)

Army Form C. 2118.

Place	Date	Hour	Summary of Events and Information	ARRIVALS	DEPARTURES	Remarks and references to Appendices
In the Field	25/12/17		Between 12 midnight and 3 A.M. three guns fired 9000 rounds between them, on POODLE and TREE Trenches		1. O.R leave to UK	
"	26-12-17		10.000 rounds were fired on POODLE and TREE Trenches between 12 midnight & 6-30 A.M.			
	27-12-17		On this date the company was relieved in the left Brigade Sector by the 12th M.G. Company, and upon relief went into billets in ARRAS. Relief commenced at 12 noon and was complete at 3-30 P.M.	1. O.R from Base Hosp. MAJOR PETTLE from leave.		
"	28-12-17		The day was spent in cleaning guns & Etc, & personal equipment. The company provided a fatigue party of 4 N.C.Os & 32 men to unload coal at ARRAS. Station, and a patrolling picquet of 1 N.C.O & 8 men.		2. O.R. to Hosp	
"						

(A7092). Wt. W12839/M1293. 750,000. 1/17. D. D. & L., Ltd. Forms/C.2118/14.

Instructions regarding War Diaries and Intelligence Summaries are contained in F. S. Regs., Part II. and the Staff Manual respectively. Title pages will be prepared in manuscript.

WAR DIARY
or
~~INTELLIGENCE SUMMARY.~~
(Erase heading not required.)

Army Form C. 2118.

Place	Date	Hour	Summary of Events and Information	ARRIVALS	DEPARTURES	Remarks and references to Appendices
In the Field	29.12.17		The company spent the day as follows:- 9 AM to 10 AM. Company drill under C. S. M. 10-15 AM to 11-30 AM Mechanism under Section Officers 11-30 AM to 12-30 P.M. Gun Drill " " 2 P.M to 4 P.M. Stripping + I. A. under Section Officers The company was paid out during the afternoon.	2 Lt Inskip, Cpl Merrick, Cpl Hicks } from Gas Course	Sgt Lynch A to XVII Corps Inf School	
"	30.12.17		The company paraded for Baths + church services in the morning. At 2 P.M. the men had their Christmas Dinner, followed by a concert.		L/Cpl Clark to XVII Corps Gas School.	
"	31/12/17		The morning was spent on the 30 yards range, when Table "C" Part I was fired. In the afternoon, guns + Etc were cleaned, and belts filled.		L/Cpl Clark to XVII Corps Gas School	

(A7092). Wt. W12839/M1293. 750,000. 1/17. D. D. & L., Ltd. Forms/C.2118/14.

pproximate British Front Line
9-9-17.
LINE
QUEANT
DROCOURT

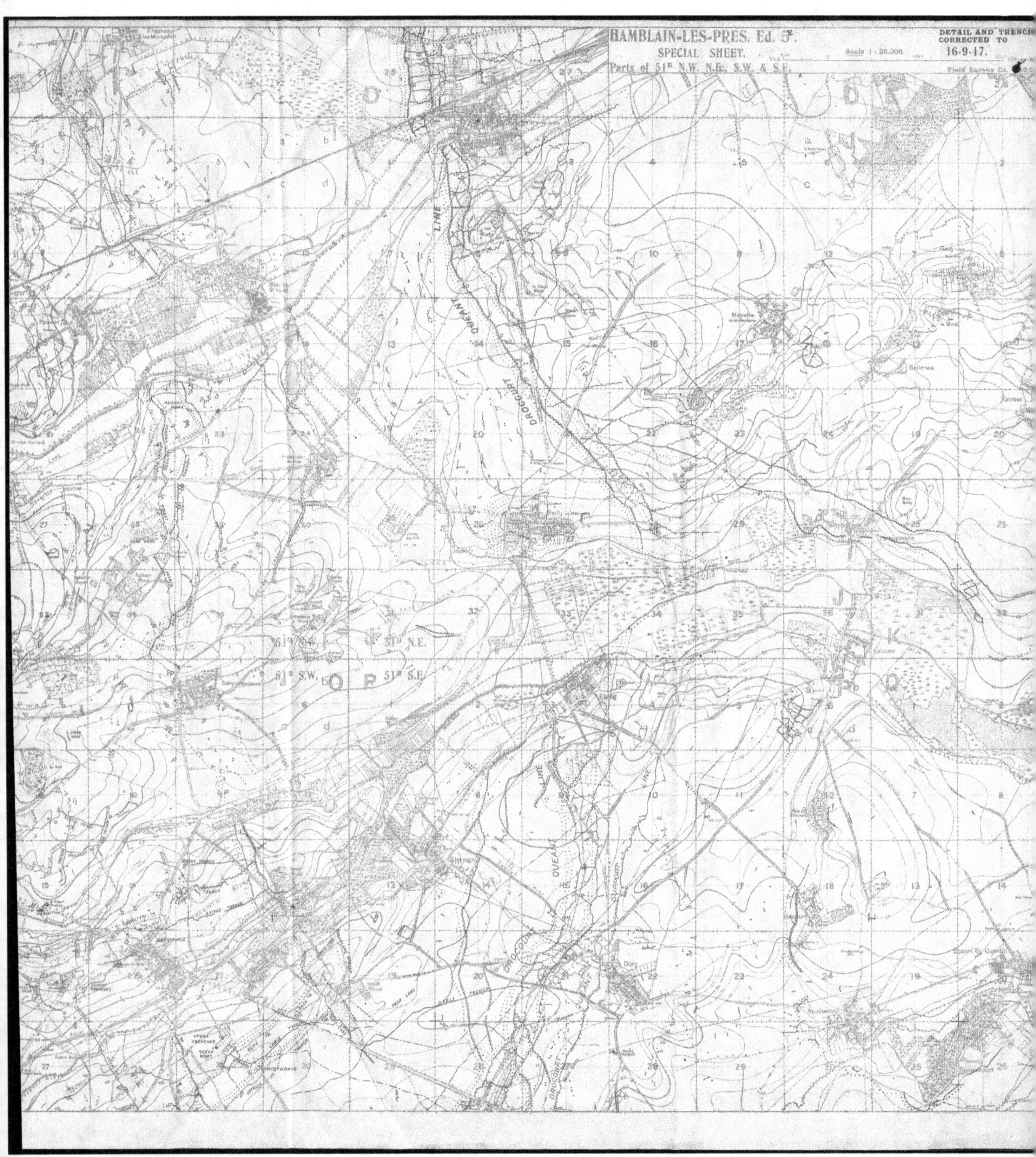
HAMBLAIN-LES-PRES. Ed. 5E.
SPECIAL SHEET.
Parts of 51B N.W. N.E. S.W. & S.E.
Scale 1 : 20,000
DETAIL AND TRENCH
CORRECTED TO
16·9·17.
Field Survey Co.
LINE
DROCOURT
QUEANT
SUPPORT
51B S.W.
51B N.E.
51B S.E.
Ecluse
Dury
Ecourt St. Quentin

WAR DIARY

4th Division

10th M. G. C.

January 1918

10th MACHINE GUN COY

ORIGINAL

WAR

DIARY

FOR MONTH OF JANUARY

FIELD.

2.2.18

R. Pettle Major.

COMMANDING 10th M.G.C.

(1)

Instructions regarding War Diaries and Intelligence Summaries are contained in F. S. Regs., Part II. and the Staff Manual respectively. Title pages will be prepared in manuscript.

WAR DIARY
or
~~INTELLIGENCE SUMMARY.~~ January 1918.
(Erase heading not required.)

Army Form C. 2118.

Place	Date	Hour	Summary of Events and Information	ARRIVALS	DEPARTURES	Remarks and references to Appendices
In The Field	1-1-18.		Map References			
			FRANCE			
			Sheet 51. B S.W. } 1/20,000			
			" 51. B N.W. }			
	1-1-18		On this date the Company was in Billets at ARRAS.			
			The following parades were carried out:-		2 O.Rs EVAC to C.C.S.	
			9 A.M. to 10 A.M. - Company drill under C.S.M			
			10-15 AM to 11-30 AM - Mechanism under Section Officers			
			11-30 AM to 12-30 P.M - Combined drill under Section Officers			
			2 P.M to 4 P.M Immediate action and Box Respirator Drill.			

(A7092). Wt. W12839/M1293. 750,000. 1/17. D. D. & L., Ltd. Forms/C.2118/14.

(2)

Instructions regarding War Diaries and Intelligence Summaries are contained in F. S. Regs., Part II. and the Staff Manual respectively. Title pages will be prepared in manuscript.

WAR DIARY
or
~~INTELLIGENCE SUMMARY.~~
(Erase heading not required.)

Army Form C. 2118.

Place	Date	Hour	Summary of Events and Information	ARRIVALS	DEPARTURES	Remarks and references to Appendices
In the Field	2-1-18		The Company paraded as follows:— 9 AM to 10 AM Company Drill under C.S.M. 10-15 " to 11-30 " Mechanism under Section Officers 12 15 PM to 4 PM Table "C" Part 1 was fired on 30x Range	2nd Lt LABES Cpl Burdett Pte Brooks Returned from XVII Corps Inf School		
	3-1-18		The following parades were carried out during the day 9 AM to 10 AM Physical Training 10-30 " to 11-30 " Mechanism 11-30 " to 12-30 PM Immediate Action 2 PM to 4 " Preparing guns etc for the trenches			
	4-1-18		On this date the Company relieved the 11th Machine Gun Coy in the Right Brigade Sector Upon completion of relief the Company was situated as follows —	1 O R from Course	Commanding Officer attached French Army 1 O.R.	DGP

(A7092). Wt. W12839/M1293. 750,000. 1/17. D. D. & L., Ltd. Forms/C.2118/14.

Instructions regarding War Diaries and Intelligence Summaries are contained in F. S. Regs., Part II. and the Staff Manual respectively. Title pages will be prepared in manuscript.

WAR DIARY

or

~~INTELLIGENCE SUMMARY.~~

(Erase heading not required.)

Army Form C. 2118.

Place	Date	Hour	Summary of Events and Information	ARRIVALS	DEPARTURES	Remarks and references to Appendices
In The Field	4-1-18 (Continued)		Company Headquarters N 10 a 8 7 No 4 Section at CORPS LINE. " 3 " Two guns in 'B' Strong Point Two guns in VINE AVENUE at O 7 a 4 5. " 2 " Two guns in SHOVEL TRENCH " " SPADE RESERVE " 1 " One gun in HOE SUPPORT Two guns in SADDLE SUPPORT One gun in HILL SUPPORT Relief was completed at 3 PM. at 9.50 PM Enemy put down a barrage along the whole Divisional Front and all Machine Guns fired in responce to S.O.S signal			
"	5-1-18		Two guns fired 3,000 rounds each on STIRRUP LANE during the night.	Sgt Tuckey from Base Depot Cpl Rodgers from M.G. Course		[initials]

(A7092). Wt. W12839/M1293. 750,000. 1/17. D. D. & L., Ltd. Forms/C.2118/14.

(4)

Instructions regarding War Diaries and Intelligence Summaries are contained in F. S. Regs., Part II. and the Staff Manual respectively. Title pages will be prepared in manuscript.

WAR DIARY
or
~~INTELLIGENCE SUMMARY.~~
(Erase heading not required.)

Army Form C. 2118.

Place	Date	Hour	Summary of Events and Information	ARRIVALS	DEPARTURES	Remarks and references to Appendices
In The Field	6-1-18		Harassing fire was carried out from 12 midnight till 6-30 AM on BEETLE TRENCH. 4,000 rounds being expended.	LIEUT. HARPER III from Base Depot. [illegible] Clarke from XVII Corps [illegible] School		
"	7-1-18		Occasional bursts of fire on S.O.S lines in the early morning by all guns.		Sgt [illegible] to M.G. [illegible] Course.	
"	8-1-18		Machine guns were quiet; single shots being fired to prevent guns freezing.			
"	9-1-18		Occasional bursts were fired on S.O.S lines during the early morning. Working party was supplied for new position in GORDON AVENUE, SOUTH of 'B' Strong point.		2nd LEINSTER 3 O.Rs to XVII Corps School	

(A7092). Wt. W12839/M1293. 750,000. 1/17. D. D. & L., Ltd. Forms/C.2118/14.

(5)

Army Form C. 2118.

WAR DIARY
or
~~INTELLIGENCE SUMMARY.~~
(Erase heading not required.)

Instructions regarding War Diaries and Intelligence Summaries are contained in F. S. Regs., Part II. and the Staff Manual respectively. Title pages will be prepared in manuscript.

Place	Date	Hour	Summary of Events and Information	ARRIVALS	DEPARTURES	Remarks and references to Appendices
In The Field	10-1-18		On this date machine gun positions on the Brigade Front were changed, and on completion of move, the guns east of CORPS LINE were situated as follows:- No 2 Section:- One gun in SPADE RESERVE at O.7.a.50.25. Two guns in SHOVEL TRENCH (one at O.7.d.05.35. (one at O.7.b.13.13. One gun from SPADE RESERVE withdrawn to CORPS LINE. No 1 Section:- One gun in DALE TRENCH at O.2.a.50.05. One gun in EAST RESERVE at O.1.d.65.26. One gun in 'D' Strong Point O.7.c.00.05. One gun in GORDON AVENUE O.13.a.00.10. No 3 Section:- One gun - N.18.a.00.40 One gun - N.18.a.47.82 One gun - N.12.c.15.80. One gun - N.12.a.50.30.	1.O.R. from leave		

RB.

(A7092). Wt. W12839/M1293. 750,000. 1/17. D. D. & L., Ltd. Forms/C.2118/14.

(6)

Army Form C. 2118.

Instructions regarding War Diaries and Intelligence Summaries are contained in F. S. Regs., Part II. and the Staff Manual respectively. Title pages will be prepared in manuscript.

WAR DIARY

or

~~INTELLIGENCE SUMMARY.~~

(Erase heading not required.)

Place	Date	Hour	Summary of Events and Information	ARRIVALS	DEPARTURES	Remarks and references to Appendices
In The Field	11-1-18		No [illegible] guns did no firing on this date		1. O.R. Leave to U.K.	
	12-1-18		No 4 Section relieved No 1 Section, relief commencing at 12 noon upon relief No 1 Section retired to positions in the CORPS LINE.			
	13-1-18		At 5 AM all guns opened fire on their S.O.S lines on commencement of enemy artillery Barrage & fired until the situation quitened down.	1. O.R. reinforcement from Hosp UK.		
	14-1-18		No Enemy action occured during the day, & no harassing fire was carried out.			
	15-1-18		Usual trench routine. The guns did no firing on this date.			

(7)

Instructions regarding War Diaries and Intelligence Summaries are contained in F. S. Regs., Part II. and the Staff Manual respectively. Title pages will be prepared in manuscript.

WAR DIARY
or
~~INTELLIGENCE SUMMARY.~~
(Erase heading not required.)

Army Form C. 2118.

Place	Date	Hour	Summary of Events and Information	ARRIVALS	DEPARTURES	Remarks and references to Appendices
In the Field	16-1-18		No firing was done, but work continued on the various new emplacements under R.E. supervision.		1. O.R. to hospital	
	17-1-18		Usual trench routine & new emplacements proceeded with. No firing took place.		1. O.R. leave to U.K.	
	18-1-18		No harassing fire on this date. Usual trench routine.	2 O.R. reinforcements from Base Depot.		
	19-1-18		The gun at O2 position in DALE TRENCH was moved to a position in SHRAPNEL TRENCH 50 yds S. of CANISTER AVENUE. No firing was done on this date.			
	20-1-18		On this date the Company was relieved by the 12th M.G. Coy and upon relief withdrew to the BOIS des BOEUFS CAMP on the CAMBRAI ROAD. Relief was complete at 3 p.m.			
	21-1-18		The day was spent in cleaning guns, gun equipment & mens equipment. New clothing was issued & the men were bathed.			[initials]

(A7092). Wt. W12839/M1293. 750,000. 1/17. D. D. & L., Ltd. Forms/C.2118/14.

(8)

Instructions regarding War Diaries and Intelligence Summaries are contained in F. S. Regs., Part II. and the Staff Manual respectively. Title pages will be prepared in manuscript.

WAR DIARY
or
~~INTELLIGENCE SUMMARY.~~
(Erase heading not required.)

Army Form C. 2118.

Place	Date	Hour	Summary of Events and Information	ARRIVALS	DEPARTURES	Remarks and references to Appendices
In the Field	22-1-18		The morning was spent inspecting anti gas appliances and overhauling, cleaning and repairing belts. In the afternoon the Sections paraded for baths at TILLOY.		3 OR to Hosp.	
	23-1-18		The following parades were carried out during the day. 9 A.M. to 10 A.M. Saluting Drill under C.S.M. 10 " to 11 " Mechanism under Section Officers 11-15 " to 11-45 " Box Respirators Drill. 12 " The remainder of the Coy paraded for baths 2 P.M. to 3 P.M. Inspection of Coy: guns, tripods, and belts, by O.C. Coy.		1. OR to Hosp.	
	24-1-18		The Coy paraded as follows 9 A.M. to 10-30 AM Overhauling of belts. 10-30 " to 11-30 " Mechanism 11-45 " to 12-30 PM Box Respirators Drill. 2 PM to 3. " Saluting Drill under C S M.			R.W.

(A7092). Wt. W12839/M1293. 750,000. 1/17. D. D. & L., Ltd. Forms/C.2118/14.

(9)

Instructions regarding War Diaries and Intelligence Summaries are contained in F. S. Regs., Part II. and the Staff Manual respectively. Title pages will be prepared in manuscript.

WAR DIARY
or
~~INTELLIGENCE~~ SUMMARY.
(Erase heading not required.)

Army Form C. 2118.

Place	Date	Hour	Summary of Events and Information	ARRIVALS	DEPARTURES.	Remarks and references to Appendices
In the Field	25-1-18		The following parades were carried out.	1. O.R. from hosp.		
			9 AM to 10 AM Arms Drill.			
			10-15 " to 11-15 " Immediate action			
			11-30 " to 12-30 PM Mechanism			
			2 PM to 3 " Explanation of indirect fire			
			A fatigue party worked all day rivetting the huts.			
	26-1-18		Two Sections worked all day revetting the huts as protection against bombs. The remainder of the Coy paraded for Arms Drill, Aiming, Instruction, Mechanism and stripping.			
	27-1-18		Church Parades during the morning at TILLOY and BOIS DE BOEUFS.	1. O.R. from French Army.		
			The C.O. returned to the Coy after a tour of duty with the French Army.	1. O.R. from leave.		

(A7092). Wt. W12839/M1293. 750,000. 1/17. D. D. & L., Ltd. Forms/C.2118/14.

(10)

Instructions regarding War Diaries and Intelligence Summaries are contained in F. S. Regs., Part II. and the Staff Manual respectively. Title pages will be prepared in manuscript.

WAR DIARY
or
INTELLIGENCE SUMMARY.
(Erase heading not required.)

Army Form C. 2118.

Place	Date	Hour	Summary of Events and Information	ARRIVALS	DEPARTURES	Remarks and references to Appendices
In the Field	28-1-18		On this date the Coy relieved the 11th M.G. Coy in the Left Sector. The morning was spent preparing guns for the trenches, and cleaning up the camp. The relief started at 4 PM on completion of relief the Coy was situated as follows			
			Company Headquarters at N. 4. b. 9. 5.			
			No 2 Section in CORPS LINE			
			No I Section. One gun H. 36. a. 50. 55.			
			One gun H. 36. a. 00. 33.			
			One gun H. 36. b. 20. 03.			
			One gun H 36. b. 5. 6			
			No 3 Section. One gun I 31. c. 47. 02.			
			One gun I 31. d. 1. 9.			
			One gun H 36. d. 75. 65			
			One gun H. 36. d 65. 50			

(A7092). Wt. W12839/M1293. 750,000. 1/17. D. D. & L., Ltd. Forms/C.2118/14.

Army Form C. 2118.

Instructions regarding War Diaries and Intelligence Summaries are contained in F. S. Regs., Part II. and the Staff Manual respectively. Title pages will be prepared in manuscript.

WAR DIARY
or
INTELLIGENCE SUMMARY.
(Erase heading not required.)

Place	Date	Hour	Summary of Events and Information			Remarks and references to Appendices
In the Field	28.11.18		No 4 Section One gun N. 6 a. 88. 63. One gun N. 6 a. 88. 41. One gun H. 36 c. 45. 25. One gun H. 36 c. 11. 41.		[illegible] to U.K.	
	29.11.18		At 3 a m the enemy put down a fairly heavy barrage on our support line for about 20 minutes. Our Artillery and Machine guns replied. Enemys Artillery was fairly quiet during the day. Our Machine guns were inactive.			
	30.11.18		Fairly quiet. Artillery on both sides doing some harassing fire. Machine guns were also quiet. Aircraft were very active on both sides owing to good visibility.			

(A7092). Wt. W12839/M1293. 750,000. 1/17. D. D. & L., Ltd. Forms/C.2118/14.

Army Form C. 2118.

Instructions regarding War Diaries and Intelligence Summaries are contained in F. S. Regs., Part II. and the Staff Manual respectively. Title pages will be prepared in manuscript.

WAR DIARY
or
INTELLIGENCE SUMMARY.
(Erase heading not required.)

Place	Date	Hour	Summary of Events and Information	Remarks and references to Appendices
In the Field	31-1-18		Very quiet day. – "HAPPY VALLEY" was shelled in the evening with gas shells, also MONCHY. Machine guns were inactive.	

[illegible] Major.
Comdg: 15th Coy: M.G.C.

(A7092). Wt. W12839/M1293. 750,000. 1/17. D. D. & L., Ltd. Forms/C.2118/14.

4th Division

10th Infantry Bde

10th Trench Mortar Battery

February to September
LESS May to July

1917

—

~~To 1919~~

CONFIDENTIAL. Vol 1

War Diary

of

10th Trench Mortar Battery

for

February 1917.

Instructions regarding War Diaries and Intelligence Summaries are contained in F. S. Regs., Part II. and the Staff Manual respectively. Title pages will be prepared in manuscript.

WAR DIARY
or
INTELLIGENCE SUMMARY.
(Erase heading not required.)

Army Form C. 2118.

Place	Date	Hour	Summary of Events and Information	Remarks and references to Appendices
CAMP 112	Feby 1st		At Camp 112	
— 18	— 3rd		Moved to Camp 18.	
"	— 5th		CAPT. SARCHET (O.C.) proceeded on special leave U.K.	
B 16 d 08 (BOUCHEVANES)	— 10th		Moved to Reserve Dugout. B 16 d 08	
"	11th–20th		Engaged in RE fatigue in trenches	
	17th		2ND LT. C. M. HUMPHRIES (2nd Seaforth Hgn) joined from 4th Army School of Mortars for attachment	
CAMP 12	21st		Moved to Camp 12	
"	26th/28th		Period of Training	
	26th		CAPT. SARCHET (O.C.) rejoined from special leave UK	

3/3/17

[Signature] Capt.
OC 10th T. M. Bty

A5834 Wt. W4973/M687 750,000 8/16 D. D. & L. Ltd. Forms/C.2118/13.

Vol

WAR DIARY

10th Trench Mortar Battery.

March 1st to 31st 1917

Instructions regarding War Diaries and Intelligence Summaries are contained in F. S. Regs., Part II. and the Staff Manual respectively. Title pages will be prepared in manuscript.

WAR DIARY
or
INTELLIGENCE SUMMARY.

(*Erase heading not required.*)

Army Form C. 2118.

Place	Date	Hour	Summary of Events and Information	Remarks and references to Appendices
CAMP 12 (CHIPILLY).	1/3/17		Training continued. 2nd/Lt. Humphries to C.C.S.	
CORBIE.	4/3/17		Battery marched to billets in CORBIE	
MONTONVILLERS	5/3/17		Battery marched to billets at MONTONVILLIERS	
BEAUVAL	6/3/17		Battery marched to billets at BEAUVAL.	
REMAISNIL.	7/3/17		Battery marched to billet at REMAISNIL.	
REMAISNIL.	10/3/17		2nd/Lt HUMPHRIES rejoined	
REMAISNIL	11/3/17		8. other ranks returned to their regiments as not likely to become efficient. 1 Officer. (2nd Lt. W. GREEN. Household Batt.) and 20 other ranks joined to complete Reserve Personnel	
REMAISNIL.	16/3/17		2nd/Lt T. G Hancox 3rd R. War Rgt proceeded to U.K on being transferred to Royal Artillery	
OURTON.	20/3/17		Battery ordered to move by bus at 4 hours notice. Marched to X roads N of BOFFLES and thence by bus to OURTON.	
ARRAS	29/3/17		Battery moved by lorry to ARRAS to join 34th Division	
ARRAS.	30/3/17		Officers reconnoitred the line with a view to putting in 8 guns to thicken 18 pounder barrage.	
ARRAS	31/3/17		Whole battery worked on new emplacements.	

10TH TRENCH MORTAR BATTERY.
No.
Date 31/3/17

[signature] Capt
OC 10th T M Bty

A5834 Wt. W4973/M687 750,000 8/16 D. D. & L. Ltd. Forms/C.2118/13.

Confidential

Vol

War Diary

of

10th Trench Mortar Battery

from

1st to 30th April 1917

W. Green.

2nd Lieut.

Commanding, 10th Trench Mortar Battery

NO 10 Trench Mortar Battery

Instructions regarding War Diaries and Intelligence Summaries are contained in F. S. Regs., Part II. and the Staff Manual respectively. Title pages will be prepared in manuscript.

WAR DIARY for April 1917
or
~~INTELLIGENCE SUMMARY.~~
(Erase heading not required.)

Army Form C. 2118.

Place	Date APRIL	Hour	Summary of Events and Information	Remarks and references to Appendices
	1st to 8th		The Battery was billeted in ARRAS being temporarily attached to the 34th Division. Each night working parties were engaged in digging 8 emplacements for the Trench mortars in the Support line near KING CRATER. On the night 7/8 4 officers and 36 other ranks moved up to a dug out in the Support line. The 8 guns were ranged on the enemy's front line on the 3rd and the 8th.	
	9th		At Zero the 7 guns had fired 600 rounds in 4 minutes. One gun could not be fired having been disabled by a piece of a German shell. Captain Sackett was wounded and went to hospital. The Battery now returned to the 4th Division and on the night 9/10th moved up to the Blue line.	
	11th		Half battery moved to sunken road near Fampoux, the remainder acted as a carrying party for the 10th M. G. Co. Heavy shelling all day caused many casualties in the Battery.	
	13th		Half battery returned to Brown line, the remainder still carrying for M. G. Co.	
	16th		The carriers returned from the M G Co and the Battery relieved the 11th T.M.B. in the line near GAVRELLE. Two guns in position both in HUDSON Trench.	
	20/21st		Battery relieved by 63rd Bde TMB (37th Division) came back to ARRAS and then by bus to DENIER	
	22nd–24th		Training at DENIER	
	25th		Battery moved to BEAUFORT	
	26th–29th		Training at BEAUFORT	
	28th		To Y huts	
	29th		To ARRAS	
	30th		To Railway cutting near FAMPOUX.	W Green 2 Lt 15 May 1917.

A5834 Wt. W4973/M687 750,000 8/16 D. D. & L. Ltd. Forms/C.2118/13.

War Diary

August 1917

10 Trench Mortar Battery

W Green
Capt
1 Sept 1917

Army Form C. 2118.

Instructions regarding War Diaries and Intelligence Summaries are contained in F. S. Regs., Part II. and the Staff Manual respectively. Title pages will be prepared in manuscript.

WAR DIARY

~~or~~

~~INTELLIGENCE SUMMARY~~.

(*Erase heading not required.*)

Place	Date	Hour	Summary of Events and Information	Remarks and references to Appendices
	1917 AUG			
In the Field near ROEUX	1		Very wet and gloomy. 40 rounds were fired in bursts on I 20 a 75 90 in conjunction with Artillery + Machine Guns	
	2		Again very wet and over cast. Men commence to dig a level path in front of the Battery dug outs in CRUMP	
	3		Wind safe S.W.15 to 20 miles per hour. Showery and gusty. Men complete the path	
	4		Rainy + close. Captain Green returns from leave. 30 rounds fired on I 20 a 90.80 Shooting was reported to be very good.	
	5.		Gloomy morning becoming afterwards very hot. Men employed detonating and carrying ammunition to the line. 40 rounds were fired on I 20 a 70 90 + I 20 a 90.80 2 Lieut R. P. Wilson 2nd Seaforth Highlanders reported for duty. 2 Lieut Lee relieves 2 Lieut Lemon in the line	
	6.		Very misty morning but the mist was dispersed by sun about noon when it became very hot. Men employed carrying ammunition to the line. Seven men of 3/10 Middlesex Regt and one man 1st Royal Warwickshire Regt reported for duty. 32 rounds were fired on enemy dug outs at I 20 b 18 58	
	7		Warm morning getting close and gloomy towards 5.30 p m when a heavy thunderstorm	

T2134. Wt. W708—776. 500000. 4/15. Sir J. C. & S.

Instructions regarding War Diaries and Intelligence Summaries are contained in F. S. Regs., Part II. and the Staff Manual respectively. Title pages will be prepared in manuscript.

WAR DIARY

~~or~~

~~INTELLIGENCE SUMMARY~~.

(*Erase heading not required.*)

Army Form C. 2118.

Place	Date	Hour	Summary of Events and Information	Remarks and references to Appendices
	1917 Aug			
In the Field near ROEUX	7 Contd		broke lasting until 8.15 p.m. The men detonated 104 rounds of ammunition	
	8		Misty morning. 180 rounds of ammunition received	
	9		Wind S 15 to 20 miles per hour Raw and cold. Bombardment on the right all day. ROEUX wood shelled.	
	10		Cool morning Wind W. Day improved and became very warm. At evening a captive balloon broke away and drifted N E into enemy lines. 60 rounds were fired on the suspected Company H.Q at I 14 d 07 07.	
	11.		Warm & windy. Heavy thunderstorm from 3.15 to 4.30 p.m. 20 rounds fired during the night on enemy front line. 2 Lieut Lee leaves to rejoin the 1st Royal Irish Fusiliers	
	12		Windy, warmer in the afternoon. Men employed carrying shells to gun positions 34 rounds were fired on junction of CRUST and CORE	
	13		Dull slight rain. Men detonating and carrying shells to front line 2 Lieut Lemon relieves 2 Lieut Wilson. 40 rounds fired on CRUST and CORE	
	14		Dull morning. Heavy thundershowers at noon. Men employed detonating ammunition 40 rounds were fired on a Machine Gun in CRUST	
	15		Dry but windy. Heavy thunder showers about 3.45 p.m. All spare men	

Instructions regarding War Diaries and Intelligence Summaries are contained in F. S. Regs., Part II. and the Staff Manual respectively. Title pages will be prepared in manuscript.

WAR DIARY

~~or~~

~~INTELLIGENCE SUMMARY~~.

(*Erase heading not required.*)

Army Form C. 2118.

Place	Date	Hour	Summary of Events and Information	Remarks and references to Appendices
In the Field near ROEUX	1917 Aug 15 (contd)		employed at night in clearing a cellar in ROEUX to make an alternative gun position. 40 rounds fired on CRUST and CORE.	
	16.		Dry but windy. Men employed in carrying to the front line and in working at night on the new position in ROEUX. 50 rounds were fired on the suspected Company H.Q I 14 d 1.7	
	17		Weather still improving. Wind W 20 miles per hour. 2 Lieut Wilson relieves 2 Lieut Lemon. Men working on the cellar at night. 50 rounds fired on I 20 a 90.70.	
	18		Dry windy. Men employed detonating and carrying to the front line. 40 rounds were fired on the enemy's advanced post on the N bank of the SCARPE	
	19		Quiet and cool in morning. Capt Green and Lieut Nelson visit the sector S of the river which we have been ordered to take over. 68 rounds were fired on I 14 C 80.20	
	20.		Weather bright clear warm. Lieut Nelson takes over 2 gun positions S of river from 11 Trench Mortar Battery. 2 Lieut Lemon rejoins the 1st Royal Irish Fusiliers	
	21		Very hot day. 2 Lieut C.G Laycock 1st Royal Warwickshire Regt, who reported for duty on the 19th inst, relieves 2 Lt Wilson in the line. 120 rounds were fired on the wire rounds the enemy Machine Gun emplacement in CRUST.	

T2134. Wt. W708—776. 500000. 4/15. Sir J. C. & S.

Army Form C. 2118.

Instructions regarding War Diaries and Intelligence Summaries are contained in F. S. Regs., Part II. and the Staff Manual respectively. Title pages will be prepared in manuscript.

WAR DIARY

~~or~~

~~INTELLIGENCE SUMMARY.~~

(Erase heading not required.)

Place	Date	Hour	Summary of Events and Information	Remarks and references to Appendices
In the Field near ROEUX	1917 Aug 22		Again very hot. 30 rounds were fired by our guns S of river at 3 p.m on ARCHIE trench in conjunction with the Machine Guns in ROEUX wood. The shooting was very successful. One German attempted to climb out of the trench and was killed by Machine Gun fire. Several direct hits on the trench were obtained and a helmet and Very lights were thrown into the air.	
	23		Cooler and strong wind. 50 rounds were fired on ARCHIE at 3 p.m by our guns S of the river in conjunction with the Machine Guns in ROEUX WOOD. Several direct hits on the trench were obtained. An enemy light T.M. ~~sed~~ shell at about 11 p.m hit one of our guns in CROFT killing the sentry and destroying 24 rounds of ammunition	
	24		Cool, some rain. An enemy working party in ANGEL trench was dispersed by a few rounds at 11 A.M. 16 rounds were fired on MG at I 20 a 75 90.	
	25.		Warm & bright. 80 rounds were fired on MG at I 20 a 75 90 + 80 rounds on enemy line opposite No 3 post. A party working in ANGEL trench was dispersed by a few rounds at 11 A.M. and 30 rounds were fired on ANGEL during the night in retaliation for hostile fire.	

T2134. Wt. W708—776. 500000. 4/15. Sir J. C. & S.

Army Form C. 2118.

Instructions regarding War Diaries and Intelligence Summaries are contained in F. S. Regs., Part II. and the Staff Manual respectively. Title pages will be prepared in manuscript.

WAR DIARY

or

~~INTELLIGENCE SUMMARY~~.

(*Erase heading not required.*)

Place	Date	Hour	Summary of Events and Information	Remarks and references to Appendices
In the Field				
near ROEUX	26		At 3.50 p.m. 40 rounds were fired on the junction of ANGEL and ARCHIE. Several direct hits on the trench were obtained. At "stand to" retaliatory rounds were fired on ARCHIE both at night and in the morning. The night was very wet. 2 Lieut R.H. Tune Household Batn reported for duty. 2 Lieut Wilson relieves 2 Lieut Laycock in the line.	
	27.		Raining all day. 15 rounds were fired on ARCHIE at 'stand to' evening and morning	
	28		Wind very strong Rain at night. 2 Lieut Tune joins Lieut Nelson for instruction At 3A.M. 26 rounds were fired on ANGEL at I 25 d 75 45 & I 25 d 82 12 A Machine Gun was reported as having been silenced. 21 rounds were fired in bursts as retaliation during the day. 10 rounds were fired on CRUST at night	
	29		Wind still strong with intermittent rain. At 11 p.m 30 rounds were fired on CRUST and at 3 AM 30 on ANGEL	
	30		Stormy and wet. Little shooting possible. 30 rounds were fired on CRUST 2 Lt Laycock relieves 2 Lt Wilson who takes the place of Lt Nelson S of river	
	31		Gloomy and slight rain. 60 retaliatory rounds were fired on ARCHIE during the night and 20 rounds were fired on the junction of CRUST & CORE	

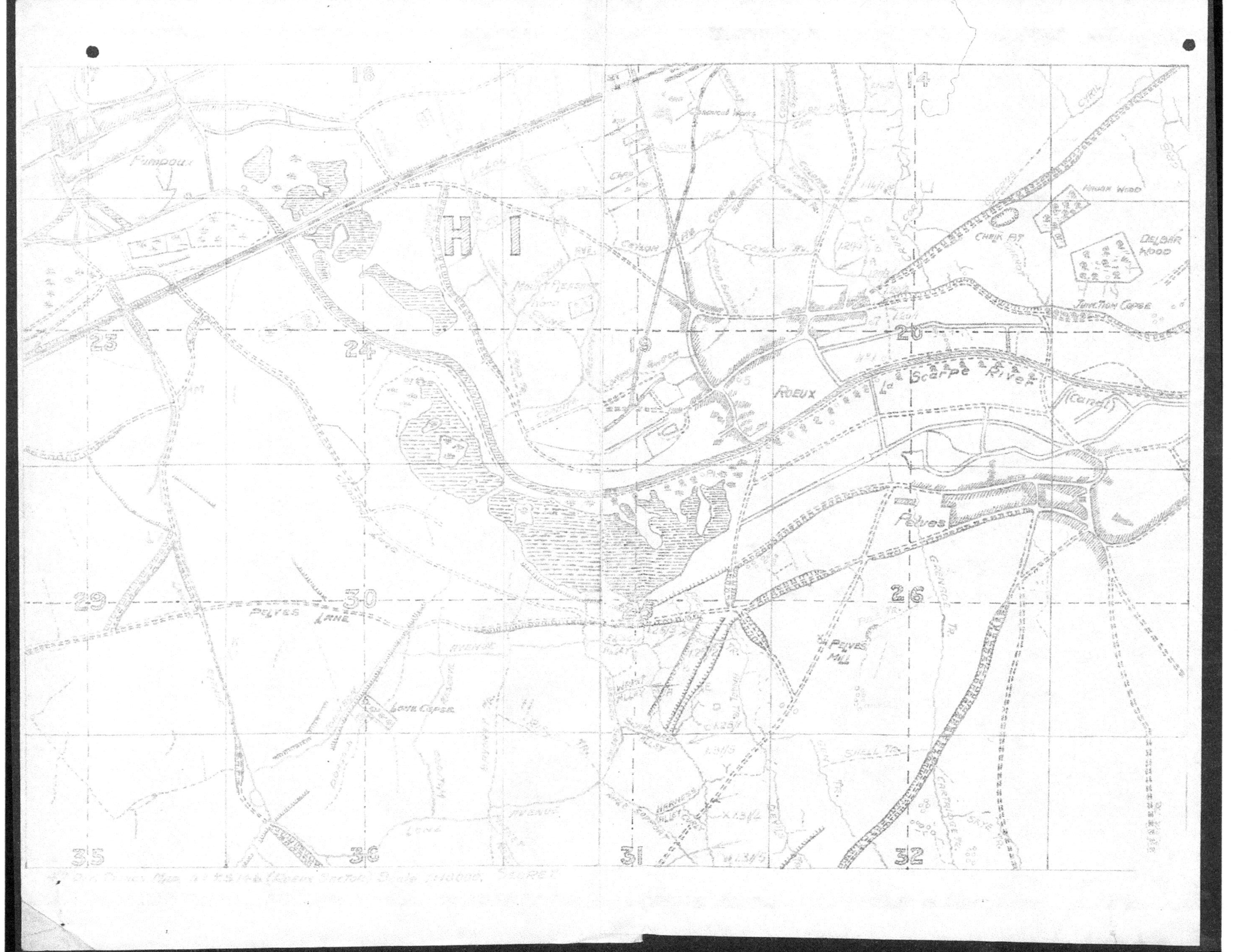

Fampoux
H
I
Scarpe River
(Canal)
Roeux
Pelves
Pelves Mill
Pelves Lane
Chemical Works
Mount Pleasant Wood
Hausa Wood
Delbar Wood
Junction Copse
Chemical Works
Lone Copse
Cyril
Chili Tr.
Ceylon Tr.
Grenade Tr.
Shell Tr.
Cartridge Tr.
Colne Tr.
17
18
14
19
20
23
24
25
26
29
30
31
32
35
36

CONFIDENTIAL.

War Dairy

10th Trench Mortar Battery.

Volume

From 1st to 30th September 1917.

I

Instructions regarding War Diaries and Intelligence Summaries are contained in F. S. Regs., Part II. and the Staff Manual respectively. Title pages will be prepared in manuscript.

WAR DIARY or ~~INTELLIGENCE SUMMARY.~~

(Erase heading not required.)

of 10th Trench Mortar Battery. Army Form C. 2118.

September 1917.

Place	Date	Hour	Summary of Events and Information	Remarks and references to Appendices
	1st		A windy day with slight rain. South of the River Scarpe 102 rounds were fired during the night on Angel Trench. A party were heard working about 2AM in Angel trench, they were fired on and dispersed. North of the Scarpe 17 rounds silenced an enemy M.G. which had been very active. About 11.30 pm an enemy T.M shell fell close to our position in front of Roeux. The sentry was buried & the entrance to the dugout blocked. All the team, the gun & 100 rounds of [illegible] shells were rescued undamaged.	
	2nd		Considerable wind all day, which is drying the trenches rapidly. Work was continued on repairing the damage of last night's shell. During the night 2/3rd, North of the River, 30 rounds were fired on the new enemy sap. South of the River, during the day & night, altogether 65 rounds were fired on Archie & Angel trenches. In the daylight shoot several direct hits were obtained and a lot of boards were thrown into the air.	
	3rd		South of the Scarpe, we fired 75 rounds along Archie & Angel trenches during the night. North of the Scarpe 60 rounds were fired in three bursts between 9 & 9.30 pm on the new sap, upon which the enemy had been reported to be working.	
	4th		Lieut Nelson went to Bellacourt to billet for the battery. In conjunction with the heavy T.M, a shoot was carried out on the hostile post & dugouts in APE trench. Several Germans bolted by the heavy were killed by our fire. At 10 pm Company in the line reported a new hostile machine-gun firing from Angel. It was silenced by 5 rounds rapid. In all 130 rounds were fired from the Southern positions. North of the Scarpe, at 10 pm we fired 20 rounds on the suspected Coy. H.Q., in the support line in front of ROEUX, where aerial observers had reported fresh activity.	
	5th		South of the Scarpe, during the afternoon we engaged the junction of Angel & Archie. 80 rounds were fired & the enemy trench was badly damaged. He retaliated with 10 rounds of light T.M shells on our battle positions. In the ROEUX sector between 11 pm & midnight we bombarded the Coy. H.Q in the support line with 64 rounds.	
	6th		We were relieved at 5.30 pm by the 45th T.M.B. after 11 weeks in this sector. On relief, the battery marched to ARRAS & were settled in their billets by 7.45 pm.	
	7th		A very warm day; the battery paraded at 4 pm and marched to BELLACOURT, arriving at 7.15 pm. All ranks very pleased at getting out of the line.	
	8th		Lieut Nelson goes on leave to the U.K. Battery spent the day cleaning & polishing up.	
	9th		Church parade in the morning; resting for the remainder of the day.	
	10th–14th		The mornings were spent, doing arms drill, P.T. & gun drill. In the afternoons we had games and sports.	

II

WAR DIARY
or
~~INTELLIGENCE~~ SUMMARY.
(Erase heading not required.)

10th Trench Mortar Battery. Sept. 1917.

Army Form C. 2118.

Instructions regarding War Diaries and Intelligence Summaries are contained in F. S. Regs., Part II. and the Staff Manual respectively. Title pages will be prepared in manuscript.

Place	Date	Hour	Summary of Events and Information	Remarks and references to Appendices
	15th		A practice attack was carried out by two of the battalions in the morning. We put up two preliminary barrages, firing 400 rounds from 4 guns. The shooting was very good & the dummy trench destroyed.	
	16th		2/Lieut W.R.S. Girard [?]; 3/10 Middx Regt reported for duty. The battery went thro' the gas chamber in the afternoon to test their box respirators.	
	17th		The practice attack of the 15th was repeated with another battn. 830 rounds were fired.	
	18th		2/Lieut Tune went to PROVEN to billet for the battery.	
	19th		The battery moved to PROVEN by rail, arriving at 7pm. Billeting accomodation very crowded.	
	20th		2/LIEUT TUNE went on leave to U.K.	
	21st-22nd		Parades, training & games each day, the weather being exceptionally fine & hot.	
	23rd		Lieut Nelson returns from leave.	
	24th-27th		Training and sports as usual. N.C.O.s were given instruction in the use of the compass & map in T.M work.	
	28th		The battery was inspected by the new Divisional General in the afternoon.	
	29th		The battery marched to PROVEN & entrained for ELVERDINGHE, from which place they marched to their camp near the CANAL bank North of YPRES. On arrival it was found that there was no accomodation in the camp & the men had to bivouac on the ground as best they could. The Area adjutant played the Good Samaritan & allowed the officers to sleep in his office floor. During the night, the enemy aeroplanes dropped several bombs in the neighbouring camps, causing numerous casualties, but fortunately there were none among our personnel. One bomb fell within 15 yds of our hut, but failed to explode!	
	30th		An open piece of ground was found, bivouac shelters obtained and a new camp formed for the battery. O.C. Battery & two subalterns went up to reconnoitre the line for the coming offensive.	

F.W. Nelson Lt & Adj
10 Trench Mortar Battery

(A7092). Wt. W12839/M1293. 750,000. 1/17. D. D. & L., Ltd. Forms/C.2118/14.

4th Division

10th T. M. B.

~~January to December 1918~~

1918 JAN — 1919 JAN

10 Trench Mortar Battery

War Diary – January 1918

W Green
Capt.

10th Trench Mortar Batty. I

WAR DIARY
or
INTELLIGENCE SUMMARY.
(Erase heading not required.)

January 1918.

Army Form C. 2118.

Instructions regarding War Diaries and Intelligence Summaries are contained in F. S. Regs., Part II. and the Staff Manual respectively. Title pages will be prepared in manuscript.

Place	Date	Hour	Summary of Events and Information	Remarks and references to Appendices
ARRAS.	JAN. 1st		The new year finds us out resting — a good beginning! The battery strength is 6 officers and 71 other ranks. It is still freezing hard and bitterly cold. All parades have to be those of movement. Battery personnel engaged on usual parades. Capt. [illegible] went up the line to interview O.C. 11 T.M.B. with a view to forthcoming relief in the Cambrai Road Sector.	All references are to MONCHY TRENCH MAP (Part of 51.B. NW. SW)
do	2nd		Slight thaw beginning in the morning, changed to hard frost again at night. Guns were re-cleaned & deficiencies made up, in readiness for tomorrow's relief.	
do CAMBRAI ROAD SECTOR	3rd		Still freezing hard. Battery paraded at 12.20 pm, reaching SHAMROCK CORNER (H. 7) at 1.45 pm. Relief in the line reported complete by 4.0 pm. 11th T.M.B. were clear by 5.30 pm. 2Lt Laycock is in on the left in DALE Tr with 4 guns & a complete 1st R.War.R. team. 2Lt Tune, in on the right in HOE Support, with a Household Battn detachment. This is the first time for 9 or 10 months that we have tried making up each detachment by regiments, as it is only lately we have had sufficient personnel to carry it out. By a new arrangement the 4 guns in & about DALE Tr will be taken over for tactical purposes by each Brigade in the line for eight days each in turn. During the night 3/4th the guns on the right fired 60 rounds on LANYARD, BEETLE & PUN trenches. The guns on the left fired 22 on the junction of HEN & FOAL trenches.	
do	4th		Still freezing. Some of the gun positions might be improved, but nothing can be done while this hard weather continues. Firing during the night took place as follows. Right guns. Harassing fire was kept up throughout the night on LANYARD Tr & about the junction of BADGER & front line. 100 rds being fired. Left guns. 64 rounds on SPOON Tr (O.8.b.5.7) half between 10 pm & 10.45 pm, & half from 5.30 AM to 6 AM. 20 " " JUNCTION of FOAL & FOX trenches.	
do	5th		Reserve personnel engaged in carrying 108 rounds to Right position. A very cold day. During the night 5/6th Right guns fired 60 rounds on LANYARD Tr at O.14.b 72.60 & 60.50, traversing 9° right & left from these points. At 9 pm. infantry reported enemy party working on junction of PUN & front line. 10 rds rapid were fired on them, & 30 other rounds at intervals on same spot up to 10.45 pm. Left guns fired as follows:- 20 on SPOON Tr. 20 on HEN. & 20 on FOX.	
do	6th		Capt. Green returns from leave. Thaw begins in heavy down pour of rain at 3 pm. Freezing again by morning. During the night 6/7 the guns on the right fired 75 rounds; 25 on each of following three targets. LANYARD Tr O.14.b 72.60., junction of BEETLE & BRACE, junction of BADGER & front line. Enemy T.M.s very quiet in this sector. Guns on the left only fired 30 rounds on SPOON Tr at O.8.b.75.30, owing to patrols etc being out.	
do	7th		Frost still holding. Reserve personnel carried 160 rounds to Right position. Right guns fired 90 rounds on the same targets as the night previous, while the left guns fired 30 rds on enemy M.G. reported at O.8.d.47.17.	
do	8th		Thawing from about 4 pm. Then it froze again about 8 pm & there was a heavy fall of snow during the night. The guns on the right fired at 2.30 am 30 rds on new enemy trench at O.14.b.41.61. & 30 on PUN Tr at O.8.d.50.60. Guns on the left fired 8 rds on SPOON Tr O.2.d.71.25. when a short round fell in our own line, fortunately no one was hurt. This is the first abnormal short we have had & was evidently due to one of the rings failing to explode. 14 other rounds were fired at 6 am. on the junction of FOAL & FOX.	
do	9th		Snow fell intermittently during the day, & no carrying was possible. About 6 pm it turned to heavy rain with wind about 20 miles per hr from the west. Right guns fired 150 rds during the night, 50 on each of following points. Enemy front line at O.14.b.41.51. & O.14.b.41.93. junction of BUCKLE & PUN. The left guns 30 rds on BOLT trench & 24 on the junction BOLT & SPOON between 4 & 5 pm.	

A5834 Wt. W4973/M687 750,000 8/16 D. D. & L. Ltd. Forms/C.2118/13.

10th Trench Mortar Battery II

Instructions regarding War Diaries and Intelligence Summaries are contained in F. S. Regs., Part II. and the Staff Manual respectively. Title pages will be prepared in manuscript.

WAR DIARY
or
INTELLIGENCE SUMMARY.

(Erase heading not required.)

January 1918.

Army Form C. 2118.

Place	Date	Hour	Summary of Events and Information	Remarks and references to Appendices
CAMBRAI RD SECTOR	JAN. 10th		A dry day with a strong wind from the S.W. The going was very bad as there was a sticky layer of mud over a still frozen surface. Reserve men carried 60 rounds to the right position & the 12 T.M.B. supplied 300 to the left. Capt Green & Lt Nelson reconnoitred the ground near VINE & PICK Trenches (behind reserve line) with a view to putting four guns into defence positions, in accordance with new Defence Scheme. During the night the guns on the Right fired 150 rounds, 50 each on STRING Tr, junction of BEETLE & LANYARD, & STRAP Tr at O.8.d 30.52, where a German post had been located. On the left, 53 rounds were fired in short burst between 4.30 & 5.30 pm on BUCKLE Tr at O.8.b.8.0.	
do.	11th		Still dry, mud as bad as ever. Half battery relief took place today. 2Lt Gerard relieved 2Lt Tune in the Right positions, & the 11 T.M.B. supplied the officer in place of 2Lt Laycock (10TMB) on the left. Under the new Defence Scheme No1 Gun in HOE SUPT was withdrawn to head quarters, this leaves us with only the two guns in HOE SUPT. as the two in Vine have passed to 11 T.M.B. During the night 25 rounds were fired on the junction of STRAP & BADGER Trenches. As soon as fire was opened the enemy sent up a white light which burst into two white stars. Immediately the enemy opened medium T.M. fire on the neighbourhood of HOE SUPT. Between 3.30 AM & 3.40 am 25 rounds were fired on the junction of BEETLE & LANYARD trenches. This also drew a few T.Ms from the enemy.	
do.	12th		During the morning we reconnoitred the houses on the outskirts of MONCHY to find a cellar for the accomodation of the crews of the guns to be put in in that vicinity, as the places chosen on the 10th were not approved by H.Q. A good cellar was found quite close to CIRCLE Tr. with two entrances, a reinforced roof, tables, chairs etc etc which should answer the purpose very well. Owing to the amount of wiring & digging that is being done at present, it is not desired to draw enemy fire more than is unavoidable, accordingly instructions have been issued that we are to reduce our fire as much as possible. During the night 12/13th from 10.50 to 11.10 pm 30 rounds were fired on M.G reported active at O.8.d.30.50. & from 4.0 am to 4.10 am 20 rounds were traversed along STRING Tr. at the Northern end. At 4.45 am the enemy put down a ragged T.M. & artillery barrage along our left battn front. Our S.O.S was sent up ten minutes later, in response to which our guns in HOE fired 70 rds on their S.O.S lines. The enemy attempted a raid on Sap 7 in O.8.b. but was driven off by L-G. & rifle fire. We suffered no casualties. At 5.5 am, a shell which fell near HOE SUPT. on bursting emitted a bright white light which lit up the ground for a radius of 100 yds at least. Everything was quiet by 5.30 am.	
do.	13th		The ground was quite hard this morning, as it froze during the night. Reserve personnel cleared out the cellar in MONCHY in readiness for the incoming teams. Our guns did not fire during the night of the 13/14th.	
do.	14th		Four inches of snow fell during the night. The day is calm but poor visibility. 70 rounds were carried to the MONCHY cellar during the morning. In the afternoon two guns were set up near the cellar & laid on their defence-lines, the team of six men & an N.C.O living in the cellar. Our other guns in HOE did not fire during the night.	

Instructions regarding War Diaries and Intelligence Summaries are contained in F. S. Regs., Part II. and the Staff Manual respectively. Title pages will be prepared in manuscript.

III

10th Trench Mortar Battery.

WAR DIARY
or
~~INTELLIGENCE~~ SUMMARY.
(Erase heading not required.)

January 1918.

Army Form C. 2118.

Place	Date	Hour	Summary of Events and Information	Remarks and references to Appendices
CAMBRAI ROAD SECTOR.	Jan 15.		Heavy rain, almost continuously from 10am, soon banished the snow and left the ground a sea of mud. The reserve personnel started to carry 93 rounds to MONCHY cellar at 9.30am & owing to the difficult ground & high wind from the S.W. did not get back till 1.30 pm. Both ourselves & the enemy were very inactive in all arms during the day & night. The rain & wind attained their greatest violence from about midnight 15/16 to 4 am 16th. Our guns did not fire during the period.	
do.	16th		No rain fell during the day, & there was a strong drying wind from the west until about 4pm when it died away. The front-line system is almost impassable in places. ~~Also~~ Nearly every ~~where~~ place that has not been revetted, has fallen in, especially the communication trenches. One of our positions in HOE SUPT. has completely caved in. Trenches are in such a bad state that orders have been issued reducing movement in the trenches to the minimum possible.	
do	17th & 18th		Dry but dull weather. The trenches still remained impassible and our mortars did not fire	
do	19th		The Battery was relieved by No 12 Trench Mortar Battery and withdrew to ARRAS The relief was carried out over the top owing to the condition of the trenches	
ARRAS	19th to 27th		The Battery was billeted in RUE EMILE BRETON and RUE DE BIETZ. The men were employed most of this time in cleaning up cellars under the Sanitation Officer and in digging a butt on the Brigade Assault Course at ACHICOURT. Little time could be given to training.	
MONCHY SECTOR	27th		The Battery relieved No 11 Trench Mortar Battery in the MONCHY SECTOR. 2 Lt Wilson with 15 men is in CHAIN SUPPORT with 2 guns in OAL? TRENCH and one gun in HIGLAND SUPPORT 2 Lt Trans? with 9 men is in ORCHARD trench with 3 guns in ORCHARD TRENCH and 2 guns in ORANGE AVENUE	

Instructions regarding War Diaries and Intelligence Summaries are contained in F. S. Regs., Part II. and the Staff Manual respectively. Title pages will be prepared in manuscript.

IV

10 Trench Mortar Battery **WAR DIARY** Jan 1918

or

~~INTELLIGENCE SUMMARY.~~

(Erase heading not required.)

Army Form C. 2118.

Place	Date	Hour	Summary of Events and Information	Remarks and references to Appendices
MONCHY SECTOR	28th to 31st		The weather was fine and parties of the Infantry were busily engaged in cleaning out the trenches and in revetting and duckboarding them. Little firing was possible but our gun pits were improved and 55 rounds were fired in retaliation for enemy activity. Owing to the condition of the trenches gum boots ~~were~~ were necessary and there was still much movement over the top. The weather continued fine with a tendency to frost and the trenches were greatly improved at the end of the four days.	

10 <u>Trench Mortar Battery</u>

War <u>Diary - February</u> 1918.

W Green Capt

28 Feb 1918.

10th Trench Mortar Battery.

WAR DIARY
or
~~INTELLIGENCE SUMMARY.~~
(*Erase heading not required.*)

February 1918.

Army Form C. 2118.

Instructions regarding War Diaries and Intelligence Summaries are contained in F. S. Regs., Part II. and the Staff Manual respectively. Title pages will be prepared in manuscript.

Place	Date	Hour	Summary of Events and Information	Remarks and references to Appendices
MONCHY SECTOR.	1st		Thick mist all day, visibility NIL. 2Lt Laycock & a team of R War R's & Middlesex relieved 2Lt Wilson in HIGHLAND SUPPORT. 2Lt Girard & a Middlesex team relieved 2Lt Tune in ORCHARD RESERVE. In the evening two guns were moved from the latter position up to DALE Tr. At 10.43 pm the S.O.S. went up on the left & our guns fired 74 rounds on their S.O.S. lines. The rate of fire was unusually slow owing to the plates sinking in the soft ground.	
do.	2nd		The guns in DALE under 2Lt Girard fired 136 rds on HEN, FOAL, FOX & LONG trenches between 8.30 & 8.45 am in support of the raid by the Brigade on our right. The ammunition was supplied by the 12 T.M.B. as owing to the short notice given us there was not time to bring it from the dump. The gun in HIGHLAND SUPt also fired 20 rounds. The day turned out very bright & clear. In the morning we supplied a fatigue party to the Durham R.E. to carry up pumps.	
do.	3rd		A clear day, good visibility. During the day reserve teams carried up 56 rounds to the line. The men in the line were engaged in improving their gun positions. At 5.30 am (3/4th) 11 rounds were fired on the junction of DEVILS Tr & FACTION Tr.	
do.	4th		Weather still clear & dry, & the trenches are greatly improved & much dryer than they have been for a long time. All the men (13) of the Household Battn in the battery left us to rejoin their Battn in SCHRAMM Bks.	
do.	5th		Another fine day. At 5.30 am the gun in HIGHLAND SUPPORT opened fire on the junction of DEVILS & FACTION TRENCHES but after the third round the base cap broke off thus putting the gun out of action.	
do	6th		Visibility exceptionally fine. The Division was relieved by the 15th Division; we were relieved by the 45th T.M.B. & returned to our usual H.Q. in ARRAS. The relief was complete by 3 pm. Lieut NELSON returned from leave to U.K.	
ARRAS.	7th		Lieut TUNE rejoined the Household Battn. 2Lt GIRARD + 16 O.R. rejoined the 11th Middlesex Regt prior to them leaving the Brigade. These departures leave the Battery strength at 4 officers & 33 O.R.	
do	8th		Morning was spent in general cleaning up of men & guns. Cpl Brown goes home on 1 month's leave to U.K. We also learn that he has been awarded the D.C.M. as well as the CROIX de GUERRE.	
do.	9th		The usual parades were held during the day & the guns given a final cleaning. Paint was obtained & the legs & howitzers were given a first coat.	
do	10th		A dry day with some wind. Church parades as usual.	
do	11th		Training began in earnest today in accordance with Brigade programme and continued during the week favoured by fine dry weather. A class of 30 men from the 1st R War. Regt, 2nd Duke of Wellington's Regt and 2nd Seaforth Hdrs assembled for instruction in T M work. 13 men from 2nd Duke of Wellington's Regt joined the Battery on 11th inst.	
do	18th		Divisional Field Day at WAILLY. Battery personnel were employed as sentries and in working the targets representing an enemy counter attack.	

A7092 Wt W128 9/M1293 750,000. 1/17. D. D & L., Ltd. Forms/C2118/14.

10 Trench Mortar Battery

Instructions regarding War Diaries and Intelligence Summaries are contained in F. S. Regs., Part II. and the Staff Manual respectively. Title pages will be prepared in manuscript.

WAR DIARY
or
~~INTELLIGENCE SUMMARY.~~

(*Erase heading not required.*)

Feb 1918.

Army Form C. 2118.

Place	Date	Hour	Summary of Events and Information	Remarks and references to Appendices
ARRAS	19th to 22nd		Training continued favoured by fine weather. On the afternoon of 22nd 4 guns were carried to a position near BEAURAINS and dug in in position ready for a practice attack at dawn	
	23rd	AM 6.15	The 2nd Duke of Wellingtons Regt and the 1st R Warwickshire Regt with the 2nd Seaforth Hdrs ~~supported~~ attacked and took an enemy position. The enemy were represented by a body of men drawn from the 2nd Seaforth Hdrs. Our guns practised a barrage for the infantry and when the objective was taken all 4 guns moved forward and dug in to defend the newly captured ground against counterattack.	
			The class which assembled on 13th inst finished this day and 17 men drawn from it were attached for duty to the Battery.	
	24th		30 men drawn from the 3 battalions assemble for a course of instruction in T M work.	
	26th		2 Lieut McLeod 1st R War Regt reported for duty with the Battery	
	27th		Lieut Nelson who went to hospital on 11th transferred to C. C. S.	
			The Battery was employed during the afternoon in improving the butts at BEAURAINS Range.	
	28th		The Battery now numbers 5 officers 59 other ranks.	

A7092. Wt W128 9/M1293. 750,000. 1/17. D. D & L., Ltd. Forms/C2118/14.

War Diary – March 1918

10 Trench Mortar Battery

W Green
Capt

31 March 1918.

10 Trench Mortar Battery

Army Form C. 2118.

WAR DIARY ~~or~~ ~~INTELLIGENCE SUMMARY~~. March 1918.

Instructions regarding War Diaries and Intelligence Summaries are contained in F. S. Regs., Part II. and the Staff Manual respectively. Title pages will be prepared in manuscript.

(Erase heading not required.)

Place	Date	Hour	Summary of Events and Information	Remarks and references to Appendices
ARRAS	1st to 15th		The Battery continued their training. The weather continued warm & bright during the whole period. Deficiencies of kit were made up and a further 14 men were attached bringing our total strength up to 75 other ranks.	
TILLOY	16th		The Battery gave a demonstration of live firing before the Divisional General. 166 rounds in all were fired. The first practice was a trench mortar barrage by 8 guns preparatory to a trench to trench attack and the second represented an advance in support of Infantry and a rapid concentration of fire on an enemy strong point. In the latter practice the guns were steadied between the firer's knees and no elevating stands were used.	
NEUVILLE VITASSE ROAD	18th		The Battery together with the batteries of the 11th and 12th Brigades gave a demonstration before a number of spectators of our own and other Divisions. 550 rounds were fired and the practices included a burst of 2 rounds per gun from 24 guns on an enemy strong point, a box barrage for a raid and rapid advance and concentration of fire without the use of elevating stands.	
ROEUX	19th		The Battery moved up by motor launch to FAMPOUX and relieved the 3rd Guards Brigade Trench Mortar Battery in the line near ROEUX. Rain continued all day but the trenches were in good condition, well revetted and duck-boarded. Lieut Laycock was in charge of the guns in the line, disposed as follows ~~in~~ two covering front system and three	

A7092 Wt. W128 9/M1293 750,000. 1/17. D. D & L., Ltd. Forms/C2118/14.

10 Trench Mortar Battery

Army Form C. 2118.

WAR DIARY March 1918 (Contd)

or

~~INTELLIGENCE SUMMARY~~.

(Erase heading not required.)

Instructions regarding War Diaries and Intelligence Summaries are contained in F. S. Regs., Part II. and the Staff Manual respectively. Title pages will be prepared in manuscript.

Place	Date	Hour	Summary of Events and Information	Remarks and references to Appendices
ROEUX	19th (contd)		covering the support system. The gun positions taken over were very poor.	
	20th		Weather improved and the two guns covering the front system were ranged on S.O.S lines.	
	21st		The enemy who had hitherto been quiet were firing heavily from 5 A.M. Gas shells were freely used. On this morning the great offensive of the enemy commenced further South. Our Mortars fired 80 rounds between 5 and 6 A.M on the enemy trench junctions in front. 2 Lieut McLeod relieved Lieut Laycock in the line.	
	22nd		The enemy offensive continued further South but our Sector was quiet. The day was very fine and warm and work was pushed forward in the construction of new gun positions.	
	23rd		The XV Division on our right evacuated MONCHY LE PREUX and rumours as to an impending withdrawal from our own Sector became current. During the night 23rd/24th the Heavy Trench Mortars were withdrawn from the sector. At 2 P.M. about 20 Germans were found in our front line which was only patrolled during the day. The enemy were quickly driven out by a bombing party and our T.M. fire.	
	24th		Enemy snipers from South bank of the river SCARPE are very active against any movement along CRUMP. The day was fine and passed very quietly in our sector.	
	25th		The sniping became worse and it became evident that our Head Quarters must be moved from CRUMP. The 6 In NEWTON Trench Mortars were withdrawn from the sector during the night 25th/26th	

W. 1128/M1293. 750,000. 1/17. D. D. & L., Ltd. Forms/C2118/14.

10 Trench Mortar Battery

Army Form C. 2118.

Instructions regarding War Diaries and Intelligence Summaries are contained in F. S. Regs., Part II. and the Staff Manual respectively. Title pages will be prepared in manuscript.

WAR DIARY
or
~~INTELLIGENCE SUMMARY~~.

(Erase heading not required.)

March 1918 (Contd)

Place	Date	Hour	Summary of Events and Information	Remarks and references to Appendices
ROEUX	26th		Our Head Quarters were moved from CRUMP to the RAILWAY EMBANKMENT west of FAMPOUX CROSSING. 200 rounds were fired at 3.5 AM in reply to the S.O.S signal sent up on our left.	
	27th		The day was dry & fine. 2 Lieut Wilson and a reserve section relieved 2 Lieut McLeod and the section who had been in the line since the 19th inst.	
FEUCHY	28th		The enemy artillery was firing heavily from 4 AM. Later their attack developed and the line held by the 11th Brigade on our left and the XVth Division on our right was broken. Our Brigade being left in the air had to retire to the army line near FEUCHY. The Battery succeeded in withdrawing without loss of personnel but one gun could not be withdrawn and was blown up. Parts of 3 other guns were also lost. Two guns were placed in position in the ARMY LINE and the remainder of the Battery personnel acted as Infantry in defence of the line. Lieut Laycock & 2 Lieut McLeod were in charge.	
	29th		The day passed quietly. 2 Lieut Wilson relieved 2 Lieut McLeod in the line.	
	30th		The day was wet. During the night 30th/31st the 1st Royal Warwickshire Regt advanced their line to take in the greater part of FEUCHY.	
	31st		2 Lieut Wilson with 6 men and one mortar move up in support of the 1st Royal Warwickshire Regt. The day passed quietly & was moderately fine	

A7092. Wt. W128 9/M1293. 750,000. 1/17. D. D & L., Ltd. Forms/C2118/14.

10 Trench Mortar Battery

War Diary April 1918

W Greene
Capt

30 April 1918

10 Trench Mortar Battery

WAR DIARY – April 1918

~~or INTELLIGENCE SUMMARY~~.

(Erase heading not required.)

Army Form C. 2118.

Instructions regarding War Diaries and Intelligence Summaries are contained in F. S. Regs., Part II. and the Staff Manual respectively. Title pages will be prepared in manuscript.

Place	Date 1918	Hour	Summary of Events and Information	Remarks and references to Appendices
near FEUCHY	April 1st		The day was fine and there was good observation. About 6 pm 4 of our observation balloons were brought down by an enemy aeroplane.	
	2nd		A very clear day and great aerial activity	
	3rd		Corporal Brain and 10 men go back to HAUTE AVESNES to be the "10% personnel" left out of action and to take the place of Corpl Atherton and 10 men who rejoined the Battery from HAUTE AVESNES on this day.	
			2 Lieut G. R. Smith 2nd Duke of Wellingtons Regiment joined the Battery on his return from leave to the United Kingdom	
	4th		2 Lieut Smith and 2 Lieut McLeod relieve 2 Lieut Wilson and Lieut Laycock in the line	
	5th 6th 7th		It is reported that the enemy are using a captured Stokes Mortar against us. About 60 rounds were fired by us each night on the enemy strong point near ICELAND TRENCH	
	8th		Heavy rain fell all day. In the evening we were relieved by the 3rd Canadian Trench Mortar Battery and the whole Brigade came by motor bus to AGNES-LES-DUISANS arriving about 1 AM on the 9th. The "10% personnel" rejoined us here.	
	9th to 11th		The weather improved and the roads, which had been very muddy when we arrived, quickly dried	
near LILLERS.	12th		The whole 4th Division moved by motor lorries to the LILLERS AREA arriving about 6 P.M. On arrival we were told that the limit of the enemys advance was not known and	

Instructions regarding War Diaries and Intelligence Summaries are contained in F. S. Regs., Part II. and the Staff Manual respectively. Title pages will be prepared in manuscript.

Army Form C. 2118.

10 Trench Mortar Battery

WAR DIARY

or

~~INTELLIGENCE SUMMARY.~~

(Erase heading not required.)

April 1918.

Place	Date	Hour	Summary of Events and Information	Remarks and references to Appendices
near LILLERS	1918 April 12th Contd		that the Battery was to spend the night on the LILLERS CANTRAINNE RD. A small farm recently deserted by its owners was found and the whole of the personnel was comfortably housed for the night.	
	13th		2 Lieut McLeod went to hospital with trench fever. Numbers of refugees were seen bringing back their property from the invaded area.	
near ROBECQ	14th		The Battery moved up the line to BELLERIVE. Lieut Laycock and 6 men go back to AMES as "10% personnel".	
	15th		The 1st Royal Warwickshire Regt and 2nd Duke of Wellingtons Regt make an unsuccessful attempt ~~to~~ to take the BOIS DE PACAUT. The Battery under 2 Lieut Wilson and 2 Lieut Smith ~~—~~ were employed to carry ammunition for these battalions. This they did successfully and without any casualties	
	16th		During the night the Battery was again employed on carrying parties for the battalions	
	17th		Four mortars were placed in position to cover PONT L'HINGES and PONT LEVIS on the right. (near HINGETTE). 2 Lieut Wilson was in charge of the gun teams	
	18th		About 1 A.M. a very heavy bombardment by the enemy began and during the morning a determined attempt by the Germans to cross the LA BASSEE CANAL was repulsed by the 2nd Seaforth Highlanders. The enemy losses were very heavy. In the afternoon a house on the canal bank was noticed to be occupied by a party of the enemy. 2 Lieut Wilson moved up a Mortar and bombarded the house. Six	

A5834 Wt. W4973/M687 750,000 8/16 D. D. & L. Ltd. Forms/C.2118/13.

10 Trench Mortar Battery

Instructions regarding War Diaries and Intelligence Summaries are contained in F. S. Regs., Part II. and the Staff Manual respectively. Title pages will be prepared in manuscript.

WAR DIARY April 1918.

or

~~INTELLIGENCE SUMMARY.~~

(*Erase heading not required.*)

Army Form C. 2118.

Place	Date April (1918)	Hour	Summary of Events and Information	Remarks and references to Appendices
near ROBECQ	18 Contd		Germans ~~were~~ bolted and were killed by rifle and Lewis gun fire. Others were thought to have been killed in the house. During the day we had 4 men wounded - one of them by a bomb dropped by one of our own aeroplanes. During the night 2 more mortars were put in to fire on PACAUT WOOD.	
L'ECLEME	19		The Battery was relieved by the 11th Trench Mortar Battery and retired to L'ECLEME	
	20		Warning is received that we are to put in 4 mortars to fire on PACAUT WOOD in connection with a forthcoming attempt, at dawn on the 21st inst, to take the wood. Capt Green 2 Lieut Wilson and 13 other ranks moved up 4 guns and 159 Stokes shells but were informed that the attack had been postponed. The night was a beautiful moonlit night but a good deal of gas was hanging about from the enemy shelling.	
	21		A fine dry day. Warning was received that the attack will take at dawn on 22nd inst. 2 Lieut Wilson and 13 men move up the line at night and	
near ROBECQ	22.		fire a 3 minute barrage at 5.15 AM on the 22nd inst. The attack was very successful and the objective, which was a drive about half way through the wood was reached without much difficulty. Four guns from each of the 11th and 12th T.M. Batteries as well as the 6 In Newton and Heavy T.M's were employed also in the preliminary barrage. The machine gun fire which held up the attack on the 15th inst was smothered by T.M. fire.	

A5834 Wt. W4973/M687 750,000 8/16 D. D. & L. Ltd. Forms/C.2118/13.

Instructions regarding War Diaries and Intelligence Summaries are contained in F. S. Regs., Part II. and the Staff Manual respectively. Title pages will be prepared in manuscript.

10 Trench Mortar Battery

WAR DIARY April 1918.

or

~~INTELLIGENCE SUMMARY~~.

(Erase heading not required.)

Army Form C. 2118.

Place	Date	Hour	Summary of Events and Information	Remarks and references to Appendices
	1918 April			
L'ECLEME	23		The Battery rested at L'ECLEME.	
	24th		We relieved the 12th T. M. B. in the left Sector of our Divisional front. Two mortars	
near ROBECQ			were taken over in RIEZ DU VINAGE. The rest of the guns were at Battery H.Q in BELLERIVE.	
			Movement during the day was almost impossible and our Mortars did not fire being laid on S.O.S lines.	
	26th		Two more mortars were placed in position in our left battalion front to fire on PIERRE AU BEURE. These mortars were also laid on S.O.S lines.	
	26th to 30th		Work was carried on by night at our gun positions but the nights were very dark and it was difficult to get much done.	
			The strength of the Battery was now 4 Officers 63 other ranks.	
			The weather fortunately continued fine and the men were able to live out in their hastily improvised shelters in the line without great discomfort. Had it rained this low lying country would have been quickly turned into a swamp.	

A5834 Wt. W4973/M687 750,000 8/16 D. D. & L. Ltd. Forms/C.2118/13.

War Diary - May 1918.

10 Trench Mortar Battery

W Green
Capt

2 June 1918.

Instructions regarding War Diaries and Intelligence Summaries are contained in F. S. Regs., Part II. and the Staff Manual respectively. Title pages will be prepared in manuscript.

WAR DIARY ~~or~~ ~~INTELLIGENCE SUMMARY.~~

(Erase heading not required.)

10 Trench Mortar Battery

May 1918.

Army Form C. 2118.

Place	Date	Hour	Summary of Events and Information	Remarks and references to Appendices
near ROBECQ	1918 May 1st		A light German Machine was found by Corporal James in a barn near the front line. It was handed in to Brigade to be sent down to the Base.	All References are to the Map FRANCE Sheet 36A SE Edition 6.
	2nd		The Battery was relieved by 11 Trench Mortar Battery and retired to L'ECLEME	
L'ECLEME	3rd 4th 5th		The Battery was resting and cleaning. The weather continued fine until the 5th when rain fell during the afternoon and evening.	
near ROBECQ	6th		The Battery under Lieut Laycock relieved the 12th Trench Mortar Battery in the right sector. The night was wet. 2 Lt McLeod went into the line in charge of 4 Mortars in PACAUT WOOD	
	7th		The morning was wet and the forward area was very sticky	
	8th		An enemy attack was reported imminent and orders were received to place 4 mortars in position in the Canal Bank to fire if the enemy should penetrate our forward defences. These 4 mortars with 150 shells were placed in position on the 9th instant	
	9th to 13th		All Teams in PACAUT WOOD and on CANAL BANK on the alert for an enemy attack which did not come. Work was carried on to improve the gun positions and to carry shells forward to them.	
	14th		33 rounds were fired with good results on the enemy posts in the orchard in Q 33a	
L'ECLEME	15th		The Battery was relieved by the 11th Trench Mortar Battery and retired to L'ECLEME	
	16th to 18th		The Battery was smartening up and cleaning in beautiful weather. On the 16th inst Private Muir of the 2nd Seaforth Highlanders attached to the Battery was tried by F. G. C. M. for accidentally wounding Private Grant on 30th of April in a cellar in RIEZ DU VINAGE. Pte Muir received a sentence of '56 days' F. P. No I	

A7092 Wt. W12859/M1293. 750,000. 1/17. D. D & L., Ltd. Forms/C2118/14.

Instructions regarding War Diaries and Intelligence Summaries are contained in F. S. Regs., Part II. and the Staff Manual respectively. Title pages will be prepared in manuscript.

WAR DIARY
or
~~INTELLIGENCE SUMMARY.~~
(Erase heading not required.)

10 Trench Mortar Battery

May 1918.

Army Form C. 2118.

Place	Date	Hour	Summary of Events and Information	Remarks and references to Appendices
near ROBECQ	1918 May 19		The Battery relieved the 12th Trench Mortar Battery in the left Sector in beautiful weather. 2Lt Wilson in charge of 3 mortars in RIEZ DU VINAGE and 2Lt McLeod in charge of 3 mortars on the left in Q 20 d.	
	20		The day was very hot. No movement was allowed by day in the forward area but at night 78 shells were carried by 13 men to RIEZ DU VINAGE. During this and the 2 succeeding nights there was very bright moonlight.	
	21		An attempt was made by a special company R.E to set on fire by the projection of oil drums of certain houses in front of our lines at RIEZ. The oil drums did not hit the houses and no fires were caused. 2 Lieut Wilson fired 34 rounds in cooperation on the left flank of the houses in order to drive into the open on the right any of the enemy driven out by the oil drums.	
	22		Again a very hot day. During the night corrugated iron was carried up to the left positions where shelters were made for the officers and gun teams to live in.	
	23		A limber load of government stores found in our Head Quarters billet and in a neighbouring farm house was sent down to be handed in to DADOS IV Division.	
	24.		Rain fell during the day. At night 12 rounds with fuzes cut to 5 seconds were brought up to each position for use against low flying enemy aeroplanes.	

Wt. W128/9/M1293. 750,000. 1/17. D. D & L., Ltd. Forms/C2118/14.

Instructions regarding War Diaries and Intelligence Summaries are contained in F. S. Regs., Part II. and the Staff Manual respectively. Title pages will be prepared in manuscript.

WAR DIARY

~~or INTELLIGENCE SUMMARY~~. 10 Trench Mortar Battery

(Erase heading not required.) May 1918.

Army Form C. 2118.

Place	Date	Hour	Summary of Events and Information	Remarks and references to Appendices
near ROBECQ	1918 May 25		The day was fine and the ground dried rapidly after the previous days rain. During the afternoon our guns registered on a farm occupied by the enemy at Q 27 a 75.10 A direct hit was obtained. At night 40 rounds were fired on the same target.	
	26		The day was fine. At night our mortars fired 90 rounds on the enemy houses and posts in front of RIEZ DU VINAGE. Many hits on the houses and outbuildings were observed.	
	27		We were relieved by No 11 Trench mortar Battery and retired to L'ECLEME	
L'ECLEME	28th to 31st		The Battery was resting and cleaning. The weather continued fine and warm Enemy aeroplanes were active at night but no bombs were dropped near the Billets occupied by the Battery. Our strength is now 5 Officers 61 other ranks.	

A7092. Wt. W12839/M1293. 750,000. 1/17. D. D & L., Ltd. Forms/C2118/14.

Army Form C. 2118.

Instructions regarding War Diaries and Intelligence Summaries are contained in F. S. Regs., Part II. and the Staff Manual respectively. Title pages will be prepared in manuscript.

WAR DIARY
or
INTELLIGENCE SUMMARY.

(Erase heading not required.)

Place	Date	Hour	Summary of Events and Information	Remarks and references to Appendices
			The 10th Trench Mortar Battery. War Diary June 1918.	

9

A7092. Wt. W12839/M1293. 750,000. 1/17. D. D & L., Ltd. Forms/C2118/14.

10th Trench Mortar Battery

WAR DIARY
or
~~INTELLIGENCE SUMMARY~~.

(Erase heading not required.)

June 1918

Army Form C. 2118.

1.

Instructions regarding War Diaries and Intelligence Summaries are contained in F. S. Regs., Part II. and the Staff Manual respectively. Title pages will be prepared in manuscript.

Place	Date	Hour	Summary of Events and Information	Remarks and references to Appendices
L'Eclème	1st		Capt Green went up the line to make arrangements re taking over from the 12th T.M.B.	
Pacaut Sector.	2nd		The battery relieved the 12th T.M.B. in the PACAUT SECTOR having 4 guns in the line under 2LT. McLeod & 4 guns in Support under 2 LT. Wilson	
"	3rd		The men at Battery H.Q. working strengthening a barn with earth & bricks etc. A few registering rounds were fired on M.G.'S.	
"	4th		Bright clear weather. During the afternoon a few ranging rounds were fired on the house at Q34C1.8. & 17 rounds were fired during the night on the same target. Men working on the shelter.	
"	5th		Capt Green & 2LT. McLeod ranged again on house at Q34C1.8. The enemy retaliated with light T.M.'S & grenatenwerfer. At night 26 rounds on same target. Anti-aircraft shells arrive.	
"	6th		Still beautiful weather. LT. Laycock goes on leave. 2/LT. Smith relieves 2LT McLeod in the WOOD.	
"	[illegible]		15 rounds were fired at 10-30 pm. on wood & house at Q 34 C 10.85. A German buoy was blown up & men who ran out engaged by Lewis guns. 26 rounds from 11-45 pm to midnight on orchard & house at Q 33 b.10.35.	
"	7th		46 rounds were fired during the night as follows:- 20 on wood & house at Q 34 C 10.85 to 95; 16 " house at Q 33 b 10.35; 10. on M.G. in orchard at Q 33 a 80.70. Gas was projected from the CANAL BANK on WOOD. at 2 am.	
"	8th		Hot day. At 4-30 the battery co-operated with 6" Newton in a shoot on house at Q 33 b 80.50 & good observation was obtained from BOORKES. Farm. One 6" was dropped short in an enemy post & shrieks were heard. Houses & M.G.'s were fired on during the night & 121 rounds in all fired.	
"	9th		Threatening rain & cooler. At 5 pm a rolling barrage by our Artillery took place on the Division front on our right. The battery co-operated by firing at the same time 90 rounds on posts in orchard, house & wood on right flank at Q 33 b 80.50. The enemy sent up lights bursting into 3 greens also one bursting into 2 reds. Our shoot was very successful. Later on the enemy strafed wood on gun positions with 5.9's & knocked everything about badly. 10 rounds were fired at 3.30 am on Q 33 b. 80.50. Enemy Aircraft was fired upon but was out of range.	
"	10th		2LT Wilson relieved 2LT Smith in the line. 40 rounds were fired from the right guns on WOOD House & neighbourhood. Some gas shells were fired about LE CAIROY at night near the Battery H.Q.	

A7092. Wt. W128 9/M1293 750,000. 1/17. D. D & L., Ltd. Forms/C2118/14.

10th Trench Mortar Battery

WAR DIARY
or
~~INTELLIGENCE SUMMARY.~~
(Erase heading not required.)

June 1918.

2

Army Form C. 2118.

Instructions regarding War Diaries and Intelligence Summaries are contained in F. S. Regs., Part II. and the Staff Manual respectively. Title pages will be prepared in manuscript.

Place	Date	Hour	Summary of Events and Information	Remarks and references to Appendices
PACOUT SECTOR	11th		The Battery fired 195 rounds - as follows: 181 from 12.42 am in conjunction with raid by the Seaforths the targets were enemy posts in neighbourhood of house Q33 b.05.35. 12 rounds on house at Q34c10.85 in reply to enemy M.G. which had troubled our right mortar during the raid. 2 rounds were fired at enemy aircraft 2 LT. Wilson went to hospital with fingers badly smashed by the gun when firing at an E.A. 2 LT Smith takes his place in the line.	
"	12th		139 rounds were fired during the night on targets in the WOOD. The enemy retaliated much with granatenwerfer & rifle grenades which were silenced in the end. Work was commenced to move the 2 left gun positions further into the wood.	
"	13th		25 rounds were fired during the day in registration of S.O.S. targets. The battery was relieved by 11 T.M.B. by 9.30 P.M. & came out to L'ECLEME A great deal of Salvage was obtained	
L'ECLEME	14th		Inspection & cleaning up.	
"	15		Training Capt. Green went to the G.H.Q. L.T.M. School	
"	16–18		Training	
RIEZ du VINAGE SECTOR	19th		The Battery relieved the 12th T.M.B. in the RIEZ du VINAGE Sector having 4 guns in the line & 4 in Reserve. 2 LT. McLeod went into the line	
	20th		5 rounds were fired on enemy posts (M.G.) at Q 21c 10.60.	
	21		45 rounds were fired on enemy posts at Q 27 a 50.50 & Q21c 20.60. The enemy retaliated on our position with 5.9s. A great deal of salvage was obtained from Mt. ~~[illegible]~~ BERNENCHON. 3 O.R. went to hospital 3 day fever started to get a hold of the men	
22nd on night	~~22~~ 23.		51 rounds were fired on enemy posts at Q 27 b.60,60 & Q 27 a 50,70 between 2 am & 4 am. & the enemy retaliated with searching fire. Fever catching hold of the men 2 LT. McLeod & his teams very sick in the line also Details very sick	

10th Trench Mortar Battery — June 1918 — 3

Army Form C. 2118.

WAR DIARY
or
INTELLIGENCE SUMMARY.
(Erase heading not required.)

Instructions regarding War Diaries and Intelligence Summaries are contained in F. S. Regs., Part II. and the Staff Manual respectively. Title pages will be prepared in manuscript.

Place	Date	Hour	Summary of Events and Information	Remarks and references to Appendices
RIEZ de VINAGE SECTOR	22nd		Positions reconnoitred in the Right position for moving the guns further back so as to be able to cover both the front line & 2nd line. 146 rounds of ammunition were carried to the forward positions from the Brigade Dump. Corpl. Tough got the Meritorious Service Medal awarded to him in the King's Birthday Honours.	
	24th		The 2 guns in RIEZ de VINAGE were moved further back to the orchard at Q26 d 24.92. 5 O.R. went to hospital with the Fever & the Details were also down with it. Lt. Laycock returned from leave. Stormy night	
	25th		2Lt. Smith relieved 2Lt. McLeod in RIEZ & Sgt. Major. Crisp relieved Corp. Parks on the left. 1 O.R. went to hospital. Lt. Laycock went to Brigade re proposed raid	
	26th		6 gun positions for the raid were reconnoitred. The new gun positions in RIEZ were improved & made good emplacements. Took 300 rounds up to the Right position at night. 2 O.R went to hospital	
	27th		25 rounds were fired in Co-operation with our Artillery who put down a creeping barrage on the Brigade left Company front at 7 pm. BELLERIVE was lightly shelled during the night. 200 Gas Projectors were fired from the left. 1 O.R. went to hospital.	
	28th		Took 150 rounds up to the right position. Men preparing gun pits & ammunition for the raid. Battery H.Q at BELLERIVE was shelled with H.E. & gas from 2 am to 2-30 am. The gas hung about for about 2 hours owing to no breeze blowing	
	29th		BELLERIVE was shelled heavily during the afternoon. The six guns were put into position ready for the raid & the men from the Reserve were taken up for the raid. BELLERIVE was again shelled at night	
	30th		The R Warwickshire Regt. made a very successful raid at 9.20 am. The battery fired 419 rounds from six guns in 17 minutes. 3 prisoners were taken & it estimated 50 killed. The enemy did not retaliate at all until the night. The barrage put up by the T.M.s was put on the flanks & beyond the objective & was most effective. The Artillery put up a very fine barrage also the Special R.E. fired a smoke barrage along PACAUT WOOD. The Reserve [illegible] Reconnoitred positions in Reserve at MT. BERNENCHON.	C. E. Laycock. Lt for O.C. 10th T.M.B. 2/7/18.

A7092. Wt. W12839/M1293. 750,000. 1/17. D. D & L., Ltd. Forms/C2118/14.

War Diary

10 Trench Mortar Battery

July 1918.

W Green
Capt
1 Aug 1918

Army Form C. 2118.

Instructions regarding War Diaries and Intelligence Summaries are contained in F. S. Regs., Part II. and the Staff Manual respectively. Title pages will be prepared in manuscript.

WAR DIARY
or
~~INTELLIGENCE SUMMARY~~.
(Erase heading not required.)

10 Trench Mortar Battery

July 1918.

Place	Date	Hour	Summary of Events and Information	Remarks and references to Appendices
L'ECLEME	1918 1 July		The Battery was relieved by the 11th Trench Mortar Battery and came back to L'ECLEME. Capt Green rejoined from the G.H.Q. course in light mortars.	
	2nd to 6th		The Battery cleaned up and had smartening drill. Twice we marched to CANTRAINNE open air swimming bath and bathed. The Battery also went through the LEVICK spray as a preventative against the "3 day fever". This illness which had been very prevalent during the last half of June had now ceased and the men who had gone away sick were returning daily.	
In the Line in PACAUT SECTOR	7th		We relieved the 12th Trench Mortar Battery in the PACAUT SECTOR. Relief was complete at 10.15 P.M. 2 Lieut Smith took charge of the guns in the line in PACAUT WOOD.	
	8th		After the Infantry relief was complete 2 Lieut Smith fired 150 rounds on the enemy posts at the edge of PACAUT WOOD. At night there was a heavy thunderstorm	
	9th		Men were kept busy carrying ammunition up into the gun pits in the WOOD. 150 rounds were fired on enemy posts, houses and machine guns. At night gas was projected by LEVIN projectors on the enemy positions in the rear part of the WOOD.	
	10.		200 rounds were fired on enemy positions. A bivouac in PACAUT WOOD caught fire and Pte WOOD of the 1st Royal Warwickshire Regt attached to the Battery was burnt to death. The fire was thought to be caused by a cigarette setting fire to a bag of blue cordite rings. Lance Corpl Woodward & Ptes Sellars & McGregor showed great pluck in rescuing Pte Wood but unfortunately he died shortly after rescue.	

A7092. Wt. W128 9/M1293 750,000. 1/17. D. D & L., Ltd. Forms/C2118/14.

Instructions regarding War Diaries and Intelligence Summaries are contained in F. S. Regs., Part II. and the Staff Manual respectively. Title pages will be prepared in manuscript.

WAR DIARY
or
~~INTELLIGENCE SUMMARY~~.
(Erase heading not required.)

10 Trench mortar Battery

Army Form C. 2118.

July 1918.

Place	Date	Hour	Summary of Events and Information	Remarks and references to Appendices
In the line in PACAUT SECTOR.	1918 11 July		Capt Green visited Brigade and was directed to prepare alternative positions for 20 mortars in PACAUT WOOD as it is proposed that the 2nd Duke of Wellingtons Regt shall shortly make a raid in this Sector. 100 rounds were fired during the night on the enemy posts.	
	12		A stormy day and a good deal of rain fell. The bivouacs in the line started letting in water so the gun teams had to rebuild them. 2 Lieut Smith fired 200 rounds during the 24 hours.	
	13		193 rounds fired to 6 A.M. 2 Lieut Smith was relieved by Lieut Laycock having fired over 1000 rounds in 6 days and having established a moral ascendancy over the enemy. A conference was held at Brigade with reference to the cooperation of Stokes mortars in the forthcoming raid. 20 mortars are to barrage the enemy front line of posts, 8 from 10 T.M.B, 8 from 11 T.M.B. and 4 from 12 T.M.B.	
	14.		The afternoon & evening were very wet. Our men were busy all day making new emplacements in the line and cleaning and fuzing shells on the dump.	
	15.		A carrying party from the 1st R. Warwickshire Regt and 2nd Seaforth Highlanders carried by up 800 rounds to the gun pits in PACAUT WOOD. Each man took 8 rounds on each journey. Work was continued on the new gun positions in the line.	
	16.		The carrying party took up 1000 rounds half in the morning and the remainder at night. Lieut Laycock was injured in the leg by a small stake and had to go to hospital.	
	17.		2 Lieut Smith took Lieut Laycock's place in the WOOD and Lieut B.R. HILLARD of the 1st R Warwickshire Regt reported for duty	

A7092. Wt W128 9/M1293 750,000. 1/17. D. D & L., Ltd. Forms/C2118/14.

Instructions regarding War Diaries and Intelligence Summaries are contained in F. S. Regs., Part II. and the Staff Manual respectively. Title pages will be prepared in manuscript.

WAR DIARY

or

~~INTELLIGENCE SUMMARY.~~

(Erase heading not required.)

10 Trench Mortar Battery

Army Form C. 2118.

July 1918.

Place	Date	Hour	Summary of Events and Information	Remarks and references to Appendices
In the Line in PACAUT SECTOR	1918 18 July		A fine day and clear but a rather high wind. All 20 mortars were reported ready by 12 Noon. The raid at 2.30 P.M was successfully carried out. 28 prisoners were taken. Our T.M barrage was reported by the raiding party to have been very successful 40 German dead were found and the enemy posts were badly knocked about. The rounds fired were as follows 10 T M B 400; 11 T M B 597; 12 T M B 248; Total 1245 The Casualties among T.M personnel were: 10 T M B Killed O.R. 4, Wounded Officers 2, O.R. 1; 11 T M B NONE; 12 T M B Wounded O.R. 1	
	19		2 Lieut Harmill reported for duty and went into PACAUT WOOD.	
L'ECLEME	20		We were relieved by 11 T.M.B and came back to L'ECLEME	
	21st to 26th		The Battery resting and training. A class for instruction in T.M work was held by 2 Lieut Mc Leod and from it 15 men were chosen as reinforcements for the Battery. The members of the class were drawn from the battalions in the Brigade.	
In the Line VINAGE SECTOR	27th		We relieved 12 T M B in the VINAGE sector. 2 Lieut Mc Leod in charge of the guns in front, the Sergeant Major in charge of the reserve guns.	
	28th		Accommodation at Battery H.Q not being sufficient to hold all our men we started work on making an elephant shelter inside an empty room of the mens billet.	

A7092. Wt W128 9/M1293 750,000. 1/17. D. D & L., Ltd. Forms/C2118/14.

Army Form C. 2118.

WAR DIARY
or
~~INTELLIGENCE SUMMARY~~.
(Erase heading not required.)

10 Trench Mortar Battery
July 1918.

Instructions regarding War Diaries and Intelligence Summaries are contained in F. S. Regs., Part II. and the Staff Manual respectively. Title pages will be prepared in manuscript.

Place	Date	Hour	Summary of Events and Information	Remarks and references to Appendices
In the Line in VINAGE SECTOR	1918 29 July to 31 July		The weather continued very hot. Work was continued on the new shelter for the men which was almost completed. About 50 rounds a night were fired by our mortars in the line. The strength of the Battery was now 3 Officers 74 other ranks.	

A7092. Wt W128 9/M1293 750,000. 1/17. D. D & L., Ltd. Forms/C2118/14.

Confidential

10th Brigade No. G/827.

10th T M Batty

AUGUST 1918

4th Division. "A"

Reference this Office No. G/827, dated 8th instant.

Herewith WAR DIARY of the 10th Trench Mortar Battery, which was forwarded to the Base in error.

[illegible] Capt

for Brigadier General.

11th September 1918. Commanding 10th Infantry Brigade.

10th Trench Mortar Battery.

WAR DIARY
or
~~INTELLIGENCE SUMMARY.~~

(Erase heading not required.)

Army Form C. 2118.

HQ 10 Infy Bde

Appx 849

Instructions regarding War Diaries and Intelligence Summaries are contained in F. S. Regs., Part II. and the Staff Manual respectively. Title pages will be prepared in manuscript.

Place	Date	Hour	Summary of Events and Information	Remarks and references to Appendices
Bellevue.	August. 1..		Battery occupied making a new dugout at Bty H. Qrs.	
			Capt Green attended court martial on Pte Hetcher at L'ECLEME.	
	2.		Rained all day. 95 rounds fired. One shot fell short & wounded a man of the 1st Roy. War. Regt.	
			Pte Hetcher sentenced to 9 month imprisonment with hard labour.	
	3.		2/Lt Harnell relieved 2/Lt McHead in the line.	
	4.		2/Lt G. R. Smith awarded the Military Cross. L/Cpl Woodward awarded the M.S.M.	
	5.		2/Lt McHead attended T.M. demonstration at Le Touquet.	
			Our line slightly advanced in PACAUT WOOD. enemy still holding post in front of RIEZ du VINAGE.	
	6	6pm	Wire received from Bde that two guns are to be attached to each Battn. in the line & 2 to be in reserve (one in RIEZ & one in Q 20 d.)	
			2/Lt McHead with 2 guns attached to 1st Roy. War. Regt. 2/Lt Harnell with two guns with the 2nd Duke of Wellington's Regt. Capt Sawley with two guns with the 2nd Seaforth Hrs.	
	7.		Our line was advanced this morning, to the 2nd Yellow line. 2/Lt McHead & Capt Sawley take guns forward. Enemy offers little resistance.	
	8.		Our line advanced again.	
	9.		Guns advanced, 62 rounds were fired on house which was holding 1st Roy. War. Regt up. Several direct hits were obtained & the house was afterwards captured without any casualties.	
			10th T.M.B relieved by 11th T.M.Bty. March to L'ECLEME to rest billets.	

A7092 Wt. W12839/M1293 750,000. 1/17. D. D & L., Ltd. Forms/C2118/14.

10th Trench Mortar Bty.

Army Form C. 2118.

WAR DIARY
or
~~INTELLIGENCE SUMMARY.~~

(Erase heading not required.)

Instructions regarding War Diaries and Intelligence Summaries are contained in F. S. Regs., Part II. and the Staff Manual respectively. Title pages will be prepared in manuscript.

Place	Date	Hour	Summary of Events and Information	Remarks and references to Appendices
L'ECLEME	August 10-15.		General Training.	
	10.		Battery marches to see the King.	
	13.		Lecture to Officers & N.C.O.s on work of R.A.F.	
	14.		N.C.O.s go to No 21 Squadron. R.A.F. for demonstration. Capt Green goes on leave.	
	15.		Battery relieves 12th T.M.Bty in PACAUT SECTOR.	
LE CAUROY.	17.		Enemy falls back. 2Lt Law reports for duty.	
	18		Enemy still falling back.	
	20		Guns advanced 2000 yards.	
	21.		2Lt Law relieves 2Lt Hamell in the line.	
	23.		Bty is relieved by 58th T.M.Bty. March to L'ECLEME to rest billets.	
L'ECLEME	24.		March to RAIMBERT. to billets. Receive orders to prepare to move the following day.	
RAIMBERT.	25		March to PERNES STATION entrain for PETIT HOUVIN.	
PETIT HOUVIN.	26		Training consisting of 3 hours per day to be carried out. Orders received to march to LE PENDU that night. Distance 21 miles.	
LE PENDU	27.		2Lt McLeod proceeds to line preparatory to taking over battery positions.	
	28.		Embus for CAMBRAI ROAD for assembly area. Owing to ARRAS - CAMBRAI ROAD being shelled, troops had to march to assembly area via BLANGY & BATTERY VALLEY. Battery move into trench on ARRAS CAMBRAI Road.	
ARRAS CAMBRAI RD	29.		Bty employed carrying ammunition to Battalions.	
	30		Ptes Robinson, Wilkinson, & Fellows wounded while carrying ammunition.	
	31.		Bty employed on carrying.	

A7092. Wt. W12859/M1293. 750,000. 1/17. D. D & L., Ltd. Forms/C2118/14.

War Diary September 1918.

10 Trench Mortar Battery

W Green
Capt
2 October 1918.

Instructions regarding War Diaries and Intelligence Summaries are contained in F. S. Regs., Part II. and the Staff Manual respectively. Title pages will be prepared in manuscript.

WAR DIARY or ~~INTELLIGENCE SUMMARY~~. - 10 Trench Mortar Battery

Army Form C. 2118.

September 1918

(Erase heading not required.)

Place	Date	Hour	Summary of Events and Information	Remarks and references to Appendices
In the Line near VIS EN ARTOIS	1918 1 Sept.		Capt Green was slightly wounded while reconnoitring a Trench Mortar position and was sent to hospital. During the night the men had very heavy carrying parties and suffered 4 casualties, one man being killed and three wounded. Our quarters were moved forward during the night in anticipation of the coming attack on the DROCOURT-QUEANT line	
	2 Sept		The attack proved successful and our men moved forward again and established a forward ammunition dump.	
MONCHY LE PREUX	3 Sept		The Battery was relieved and moved to trenches near MONCHY LE PREUX	
AVERDOINGT	4 Sept		Battery went by bus to AVERDOINGT. Our mortars had to be carried four kilometres by the men as the bus drivers refused to go past a point on the ARRAS - ST POL Road.	
	5th to 18th Sept		The Battery was in training at AVERDOINGT. The weather was very unsettled and the barns, in which the men were billeted, were leaky. Capt Green returned from hospital on the 12th inst. A football competition for a cup presented by the Brigadier General Commanding was arranged but the competition had to be abandoned as our time out of the line proved shorter than anticipated.	
In the line near ETERPIGNY	18th		The 10th Brigade left AVERDOINGT in motor buses and relieved the 167th Brigade in the line. 2 Lieut Law went into the line in charge of 4 mortars, 2 covering approaches through LECLUSE and 2 covering approaches through ETAING. We took over Head Quarters from the 167 T.M.B close to ETERPIGNY. Owing to the floods caused by the enemy having dammed the rivers SENSEE TRINQUIS & SCARPE, the enemy is almost everywhere out of range of our mortars	

A7092. Wt. W12839/M1293. 750,000. 1/17. D. D. & L., Ltd. Forms/C2118/14.

Instructions regarding War Diaries and Intelligence Summaries are contained in F. S. Regs., Part II. and the Staff Manual respectively. Title pages will be prepared in manuscript.

WAR DIARY

or

~~INTELLIGENCE SUMMARY.~~

(*Erase heading not required.*)

Army Form C. 2118.

– 10 Trench Mortar Battery

September 1918.

Place	Date	Hour	Summary of Events and Information	Remarks and references to Appendices
In the Line near ETERPIGNY	1918 Sept 19th & 20th		Work was carried on each night on new gun pits near ETAING and the dug out at Battery Headquarters was improved and bunks were put in it. There is a large quantity of wood available as there are very many abandoned German huts in ETERPIGNY.	
	21st		2 Lieut Law fired 16 rounds on a German post in front of LECLUSE	
	22nd to 27th		Infantry patrols were active in investigating the depth of the water in front of our positions and in making reconnaissance for bridgeheads in case we should advance. During the period Corporal Brain D.C.M and 4 other ranks of the 1st Royal Warwickshire Regt left us to join a light Trench Mortar Battery which was being formed in the 25th Division.	
	27th		2 Lieut McLeod went into the line near LECLUSE to be ready to go forward with two gun teams in case the enemy should withdraw or be driven back by operations further South	
	28th		2 Lieut Law fired 5 rounds on a sniper's post near SAILLY EN OSTREVENT	
	29th		Corporal Parkes & 2 gun teams moved into ECOURT ST QUENTIN to relieve 2 teams of 167 Trench Mortar Battery there.	
near MONCHY LE PREUX	30th		The Battery was relieved by the 11th Trench Mortar Battery and came to ORANGE HILL near MONCHY LE PREUX. Our strength is now 4 officers and 58 other ranks.	

War Diary

October 1918.

10 Trench Mortar Battery

W Green
Capt

31 Oct 1918.

Army Form C. 2118.

Instructions regarding War Diaries and Intelligence Summaries are contained in F. S. Regs., Part II. and the Staff Manual respectively. Title pages will be prepared in manuscript.

WAR DIARY or ~~INTELLIGENCE SUMMARY~~.

(Erase heading not required.)

10 Trench Mortar Battery

October 1918.

Place	Date	Hour	Summary of Events and Information	Remarks and references to Appendices
ORANGE HILL near MONCHY LE PREUX	1918 Oct: 1st to 4th		The Battery was in Reserve living in bivouacs. The nights were very cold. On the 2nd we went to St Catherines near ARRAS for baths.	
WANQUETIN.	5th		The Battery marched to WANQUETIN where the men were billeted in barns and the officers in civilian houses. In the village there is a CINEMA run by a Canadian Division. It is open to all troops every evening.	
	6th to 10th		Training took place in the area around the village. On the 9th there was a Brigade Field Day between BERNEVILLE and the WAGNONLIEU - GOUY SWITCH in front of GOUY. The attack was carried out by the 1st Royal Warwickshire Regt and the 2nd Seaforth Highlanders and the defence was represented by the 2nd Duke of Wellingtons Regt. Two mortars with teams under 2 Lieut Harrell advanced with the 1st Royal Warwickshires and two mortars with teams under 2 Lieut Law accompanied the 2nd Seaforth Highlanders.	
ST. OLLE	11th		The Battery moved with the Brigade by lorry to ST OLLE near CAMBRAI. We were billeted in houses	
NAVES	13th		We marched to NAVES where we were billeted in the RUELLE DE L'EGLISE.	
	14th to 17th		Training was carried on at NAVES and forward routes to the line reconnoitred	
VILLERS EN CAUCHIES	18th		We marched to VILLERS EN CAUCHIES and at night reconnoitred our front line which ran along LA SELLE RIVER through SAULZOIR. The enemy shelled VILLERS EN CAUCHIES heavily ~~with~~ with gas during the early part of the night.	
	19th		We prepared 420 Stokes shells in order to barrage the enemy posts in connection with	

A7092 Wt. W128 9/M1293 750,000. 1/17. D. D. & L., Ltd. Forms/C2118/14.

Instructions regarding War Diaries and Intelligence Summaries are contained in F. S. Regs., Part II. and the Staff Manual respectively. Title pages will be prepared in manuscript.

WAR DIARY
~~or~~
~~INTELLIGENCE SUMMARY~~.
(*Erase heading not required.*)

10 Trench Mortar Battery

October 1918.

Army Form C. 2118.

Place	Date	Hour	Summary of Events and Information	Remarks and references to Appendices
VILLERS EN CAUCHIES	1918 Oct 19th contd		an attack on the morning of the 20th. In the evening we learnt that the enemy had evacuated SAULZOIR and so the attack had to be postponed.	
	20th		Many civilians came down from SAULZOIR. They had lived in cellars during the period that the place had been under fire. Amongst them were a few young men of military age who had concealed themselves when ordered by the Germans to go back for work behind their lines.	
	21st		An attack was carried out on the enemy positions in front of SAULZOIR. These were captured and our patrols reached the edge of VERCHAIN. In the afternoon the	
SAULZOIR			Battery moved to SAULZOIR. Our mortars were pushed up by the men on hand-carts which the civilians had used to carry off their belongings from the town to a place of safety.	
	22nd		Four mortars with teams under 2 Lieut Harnell were placed in position in front of SAULZOIR to cover the roads of approach to the town.	
	23rd		Four mortars were moved forward to barrage the enemy's posts in VERCHAIN in connection with a projected attack on the following morning.	
	24th		The attack took place at 2 AM. VERCHAIN was taken and our line was carried forward to the heights E of the town. Lieut McLeod who was in charge of two of our Mortars was slightly wounded in the face and went to hospital. During the barrage we fired 170 rounds. 2 Lieut Harnell moved 4 guns forward to the Eastern end of VERCHAIN to cover the approaches to the village.	
	25th		2 Lieut Harnell was relieved by the 12th Trench Mortar Battery and withdrew to Battery Headquarters	

A7092. Wt. W12839/M1293. 750,000. 1/17. D. D & L., Ltd. Forms/C2118/14.

Instructions regarding War Diaries and Intelligence Summaries are contained in F. S. Regs., Part II. and the Staff Manual respectively. Title pages will be prepared in manuscript.

WAR DIARY

~~or~~

~~INTELLIGENCE SUMMARY.~~

(Erase heading not required.)

10 Trench Mortar Battery

October 1918.

Army Form C. 2118.

Place	Date	Hour	Summary of Events and Information	Remarks and references to Appendices
SAULZOIR	1918 Oct 25 (Contd)		at SAULZOIR. The men improvised baths with tubs which they found in the houses and clean clothing was issued from the Divisional stores.	
	26th to 31st		Training was carried out. A supply of beer was obtained through the Expeditionary Force Canteens from French Breweries and issued to the men on payment at the rate of 8d a litre. Forward routes to the line were reconnoitred. Many civilians returned to SAULZOIR during the period. A cinema was run for the troops in a barn formerly used by the enemy for the same purpose. The strength of the Battery is now 3 Officers 58 other ranks.	

A7092. Wt. W12839/M1293. 750,000. 1/17. D. D & L., Ltd. Forms/C2118/14.

War Diary

—

10 Trench Mortar Battery

—

November 1918

W Green
Capt
1 Dec 1918.

Instructions regarding War Diaries and Intelligence Summaries are contained in F. S. Regs., Part II. and the Staff Manual respectively. Title pages will be prepared in manuscript.

WAR DIARY ~~or~~ ~~INTELLIGENCE SUMMARY~~.

November 1918.

Army Form C. 2118.

(Erase heading not required.)

Place	Date	Hour	Summary of Events and Information	Remarks and references to Appendices
SAULZOIR	1st to 5th		The Battery was in Billets and training was carried on during the day. The civilians continued to return to their homes	
PRESEAU	6		The Brigade marched to PRESEAU in a heavy downpour of rain. Many of our men and many Germans still lie unburied round the village. In the sunken roads there are numbers of heavy and light Machine Guns taken in the recent fighting and there are several tanks and field guns still unsalved.	
	7th to 9th		The two first days were very wet but the 9th was fine and sunny. The battalions were busy salving machine guns and enemy material. Our men brought in a German light Minenwerfer and an Anti-tank rifle.	
	10th		The Minenwerfer and Anti tank rifle were cleaned and the men of the Battery were instructed in their use. About 8-30 P.M word was received that the Germans had accepted General Foch's terms for an armistice. Bonfires were lit and great numbers of VEREY lights were sent up from all over the village and the bands of the Battalions played.	
	11th to 18th		The civilian inhabitants who were evacuated by the Germans begin returning to their homes. Our men put in a lot of work helping them to fix up their houses. Preseau was badly knocked about by bombardment and many of the houses are in ruins. The people for the first day or two of their return lived principally	

A7092. Wt. W12859/M1293. 750,000. 1/17. D. D & L., Ltd. Forms/C2118/14.

Army Form C. 2118.

Instructions regarding War Diaries and Intelligence Summaries are contained in F. S. Regs., Part II. and the Staff Manual respectively. Title pages will be prepared in manuscript.

WAR DIARY

~~or~~

~~INTELLIGENCE SUMMARY~~.

(Erase heading not required.)

November 1918.

Place	Date	Hour	Summary of Events and Information	Remarks and references to Appendices
PRESEAU			on the rations which the soldiers shared with them. Luckily the weather kept dry as there were very few roofs in the village without holes caused by shelling	
VALENCIENNES	19th		The Brigade moved to VALENCIENNES by march. The Battery was billeted in RONZIER BARRACKS and Battery HQ was in No 26 RUE DE L'INTENDANCE	
	20th to 30th		Training was carried on and the Brigade was inspected by the Divisional General and the Army Commander. There were few shops open in the town and those that were open had little stock. Civilian evacuees poured into the town at the rate of 1200 a day and numerous soldiers of all the allied nations who had been prisoners came into the town.	
			The Battery strength at the end of the month was 3 officers & 45 other ranks. All personnel surplus to establishment were returned to their Units on the 13th	

A7092. Wt. W12839/M1293. 750,000. 1/17. D. D & L., Ltd. Forms/C2118/14.

War Diary - December 1918

---

10 Trench Mortar Battery

W Green
Capt
5 Jan 1919.

Instructions regarding War Diaries and Intelligence Summaries are contained in F. S. Regs., Part II. and the Staff Manual respectively. Title pages will be prepared in manuscript.

WAR DIARY - 10 Trench Mortar Battery

~~or INTELLIGENCE SUMMARY~~.

(Erase heading not required.)

December 1918.

Army Form C. 2118.

Place	Date	Hour	Summary of Events and Information	Remarks and references to Appendices
VALENCIENNES	1918 Dec 1st to 31st		The Battery trained for 2 hours each day and had one hour's educational training. The latter was taken up by the men in a very perfunctory way. Two men went home during the month for demobilization as coal miners. The Battery competed in the football competition for a cup presented by Brigadier General J. Greene D.S.O. beating a team from the 9th Field Co R.E but losing to 'A' Co 2nd Seaforth Highlanders. Nine men from the Battery were attached to a Brigade Salvage Party during the month and cleared up the area around MAING. At the end of the month our strength was 3 Officers 44 other ranks.	

A7092. Wt. W12839/M1293. 750,000. 1/17. D. D & L., Ltd. Forms/C2118/14.

War Diary <u>January 1919</u>

10th Trench Mortar Battery

G. Harnell Lt.
for O.C.
10th T.M. Bty.

Instructions regarding War Diaries and Intelligence Summaries are contained in F. S. Regs., Part II. and the Staff Manual respectively. Title pages will be prepared in manuscript.

WAR DIARY
or
~~INTELLIGENCE~~ SUMMARY.

(*Erase heading not required.*)

10th Trench Mortar Battery
January 1919

Army Form C. 2118.

Place	Date	Hour	Summary of Events and Information	Remarks and references to Appendices
VALENCIENNES	1919 1st to 5th/1/19		Battery at Valenciennes, Parades & Training as usual.	
BINCHE	6/1/19		Battery moved by Motor Lorries to BINCHE.	
	7th to 31st/1/19		The Battery personnel were billeted in private houses & were very comfortable. Demobilization proceeded slowly.	
			At the end of the month the strength of the Battery was Officers 3. Other Ranks 34.	

A7092. Wt. W128 9/M1293 750,000. 1/17. D. D. & L., Ltd. Forms/C2118/14.